Translating Happiness

Translating Happiness

A Cross-Cultural Lexicon of Well-Being

Tim Lomas

The MIT Press
Cambridge, Massachusetts
London, England

First MIT Press paperback edition, 2019

This book was set in ITC Stone Sans Std and ITC Stone Serif Std by Toppan Best-set Premedia Limited. Printed and bound in the United States of America.

Library of Congress Cataloging-in-Publication Data

Names: Lomas, Tim, 1979– author.
Title: Translating happiness : a cross-cultural lexicon of well-being / Tim Lomas.
Description: Cambridge, MA : MIT Press, [2018] | Includes bibliographical references and index.
Identifiers: LCCN 2017029082 | ISBN 9780262037488 (hardcover : alk. paper), 9780262537087 (pb.)
Subjects: LCSH: Language and emotions. | Well-being—Psychological aspects. | Interpersonal relations. | Happiness. | Psycholinguistics.
Classification: LCC BF582 .L66 2018 | DDC 158—dc23 LC record available at https://lccn.loc.gov/2017029082

10 9 8 7 6 5 4 3 2

Contents

Preface

I can remember vividly the moment when I first had the notion to create a positive cross-cultural lexicography, the project on which this book is based.[1] It was a summer day in 2015, and I was standing in my parents' kitchen in London, chatting with my mum. In retrospect, though, its seeds were planted years before, way back in 1998.

I was nineteen and had gone to teach English in China for six months before starting university. The adventure was every bit as eye-opening and horizon-expanding as you might expect for a naïve, unworldly young man like me. It was challenging at every turn, testing my skills and character to the limit. But at the same time, it was thrilling and intoxicating. My world was enriched daily as I encountered new and unfamiliar people, practices, experiences, sights, sounds, tastes, and, above all, ideas. I was especially intrigued by the Taoist and Buddhist monasteries, and I sought out books and people who might explain these traditions, unknown and mysterious to me.

I soon became bewitched by terms such as *Tao** and *yīn-yáng, nirvāṇa*, and *saṃsāra*. The meanings of these concepts were opaque at best, in fact mostly unfathomable. But they seemed deeply significant. I was struck, unnerved even, by the realization that these words lacked an exact English equivalent. But they were not just untranslatable. They seemed beyond my linguistic and cognitive universe. I was radically challenged. I became

---

*A glossary of all terms from the lexicography that appear in the book can be found at the end of the main text. The glossary includes a romanized version of each word, together with the word in its original script (if applicable); a phonetic pronunciation guide; and a brief definition.

aware, really for the first time, that some concepts and practices which belong to cultures not my own are veiled to me.

This realization stayed with me as I entered university in Edinburgh to study psychology. I found the field fascinating, and during my studies was introduced to a wealth of interesting ideas and theories. But I still felt that the concepts I had encountered in China remained outside my frame of reference, indeed beyond the ken of Western psychology. One would be unlikely to find even a passing reference to *nirvāṇa* in a textbook, let alone a serious analysis of it.

Why, I wondered? In numerous cultures, the state of *nirvāṇa* is considered the peak of human development. It couldn't be unimportant to psychology. However, academic psychology, as I was learning it, seemed at best incomplete. It is rooted—understandably, given the context in which it emerged and developed—in philosophies and epistemologies that are and have been dominant in Western cultures. This is fine, as far as it goes. But it does mean that psychology has largely overlooked the deep insights into the mind that other cultures have cultivated over the centuries.

(Following Edward Said's warnings about Orientalism[2]—his critical term for the construction of "the East" in a way that homogenizes and moreover disparages Asians, Middle Easterners, and North Africans as "Other"—I hesitate to use the terms "Eastern" and "Western," and moreover to ascribe particular concepts and attributes to these two hemispheres. That said, these labels have a ring of truth for me, capturing my initial unfamiliarity with ideas I experienced as culturally "other"—in an essentially positive way, I hasten to add.)

My impressions of psychology's cultural bias lingered. After some years working as a musician and a psychiatric nursing assistant, in 2008 I obtained a PhD scholarship to study the impact of meditation on men's mental health. It was a dream project, since after my return from China I had personally developed a meditation practice and a keen interest in Buddhism. Moreover, the PhD brought me into further contact with concepts and practices that were culturally unfamiliar to me but seemed relevant to psychology.

My study centered on a group of meditators in London. In a spirit of ethnography, I joined their Buddhist community. I found myself dwelling further on terms that could be regarded as untranslatable, and on the phenomena they signify. For instance, my study participants attested to the importance of the *saṅgha*, a Pāli word for community, generally used within Buddhism to denote an established group of practitioners. *Saṅgha* provided the warmth of connection and friendship, but it was also a "community of practice."[3] The men felt it was pivotal in introducing them to new ideas, activities, and "ways of being" that were beneficial to their well-being.[4] One of these was the meditative and behavioral cultivation of *mettā*, a Pāli term usually rendered in Western contexts as "loving-kindness."[5] Of particular fascination to me was that untranslatable terms such as *mettā* were not merely intellectual curiosities. These men were engaged in a heartfelt effort to bring these concepts into the center of their lives, where they would be part of everyday discourse and influence their behavior.

The possibility of thoughtfully harnessing untranslatable words in this way would have a strong effect on my subsequent conception of the lexicography presented in this book. That project, however, would wait another few years. I wrapped up my PhD in 2012 and soon after gratefully took up a lectureship at the University of East London in the arena of positive psychology. I felt at home in this exciting and relatively new branch of academia—developed since the late 1990s—which can be regarded as the science and practice of improving well-being.[6] I spent the next couple years immersing myself in the field, which proved a garden of delights. That brings me back to my parents' kitchen.

I had just returned from the biennial International Positive Psychology Association conference, where I enjoyed a week of fascinating talks and inspiring conversations. Ideas were bubbling away in my mind. One presentation in particular made a mark on me. It was a talk by a Finnish researcher, Emilia Lahti, on the concept of *sisu*, which she described as a form of extraordinary inner courage and determination in the face of adversity. *Sisu*, she explained, was understood in Finland as a quality integral to its culture and people, enabling them not only to survive but also to thrive in the face of hardships encountered over their long history. But Lahti also suggested *sisu* was not only a strength manifested by, or available to, Finns. It was potentially within reach of all people, regardless of their background, even if their own language lacked a term to signify it.

When I got to my parents' house, my mum asked about the conference. With much enthusiasm, I told her about *sisu*—and its intriguing lack of a precise English equivalent, even as there are conceptually similar terms. The train of conversation led us to reflect that most languages may have similarly untranslatable words. I now know that there is a considerable academic literature on this topic. However, being a psychologist rather than a linguist,* at the time I wasn't aware of the concept of untranslatability per se, notwithstanding my earlier experiences in China. As such, this conversation yielded something of an epiphany. My mum and I spent a while drumming up possible examples from among our own pool of languages: we both speak French, though my skill is sadly limited and fading fast; my mum is fluent in German, and has some knowledge of Arabic; and I have an abiding interest in Chinese, courtesy of my formative months there, as well as Sanskrit and Pāli, thanks to my interest in Buddhism.

At some point during this conversation, the thought occurred that it would be wonderful to collect as many untranslatable words as possible—doing so in a respectful and appreciative spirit that does justice to the richness of the terms and the cultures that created them. Given my professional and personal interests, I hoped to focus on well-being. In this way was the idea for a positive cross-cultural lexicography born, although the term "lexicography"—the compiling of dictionaries—did not present itself to me until sometime later. We realized immediately that, were I to undertake this endeavor alone, it would be very limited in scope. Rather, I would need to harness the collective wisdom of a global community of speakers, each of whom could bring unique lexical and cultural knowledge to bear. I imagined a crowd-sourced platform, which people from around the world could use to create the lexicography together.

However, at that point, I didn't have my own website, let alone a way of attracting attention and contributions to it. I would need a catalyst to jump-start the endeavor, so I embarked on an initial quest for words myself. Using the "quasi-systematic" search procedure I detail in chapter 1, I obtained a modest but promising haul of 216 terms. I then analyzed these thematically and published the results in the *Journal of Positive Psychology* in January 2016.[7] At the same time, I created a website (not an easy task for a

---

*This background should be borne in mind throughout the book. I am writing from the perspective of psychology, not linguistics. Although the book is cross-disciplinary in nature, I am a psychologist engaging with language, rather than a linguist engaging with psychology. As such, apart from the first chapter—in which I set out a perspective on language and untranslatable words specifically—I shall mainly be interpreting and discussing the project through the lens of psychological concepts and theories.

neophyte such as me), which included a platform for what I hoped would soon become the burgeoning lexicography.* There was certainly something of an "If you build it, they will come" spirit animating my efforts.

Quite soon the outcome I had been hoping for began to crystallize. The paper received some positive coverage in high-profile publications, such as the *Psychologist* in the United Kingdom, and the *New Yorker* and *Scientific American* in the United States. These articles provided the spark the project needed. My website started to receive visitors from many different countries, who generously suggested words and recommended ways to refine existing definitions. (I am always conscious that my definitions are partial, provisional, and improvable. The project is the epitome of a work-in-progress.) The list has since grown to about 900 entries over the past year and a half. That leaves a long way to go: the list currently includes samples from nearly one hundred languages, a tiny minority of the 7,000-odd "living" languages in the world.[8] And that's before you get to the further complexity of regional dialects and linguistic subcultures.

Still, it's a decent start. Moreover, it's a start that encourages my belief in the project. My hope is that the lexicography could help foster cross-cultural appreciation, both in academic psychology and in society more broadly. The lexicography showcases the richness of cultural diversity and the unique contributions different languages can make to our understanding of the world. At the same time, I also believe the lexicography can be a powerful reminder of our common humanity: despite our apparent differences, most of us share similar feelings, dreams, hopes, and loves. As I reflect on the words and their meanings, I find many that resonate: I *know* the feeling or experience in question, even if I hadn't previously been able to put a name to it.

This brings me to my final point regarding the potential of the lexicography: I believe it has the power to enrich people's emotional understanding and experience. Untranslatable words are not merely intellectual curiosities or informative vis-à-vis the culture that created them. Rather, just as learning another language can be a valuable endeavor, I submit that we can personally engage with these words—in a way that is sensitive to their cultural origin and significance—using them to give voice to feelings and experiences we may have had, but which were previously unconceptualized

*See http://www.drtimlomas.com/lexicography.

and unarticulated. In fact, this kind of "borrowing" is central to language development. As I explore in chapter 1, as many as 41 percent of English words appear to have been brought in from other languages, often because these words filled what Adrienne Lehrer calls a "lexical gap": "the lack of a convenient word to express what [the speaker] wants to speak about."[9]

The experiential value of untranslatable words does not end with convenience, though. Like the meditators I studied, we can all, by encountering new words, find our way to *new* feelings, behaviors, and activities. A word that signifies an unfamiliar aspect of life is an invitation to inquire into the phenomenon it specifies and to explore the possibility of bringing it into one's life. A beautiful example of this process is the West's recent surge of interest in mindfulness. Millions have been engaged in an experiential exploration of *sati*, the Pāli term for which mindfulness is a somewhat imperfect "loan translation," as I discuss in chapter 2. I am hopeful that people will engage with other terms in this lexicography in a similar way. In this manner, experiences of well-being that have been "hidden" to them— either vaguely known but veiled by lack of a signifying word, or completely unknown and shrouded in darkness—may become visible.

Which brings me to this book. I am thrilled and honored to have the opportunity to publish with the MIT Press. The lexicography on my website is an evolving resource, which I hope people will find interesting and useful. However, in terms of setting out the conceptual and theoretical case for the project, there is no better forum than a monograph, and no finer publisher than MIT. I have many goals for the book. I want to set out the theory behind the lexicography. I would also like to analyze a good selection of its words in some depth, exploring connections between them and existing psychological concepts, and in the process enriching the current nomological network in Western academic psychology (i.e., the constructs comprising the field).[10] I further aim to put forward ideas for future research and for testing my propositions. Finally, I hope readers will think about how they can use these words to enrich their own emotional understanding and experience.

It remains to thank some special people without whom this book would not have been possible. First, Kate, my wife, soul mate, and best friend. Aside from providing continual love and support, of which I rarely feel deserving, she also listens with patience to my random ideas and digressions, and tolerates my restless mind and messy habits. I'm ever grateful for the eternal sunshine and warmth she brings to my life. Similarly, I would be nothing without my wonderful family, who are always my rock of support, and my closest and dearest companions. And a particular thank-you goes to my mum, the co-creator of the project. On that note, a grateful shout-out also goes to Emilia Lahti.

I'm ever thankful to a whole cast of people who helped build, energize, and disseminate the lexicography and then facilitated the development of this book. I'm grateful to Jon Sutton and Christian Jarrett at the *Psychologist*, Emily Anthes at the *New Yorker*, and Steve Mirsky and Gareth Cook at *Scientific American*, who thoughtfully propelled my initial article to public attention. Thanks also to Joana Patrasc and Maynard Russell, who generously gave their time and skills to create the interactive online lexicography. With respect to the book itself, my immense gratitude goes to Amy Brand, Phil Laughlin, Anne-Marie Bono, Judy Feldmann, Simon Waxman, Yasuyo Iguchi, and all the team at the MIT Press, who took a chance on me and provided the best academic platform I could wish for to substantiate the project. Thanks too, as always, to my fantastic agent, Esmond Harmsworth, who has continually been a source of guidance and support in realizing the book. The writing process was greatly helped by a team of bilingual experts, who advised on my interpretations and definitions of some of the words. These include Antonella Delle Fave, Itai Ivtzan, Francisco José Eiroa-Orosa, Paul Wong, Oscar Kjell, Natalia Gogolitsyna, Yannis Fronimos, Nico Rose, Seph Fontane Pennock, and Nick Brown, the last of whom also graciously read through an early draft of the book. Of course, any errors or inconsistencies in my treatment of the words are my fault alone.

Finally, my heartfelt thanks to everyone who has contributed to the lexicography: my family, friends, colleagues, students, and all those people whom I've never met but who nevertheless have generously written to me offering suggestions, advice, and enthusiasm for the project. You give me faith to continue working on it, knowing that my efforts are appreciated. Thank you so much to all of you; I would be nowhere without you. And to everyone, I hope that you enjoy the book.

1 Mapping Well-Being

This is a book about words and the influence they wield over our lives, particularly our well-being.* It is also a book about how certain dimensions and experiences of well-being can be hidden from us because we lack the words to identify and understand them. Finally it is a book about the possibility of discovering these "missing" words through engaging with other languages. For, oftentimes, another culture has identified and named the phenomenon in question. Others have a word for it, even if we don't, which makes these words untranslatable, in common parlance.

Such words are not merely intellectual curiosities. The spirit here is not "How strange that x have a word for y," as if we were idly perusing a catalog of foreign lands with no intention of visiting. Rather, the animating principle behind this book is that such words may be valuable to us personally— as academics seeking to better understand well-being, and as people trying to live the best lives we can.

Roughly speaking, aside from providing appreciative insights into the culture that created them, the potential value of untranslatable words with respect to our own lives is twofold: (a) they can help us understand and articulate experiences with which we may already be vaguely familiar but for which we lack a corresponding concept; and (b) they can lead us to seek out and cultivate new experiences, with the possibility of expanding and enriching our existential horizons. This chapter will elaborate upon these points, laying out the theoretical foundation for the book, and elucidating

---

*I do not explicitly define well-being here at the outset because this book is about arriving at a better, more nuanced and comprehensive, understanding of well-being. This understanding will be elucidated throughout the book and summarized in the concluding chapter. Suffice it to say, I use well-being here as an overarching term, encapsulating all the ways in which people might hope to be well.

how untranslatable words can improve our understanding and experience of well-being. First though, to help readers appreciate the value of such words, I will outline my perspective on words generally.*

The premise of this book is that words provide a map that can help people navigate their existence. The map is not a new metaphor in this context. The image was previously the great insight of Alfred Korzybski, creator of general semantics, a school of thought aimed at understanding and improving language use. Korzybski likened reality to physical terrain and language to a map charting it. This was a generally precise relation. "A map is not the territory it represents," he wrote, "but, if correct, it has a similar structure to the territory, which accounts for its usefulness."[1] In other words, just because a person knows the word "love," for example, that does not mean they know experientially what it is like to *be in* love, with all the depth of feeling that involves. Nevertheless, so long as language is not mistaken for the reality it signifies, it can offer a helpful guide.

If language functions like a map, with words constituting specific features of this map, this leads us to a foundational point: not all maps are the same, since languages differ in how they delineate the world. These differences are revealed most starkly by untranslatable words, the central focus of this book. Crucially, though, these divergences between linguistic maps are not necessarily an epistemological problem; they may be very useful. For, by comparing maps and seeing how other cultures have configured theirs, we may be able to further develop and refine our own. And as we do, our understanding and appreciation of the world may be enriched accordingly.

In this chapter, I introduce these ideas over three main sections, thereby elucidating the theoretical basis of this book and the lexicography it describes. The first section expands upon the idea that language functions like a map, suggesting that in so doing it facilitates a form of "experiential cartography." The second section raises the possibility that we have much to gain from studying the maps (i.e., languages) of other cultures,

---

*Throughout, I use "words" to encompass morphemes (the smallest linguistic unit that can carry meaning) and lexemes (the basic lexical unit of language, usually a word or several words, involving an abstract unit underlying a given set of inflected forms). I also often use "words" as a synecdoche for "language," which can be regarded as a system of words.

particularly their untranslatable words. In the third section, I argue that such words can enrich our understanding and experience of well-being.

Experiential Cartography

The central metaphor in this book is cartography, the making of maps. To appreciate this metaphor, consider the phenomenon of real-world cartography. We find ourselves immersed in an environment of near incomprehensible scale and complexity. Setting aside the infinite scale of the cosmos, we inhabit a planet boasting a land mass of nearly 58 million square miles, an astonishingly large terrain which nevertheless comprises less than 30 percent of Earth's surface.[2] The most viable way to get any cognitive purchase on this vast physical milieu, to reach any form of genuine comprehension, is to map it.

Cartography has been a constant throughout human history. Drawings speculatively identified as charts of visible star constellations were etched onto cave walls at Lascaux in France as far back as 16,500 BCE.[3] It is apparently a deep human impulse to capture the environment in graphic form, transposing the three-dimensional world into meaningful two-dimensional (flat) or three-dimensional (model) representations. This endeavor has enabled societies to prosper in numerous ways, from navigating to other lands, to accounting for and managing their own territories.[4] Explorers would chart far-flung regions for compatriots back home and future travelers. And mapmakers of all sorts have taken advantage of one of the most powerful features of cartography: the principle of scalable granularity.[5] This refers to the capacity of maps to take on comparable levels of complexity irrespective of the actual size of the terrain represented. Thus, a country might produce maps of its territory as a whole, yet it is possible to generate equally detailed maps of specific locales within. An architect, say, can configure an area no bigger than a single building.

Words perform a function comparable to that of maps, helping people represent their world. In saying that, I do not just mean the physical world, as charted by conventional maps. I also mean our internal, subjective world of thoughts and feelings. I shall refer to these two worlds collectively as our experiential world.

In representing the experiential world, languages do not merely share superficial similarity with geographical maps but also replicate many of the deep features that make them so powerful. These include the capacity to (a) signify a world comprising multiple dimensions, (b) create boundaries to delineate this world, (c) show how different parts of the world stand in relation to one another, (d) capture aspects of reality using scalable granularity, and (e) guide understanding of familiar and unfamiliar environments. I will briefly touch upon these points in turn, which I conceptualize as five principles underpinning maps and words alike.

The Dimensionality Principle

The first point of similarity between maps and words is their ability to signify a world comprising multiple dimensions, which I call the dimensionality principle. Conventional geographical maps can render the complex, three-dimensional topology of the physical world in a simplified but proportionally accurate two-dimensional representation. Maps also can encode dimensions beyond the standard three of physical space. For instance, maps produced by the Malaria Atlas Project, detailing the global burden of the disease, account for time parameters.[6]

Words possess a similar capacity, signifying the world around us by attaching labels to salient features of this world. This claim is not without its caveats and complexities: philosophy abounds with debates about the nature of reality and the extent to which it can be perceived and appraised. However, notwithstanding solipsistic forms of subjective idealism associated with scholars such as Edmund Husserl,[7] most thinkers agree that: there is a world that exists independently of people; people can become aware of and understand this world to an extent; awareness and understanding are mediated by psychological and social processes; and language is prominent among these processes. As with maps, then, a key function of words is to help us conceptualize the physical world. This includes delineating the configuration of objects in space—via orienting words (e.g., top, north), and labels for objects (e.g., coast, mountain)—and specifying properties of the world (e.g., color, temperature).

Along with the external physical world, words also represent the internal phenomenological world of qualia. Like the external world, the internal possesses multiple dimensions. Consider an influential neuropsychological model in consciousness studies, the state-space paradigm developed by Juergen Fell.[8] This model is situated within the broader neural correlates of consciousness (NCC) approach, a contemporary way of engaging with the perennial mind-body problem.[9] The NCC approach is based on a premise of psychophysical isomorphism—that is, states of mind are accompanied by analogous neurophysical states. At this relatively early point in our understanding of the brain, knowledge is not sufficiently advanced to definitively ascertain directional causality—whether the brain "causes" the mind, or vice versa—or resolve the ontological mind-body problem—*how* NCCs are connected to conscious states. Rather, the NCC approach just aims to chart the neurophysiological correlates of mental states.

The state-space model is one way of conceptualizing this correlation. It invites us to view both subjectivity ("the mind") and brain activity ("the body") as state-spaces of n dimensions (i.e., comprising any number of dimensions). Thus, the n-dimensional state-space of the mind encompasses every possible quale: all thoughts, feelings, emotions, sensations, perceptions, and any other phenomena that a human is capable of experiencing.[10] A given experiential state will therefore occupy a "location" somewhere in this n-dimensional phenomenological state-space of the mind. The theory holds that this location will correlate with a comparable location in the n-dimensional physiological state-space of the brain.

Consider, for example, a subjective feeling of pleasure. According to the state-space model, this experience is constituted by the configuration of a person's mental state-space along many dimensions, including valence (how enjoyable the feeling is), intensity (how strong), duration, frequency, significance (how meaningful), and so on. A given mental state-space configuration correlates with an analogous neurophysiological state-space configuration pertaining to neural processes, such as the activation of specific brain regions and the release of certain neurotransmitters. Should the configurations change in any way—say, a reduction in subjective intensity, accompanied by a concomitant attenuation of the analogous brain-state dimension—the feeling of pleasure would change, shifting perhaps from a state we might refer to as "joy" into a less aroused state identified as "contentment."

As that last sentence indicates, words are capable of capturing and representing specific configurations of our n-dimensional experiential world (which, to reiterate, comprises both the internal state-space of our subjectivity, and the external state-space of the world around us). That is, words enable us to map this world, a process I refer to as experiential cartography. This process begins with drawing boundaries, as the next principle elucidates.

The Boundary Principle

I call the second point of commonality between maps and words the boundary principle: both delineate the world by imposing boundaries upon it. In the case of geographical maps, territory is made comprehensible by the imposition of borders, which, for example, circumscribe nation-states. The lines drawn are frequently arbitrary (though not always, e.g., in the case of coastlines), based on political agendas (and associated power dynamics), and exist due to flexible social conventions. Nevertheless, such lines are real in their effects. For example, they determine the territory to which a given people is granted claim. A similar process happens with words. One way in which language renders our experiential world comprehensible is by demarcating boundaries, carving up its complexity into cognitively digestible pieces. This involves the delineation of objects (via nouns and pronouns), processes (verbs), qualities (adjectives and adverbs), relationships (prepositions and conjunctions), and communicative acts (interjections).

To appreciate how this process of boundary imposition works with respect to the external world, imagine a person who finds herself in a new city, on an unknown street. Her senses are bombarded by thousands of unfamiliar stimuli. And yet, she is not completely bewildered. Based on past experience, her mind is able to parse the scene into comprehensible components. In this she is aided in no small part by language, which enables her to apply labels to what she encounters: man, woman, pavement, road, car, shop, restaurant, and so on.

We likewise segment our internal world. To return to the example of pleasure, we become accustomed to demarcating a particular configuration of valence, intensity, duration, and so on as "joy," and a related but different configuration as "contentment." To be more accurate, it is not so much that we identify a particular *point* within this n-dimensional space as joy or as contentment. Rather, we draw boundaries within a given dimension, creating a localized *range*. The several ranges thereby produce a *region* of state-space corresponding to one or another experience. Thus joy might encompass a range of values toward the excitable end of the intensity spectrum, whereas a more muted span of values might be designated as contentment. Of course, words can be defined in different ways by different people and, indeed, by the same person at different times. These regions therefore are not precisely demarcated. It is better to think of them as a hazy cloud of probabilities, arising from the overlapping definitions people ascribe to the word in question.

In considering this drawing of boundaries, one point is especially important—a point made with particular eloquence by that broad school of thought known as social constructionism.[11] Linguistic boundaries, like territorial ones, are drawn in somewhat arbitrary fashion. They are subject to convention. This is easy to appreciate when the boundaries are fuzzy or occluded: the distinction between a restaurant and a café, say, is not obvious or pre-given. It is a boundary that different cultures and people draw in their own ways, or not at all. Similarly, when it comes to feelings, it may not be clear how joy differs from elation. The subjective state-spaces represented by these words are not self-evidently demarcated but rather are determined by convention.

One of the great insights of constructionism is that even categories that many people and cultures take for granted as "natural"—such as sexual distinctions separating people into men and women—are to an extent socially created.[12] As with maps though, these constructed boundaries are still powerful, regulating lives in important ways. The challenges faced by people who do not align with binary sexual categories attest to this.[13]

What is important for our purposes is that, because language reflects processes of social construction, there are potentially many ways of carving up the experiential state-space using words. Moreover, we'll find that different cultures do indeed carve it up in varying ways. The conceptual and experiential possibilities that these differences offer—specifically, experiences of well-being influenced by the varied construction of language across cultures—are at the heart of this book.

The Network Principle

We've seen that both words and maps are able to delineate and represent n-dimensional state-space (the dimensionality principle), doing so by demarcating boundaries within it (the boundary principle). This brings us to the third point of similarity between maps and words: the network principle.

This refers to the notion that both maps and words are configured structurally as networks. Their elements do not make sense in isolation, obtaining meaning only from their situation relative to each other. In geo-graphical maps, the elements form one interrelated schematic, charting the lay of the land as a whole. This enables people to see how territories inter-sect and how elements are configured within those territories. That lan-guage is similar was the great insight of Ferdinand de Saussure, the founder of structuralism.[14] He argued that words, and the phenomena they signify, derive meaning from their position within networks of other linguistic signs.[15] The concept of man, for instance, only makes sense in relation to oppositional terms that help to define it, such as woman, boy, and animal, with each of these juxtapositions framing the idea of man in a slightly dif-ferent way. As Claude Lévi-Strauss put it, "Looking beyond the empirical facts to the meaning between them" is "more intelligible" than analyzing phenomena in isolation.[16]

In early structuralism, language networks were largely regarded as fixed. However, this perspective was superseded by poststructuralism, which rec-ognized the dynamic nature of these networks. Influential theorists such as Jacques Derrida argued that meaning is not static[17] but, as Geneviève Rail puts it, "slippery and elusive"[18]—open to multiple and shifting interpreta-tions. To return to the example of sex categories, this slipperiness is seen in the way that dichotomies such as man and woman are increasingly con-tested in today's more gender-aware cultural climate.[19] But even if mean-ings are fluid, they still form within a network of relations.

This interrelatedness of words has three key features. The first could be called their proximity aspect. This refers to the idea that conceptually simi-lar words signify phenomena situated near one another within state-space. For instance, contentment, joy, and bliss all occupy the broader realm of positive emotions. People often have a folk understanding of this proximity aspect, an intuitive sense of how words relate to each other conceptually and how similar or dissimilar they are to one another.[20] It is then the task of fields such as psychology to map this conceptual space by means of a nomological network.[21]

Words are also related hierarchically, just as the brain itself organizes information.[22] Actually, hierarchy is not quite the right word, since this has connotations of top-down rule, whereby higher-level elements dominate lower-level ones. A preferable term, coined by Arthur Koestler, is holarchy.[23] This notion derives from another of Koestler's neologisms, *holon*, which was adapted etymologically from the Greek *holos*, meaning all or whole, and the suffix *on*, suggestive of a part or particle. Koestler proposed *holon* to reflect the idea that everything in existence is simultaneously a whole and a part. For example, a person is a whole being yet part of a family; a family is a whole unit yet part of a community; and so on. Each element in any system is a holon: a whole unit relative to the level beneath it, as a family is with respect to its members, and a constituent part relative to the level above it, as a family is with respect to the community. Thus a holarchy refers to this arrangement in which holons are embedded within larger holons, which are in turn nested within still-larger holons.

So, to rephrase the sentence above, the second aspect of the interrelatedness of words is that they—and the phenomena they refer to—can generally be arranged into holarchies. Contentment, joy, and bliss can all be aggregated into the broader category of emotions—which itself can be grouped with categories such as thoughts, sensations, and perceptions into an overarching category of qualia. In terms of my state-space metaphor, each broader category covers a larger area of n-dimensional space than the finer-grained categories encompassed within it. Thus, qualia spans a larger area of state-space than emotions, which in turn covers more ground than specific emotions such as contentment or joy. In the context of this book, our overarching category of concern is well-being. This encompasses a very broad region of state-space, which includes feelings (discussed in chapter 2), relationships (chapter 3), and personal development (chapter 4). It is possible to arrange state-space holarchies in any number of ways according to one's agenda and priorities.

Finally, words do not only make sense in relation to concepts that are close to them in state-space (the proximity aspect), or in relation to their location within various holarchies (the holarchical aspect). Words also derive meaning from the complex associations they form with other words. Here I'm picturing a vast, intricate web of links, in which each region of state-space—as represented by a word—is connected with many other different regions. A good analogy might be neural networks, in which each of the approximately 100 billion neurons in the average brain is connected to as many as tens of thousands of other neurons, generating up to 1,000 trillion synaptic links.[24] Something similar occurs with words. This I call the "web aspect" of the network principle. Words come to be associated with a complex pattern of other signifiers, which helps give them their meanings.[25] This happens at a cultural and an individual level. For instance, in the

United States, the place-name Gettysburg has accrued a weighty network of connections to culturally important concepts relating to the American Civil War, which freights the word with significance. On a personal level, as individuals grow up, each forges idiosyncratic systems of associations with respect to specific terms. For example, we all come to associate happiness with a unique set of phenomena—certain people, places, actions, objects, and so on—whose salience is a product of personal experience.

The Granularity Principle

The notion of a holarchically arranged network brings us to the fourth principle: scalable granularity. As we saw earlier, this refers to the way maps can take on comparable levels of complexity irrespective of the size of the terrain represented, in a way somewhat analogous to Mandelbrot's fractals.[26] Google Maps makes this process vivid: as one zooms in on an area, the map's granularity increases accordingly.

Language possesses similar power. To appreciate this, imagine a child entering school. He will gradually be introduced to a global cognitive map of phenomena, which will become increasingly familiar and more detailed over time. One "continent" may be the arts, another science, a third history, and so on. At first, these continents may lack any internal differentiation; the child has just a vague sense that art differs from science in some way. Soon though, he will begin to draw rudimentary boundaries separating the continents: music, painting, and dancing within the arts; biology, chemistry, and physics within science; and so on.

Essentially, the child is learning to recognize and create holarchies. Moreover, the principle of scalable granularity means it is possible to create increasingly fine-grained differentiations within these holarchies, repeatedly introducing new levels of complexity. The child may become passionate about music, for instance, and begin to zoom in on this area, learning to segment it according to music styles—classical, rock, reggae, and so on. Before starting school, these distinctions would probably not have been apparent conceptually or even perceptually; the child would have been able neither to recognize and label a particular style nor even, perhaps, to register the difference between them aurally. Maybe he had the inchoate intuition that songs heard differed in some indefinable way. But all that he was likely aware of was a vague region of experience labeled "music."

However, as the child develops, he learns to zoom in perceptually and mentally, becoming cognizant of ever more precise distinctions.

This process of zooming in can continue almost indefinitely. An interest in classical music may lead our student to learn to delineate different forms, from baroque to avant-garde. He may go on to study classical music at university, a context in which these distinctions would become yet more fine-grained. He will learn to distinguish aurally between sounds (recognizing a major from a minor seventh, say) and to identify and critique the work of different composers. He will also acquire terminological fluency enabling description of differences among pieces, from *allegro* to *andante*. Indeed, mastery of the granular terminology of a topic could be regarded as the essence of expertise.[27] This point is central to the book, which is based on the premise that, by learning new vocabulary relating to well-being, people can cultivate greater expertise with respect to it.

The Guidance Principle

This notion of zooming in toward greater levels of expertise brings me to the final parallel between maps and words. I call it the guidance principle. Maps and words both constitute guides to existence. Geographical maps help people navigate their current surroundings and venture into new territory. Words have the power to do something similar. For a start, they enable us to orient ourselves with respect to what we are currently experiencing. Consider the condition alexithymia, whereby a person is unable to recognize or verbalize emotions.[28] Both an alexithymic and a person else considered to possess high emotional differentiation might experience comparable feelings—intense joy, frustrated anger, and so on. However, whereas the alexithymic may be confused and even bewildered by his feelings, the high-differentiation individual has a precise awareness of what she is experiencing and is able to accurately identify her qualia. It is as if both people are in the same geographical location, but while the second benefits from a highly detailed map, the first has nothing more than a vague outline.

Furthermore, just as maps enable adventurers to travel to new lands, so too can words help us explore novel experiential realms. They alert us to phenomena we might not have previously encountered, or even been aware of, and can invite us to engage with these. Return to the example of the student becoming acquainted with classical music. There is a vast wealth of words pertaining to this genre—names of composers, historical periods, terms for musical styles and motifs. To a child with little appreciation for classical music, most of these words would be meaningless—signs whose referents are unknown. Encountering these words would be like glancing at a map of a foreign country he had never even heard of. But, just as the map may entice and even enable a visit to this distant land, so too might these music-related words invite our student to explore the world of classical music. In accepting the invitation, he would open himself up to a new realm of experiences, encountering a range of unfamiliar stimuli (e.g., musical pieces) and concomitant qualia (e.g., feelings). It is my contention that the words featured in this book likewise invite and enable people to experience phenomena relating to well-being that had hitherto been unfamiliar to or hidden from them.

Now, having elucidated the deep parallels between language and geographical maps, we can return to a key point: languages differ in how they chart the experiential world. As we shall see, this diversity opens a wealth of possibilities in terms of how we experience and understand life.

The Impact of Language and Culture

Having outlined a cartographic model of language, I can now address the point at the heart of this book: different languages carve up and map experiential state-space in different ways.* For as the world's cultures and countries have developed language systems, they have had cause to create subtly different configurations of boundaries. This in turn affects how people in those cultures experience and understand the world. This claim has come to be known as the Sapir-Whorf hypothesis.

*This is not only true for broadly constituted languages associated with particular nations, such as French, but also for the myriad dialects and speech communities within these languages. That is, a broad definition of language is "the words, their pronunciation, and the methods of combining them used and understood by a community." By this definition, even within a nationally identifiable language, such as French, are many different languages, overlapping, but nonetheless differing in subtle ways. These include regional dialects and the jargon generated within specific subcultures. However, while I aim to bear this internal diversity in mind, I largely keep the discussion at a more macro level, referring to languages associated with whole nation states (e.g., French) and large cultural groupings (e.g., the Inuit).

The Sapir–Whorf Hypothesis

The notion that culture, via language, influences thought has a long pedigree. This "linguistic relativity" principle traces back at least as far as the philosophers Johann Gottfried Herder (1744–1803) and Wilhelm von Humboldt (1767–1835).[29] Herder was at the forefront of a Romantic nationalism that celebrated the uniqueness of the German "spirit" and valorized the German culture in which it was manifest. Crucially here, he attributed to language a pivotal role in the creation of this spirit. His seminal "Essay on the Origin of Language" helped to instantiate the idea of an intimate and unique relationship between a given people's language and psychology.[30] Humboldt's philological study of the Basque language reinforced the point.[31] Both scholars theorized that differences in the mentalities of individual cultures derive in part from the nature of their language, which in turn is shaped by variables such as climate and geography.

Later, these ideas found their most influential articulation through the work of anthropologist Edward Sapir[32] and his student Benjamin Lee Whorf.[33] They argued that language plays a constitutive role in the way people experience, understand, and even perceive the world.[34] As Whorf put it in 1956, "We dissect nature along lines laid out by our native languages. … The world is presented as a kaleidoscopic flux of impressions which has to be organized … largely by the linguistic systems in our minds."[35] Whorf's dissection is the process of drawing boundaries, demarcating distinct regions of state-space.

As with many influential theories, the Sapir–Whorf hypothesis has generated considerable debate over the years, and has been adapted and construed by scholars in various ways. One question is just how strong claims of this sort ought to be. The strong-form hypothesis is effectively linguistic determinism, whereby language is seen as constitutive of thought. Relatedly, cognitive psychologists such as Lev Vygotsky and Valentin Voloshinov[36] have argued for the inescapable intertwining of language and thought (albeit in a reciprocal, mutually constitutive way, rather than the former simply "determining" the latter). Voloshinov argued that the mind is fundamentally semiotic in nature, and that "outside the material of signs there is no psyche." Sapir and Whorf also tended toward a strong stance. For example, Whorf assessed that, because the grammar of the Hopi language appeared to forego a linear sense of past, present, and future, the Hopi people experience time differently from Western peoples. Articulating

Sapir and Whorf's position, Penny Lee submits that there is "little point in arguing about whether language influences thought or thought influences language for the two are functionally entwined to such a degree in the course of individual development that they form a highly complex, but nevertheless systematically coherent, mode of cognitive activity which is not usefully described in conventionally dichotomizing terms as either 'thought' or 'language.'"[37]

The strong, determinist perspective has been challenged by critics arguing in various ways for greater universality in human experience, irrespective of language or culture. For instance, Steven Pinker has countered that the Hopi experience of time does not differ greatly from that of Western peoples, in part because the brain innately perceives and organizes phenomena linearly.[38]

A milder form of the Sapir–Whorf hypothesis, known as linguistic relativism, is more widely accepted.[39] This form simply holds that language *shapes* thought and experience, without determining it. This is my own position. As elucidated below, I contend that we can experience phenomena in the absence of language. That is, even if we lack the linguistic tools (e.g., a specific word) to identify and conceptualize something, we can still experience it. That said, these tools—untranslatable words, say—are cognitively useful, enabling better understanding of the phenomenon in question.

Against my view, a strong determinist might argue that we cannot consciously experience a phenomenon without a way of representing it in language. This appears to be Steven Katz's stance with respect to spiritual experiences, for example.[40] He takes issue with the claim, associated with Aldous Huxley,[41] that there is a common core of mystical experiences accessed by contemplatives across cultures. Katz argues that it is impossible to have a "pure" spiritual experience—say, of a divine presence—unmediated by conceptual or cultural baggage. Every experience is necessarily filtered through the semiotic prism of conceptual thought. However, scholars such as Donald Evans and Richard King disagree.[42] They argue that even if, after the event, people conceptualize and interpret spiritual experiences using culturally situated language, the event itself may be experienced directly, without conceptual mediation.

Indeed, King argues that any experience, not just mystical ones, can be unmediated. Even a mundane act such as drinking coffee, though mediated by cultural factors and personal expectations, "cannot be reduced to those factors alone." Picture someone unfamiliar with the notion of coffee, consuming the beverage for the first time. Though she has no term for or experience with the drink, she will still have a direct sensory experience of its taste. Using the principles elucidated above, we might say she is entering a new region of experiential state-space. She has not yet learned to demarcate this space, thereby creating a region labeled "coffee." After the event, as she inquires into a signifier (i.e., a word) for this new referent (i.e., the experience of drinking coffee), the region becomes circumscribed and labeled accordingly. As time goes by, she may link coffee to a network of associations—with pleasure or energy, for instance—that color the experience of drinking it. But the initial taste was purely a sensory event requiring no cultural mediation through language.*

However, even if people can experience phenomena for which they lack a conceptual label, the milder version of the Sapir–Whorf hypothesis may still apply. Though pure sensory experience is possible, culture, via language, can influence that experience.

Language and Culture

A key way in which language shapes experience is through the boundaries it creates within the experiential world. Crucially, languages all differ in this respect, which influences how their speakers experience and understand their lives. For a start, by demarcating a region of state-space and labeling it with a word, language creates salient objects. While it is possible to notice and experience those objects even if one's attention hasn't been guided by language, this outcome is arguably less likely. For instance, as I discuss in more detail in the next chapter, speakers of Japanese have developed a range of aesthetic concepts—*wabi-sabi*, famously—to express appreciation of ephemerality and the passage of time. In theory anyone could have a

---

*The sensory nature of this experience has further implications for language. It is often suggested that so-called mystical experiences are ineffable, since they cannot be adequately expressed in words. But this arguably applies to all experiences. Until our hypothetical coffee-drinker tried the beverage for the first time, there would be no way to accurately convey to her the nature of coffee's taste. We would have to rely on familiar, but generic, gustatory qualities such as bitterness and heat. If she had heard the term "coffee" before, without encountering the relevant region of state-space (i.e., drinking it), this word would be an empty signifier, a label whose referent is experientially unknown. This point applies to all aspects of existence, from the feeling of love to the smell of a rose.

well-developed sense for this particular aesthetic, but one is more likely to encounter, recognize, and cultivate such values within a culture that has expressly identified them. Thanks to its demarcating language, Japanese speakers have the conceptual tools with which to represent and articulate these time-based aesthetics and so develop a richer and more sophisticated understanding of them. Non-speakers may of course have an intuitive appreciation of such aesthetics, but, without concerted attention guided by language, gain at best a vague, inchoate sensitivity to them.[43]

But *why* do languages differ in how they carve up the world? According to Anna Wierzbicka, one of the foremost scholars in this area, many of these differences can be attributed to the nature of the culture that created and/or uses the language in question.[44] Here I use the term "culture" in the broadest possible sense, following Margaret McLaren, who defines it as "the way we are, both physically and mentally."[45] The "we" could be found at any scale, from the supranational (e.g., the West) to a local neighborhood.* Culture encompasses the ways in which group members conduct their lives, manage their relationships, express their thoughts and feelings, arrange work (i.e., modes of production), and so on. Culture also refers to the way in which groups engage with and respond to myriad factors that influence their existence—factors both nonhuman (e.g., geography, climate) and human (e.g., the group's history and traditions, relationships with other groups). Although cultures are not isolated monads—a point to which I will

---

*All people possess an idiosyncratic lexicon, derived from their membership in a unique set of cultural groupings. Since cultural units can be identified at various scales, it follows that individuals may belong to or identify with a number of cultural groups situated at these varied scales. And if each of these cultural groups is regarded as having its own language—or its own niche within, or version of, a widely shared language such as English—then individuals may well be versed in multiple languages. (That's aside from potentially being bi- or multilingual, e.g., fluent in English and French.) For example, I am affiliated with at least four English-speaking cultural groups, each of which contributes to a distinct lexicon within the broad context of English. At a macro-level, I am a citizen of the English-speaking West. On a more micro-level, my language use has been shaped by my experience growing up in London in the 1980s and 90s. I am also part of the transnational community of psychologists, through which I've been inducted into certain terminology and forms of discourse. Finally, my longtime immersion in music has endowed me with concepts and idioms particular to that art. My lexicon is thus the product of terms I have acquired from these varied affiliations.

turn shortly—it is fair to say that a relatively stable set of attributes defines individual groups and binds the people within. Language is one source of these ties; as Wierzbicka notes, "There is a very close link between the life of a society and the lexicon of the language spoken by it."[46]

Consider a famous—or possibly infamous—example of the intersection of language and culture: the notion that "Eskimos" have many different words for snow.* This claim has reached the status of an urban legend, while also attracting criticism for being misleading and promoting a mis-understanding of the nature of language.[47] The intricacies of the debate around this topic shed light on whether languages do indeed carve up the experiential world in unique ways.

The apparently unusual diversity of Eskimo words for snow was first described by the pioneering anthropologist Franz Boas, Sapir's mentor. In his 1911 *Handbook of American Indian Languages*, Boas noted four different Eskimo words for varieties of snow: *aput* (snow on the ground), *gana* (falling snow), *piqsirpoq* (drifting snow), and *qimuqsuq* (a snow drift).[48] Whorf later added three more terms, leading to all manner of imaginative expansions, until some reports suggested there are as many as 400 different Eskimo words on this theme.[49]

Amid such runaway inflation, Geoffrey Pullum describes the whole notion as a "hoax."[50] Yet the situation is perhaps a little more nuanced. The

---

*Eskimo is an umbrella term for the indigenous peoples of the northern circumpolar region, including Eastern Siberia, Alaska, Canada, and Greenland. These peoples are usually differentiated into two main groups: the Inuit of Canada and Greenland, together with the Inupiat of Alaska; and the Yupik of Alaska and Eastern Siberia. Collectively, their languages and those of the Aleutian Islands are referred to as Eskimo-Aleut languages. Although the term "Eskimo" is generally acceptable in Alaska, elsewhere it is regarded as contentious and even derogatory, with "Inuit" usually being preferred in Canada and Greenland. The Alaska Native Language Center puts forward a possible explanation for these divergences. It is widely thought that the appellation "Eskimo" was imparted by outsiders, meaning "eater of raw meat" (although some linguists now believe it may derive from an Ojibwa word meaning "to net snowshoes"). As such, in Canada and Greenland, the indigenous term "Inuit"—which means simply "people"—is preferred. Yet whereas in Canada and Greenland the indigenous peoples are in fact Inuit, the United States is home also to Inupiat and Yupik, hence perhaps the preference for the more encompassing "Eskimo." Thus, discussions on this topic tend to refer to Eskimos (rather than Inuit). Consequently, in keeping with standard practice, I shall also use that term here, although these nuances should be borne in mind.

issue comes down to what we mean by a word. As Pullum notes, Eskimo-Aleut languages are agglutinative, meaning that complex words are easily created by combining morphemes. For example, the West Greenlandic word *siku*, meaning ice, can be combined with other morphemes to create many compounds, such as *sikuliaq* (pack ice), *sikuaq* (new ice), and *sikurluk* (melting ice). An agglutinative language could, in theory, have almost an unlimited range of words pertaining to snow.

As Pullum sees it, this means that, even if Eskimos technically have many different words for snow, they do not necessarily possess greater lexical complexity in this arena than do English speakers. The difference is just that, in English, we use adjectives rather than agglutination, creating compound phrases such as "melting snow."

But while Pullum is technically correct, I disagree in pragmatic terms, as the size and scope of a lexicon ultimately are determined by usage. Yes, both Eskimo and English speakers can articulate many terms relating to snow and ice, the former through agglutination, the latter through adjectival phrases. But that doesn't mean English speakers do so in practice. Eskimo culture is influenced by a physical environment dominated by snow and ice in a way that most English-speaking cultures are not. As such, Eskimo-Aleut languages contain many more snow-and-ice words in common usage than does English. In his analysis of the North Sami language of the Arctic and sub-Arctic, for instance, Ole Henrik Magga points out that knowledge of snow and ice is a "necessity for subsistence and survival."[51] Magga estimates that there are over a thousand such lexemes in common usage. By contrast, snow and ice are not a significant factor in the geography where English first developed. As a result, terms for snow and ice are not prominent in English as it is mostly used, even if, theoretically, such terms could proliferate in English-speaking cultures. However, in English-speaking contexts where snow and ice *are* prominent—for instance in subcultures centered on skiing or snowboarding[52]—then the lexicon may be enriched accordingly.

But overall, this general difference between Eskimo-Aleut and English languages nicely illustrates the cartographic principles at the heart of this book. Both Eskimo and English-speaking cultures can, in theory, access a similar state-space, here concerning the ability to perceive or identify different types of snow and ice. However, due to cultural factors (e.g., geography), these cultures do not carve up the state-space in the same way.

As snow and ice are of existential importance in Eskimo cultures, speakers of Eskimo languages find it prudent to impose many more boundaries on this state-space—per the principle of granularity—thereby allowing finer-grained distinctions. Conversely, it strikes me that English speakers have developed a particularly rich lexicon with respect to rain, which befits the climatic conditions of places like the United Kingdom.

I think it's therefore reasonable to assert that cultures linguistically parse the world in idiosyncratic ways that differentially influence how people in those cultures experience and understand life. But cultures are not hermetically sealed, nor are they fixed in time. They are, as Wierzbicka puts it, "heterogeneous, historically changing, interconnected, and ... 'continually exchanging materials.'"[53] Thus the linguistic boundaries that cultures impose are not static either. These boundaries constantly evolve in part through individual cultures' interactions with each other. A fascinating example of such exchange, central to this book, is words.

Borrowing Words

When people strive to describe the cultural dynamism of the United States, they often choose the metaphor of a melting pot, evoking the intermingling of people from all parts of the globe. Less commonly noted is that English itself is such a melting pot, borrowing and assimilating words from multiple languages in ways that undoubtedly leave it enriched, that is, capable of delineating the world with greater nuance and detail.* Indeed, the language itself came into being through borrowing and has continued to evolve that way.

The roots of English lie in Proto-Germanic languages, which are part of the broader Indo-European language family. Although the historical details are speculative and much debated, Anthony Grant suggests that these Proto-Germanic languages began to diversify from the Indo-European tree around 500 BCE. Northwest Germanic split off first, followed a few hundred years later by West Germanic.[54] It was from the latter that English began to emerge around the fifth century CE, when the British Isles were invaded and settled by three Germanic tribes: the Angles, Saxons, and Jutes,

---

*This point applies to most languages, as do most other principles and ideas discussed in this book. However, the book is written from the perspective of English, so the discussion centers there.

together with a smaller number of Franks and Frisians.[55] As these groups attained dominance in England, their West-Germanic language supplanted those of Roman Britain, namely Latin and Brittonic.[56] Subsequently, this imported language evolved through three main phases: Old English (ca. 450–1100 CE), Middle English (ca. 1100–1500), and Modern English, itself split into early (ca. 1500–1800) and late periods (1800–).[57] One feature of this evolution was lexicalization: adding new words and phrases to the corpus of vocabulary.[58]

Sometimes lexicalization involves coining new words. This occurs when morphemes are combined in novel ways (e.g., "Brexit"). It also occurs when existing words are creatively adapted, as in the case of "boredom," which entered English in 1852 when Charles Dickens deployed the verb "to bore"—to pierce or wear down—to depict Lady Dedlock's apathetic state in his novel *Bleak House*.[59] Often though, words arrive through borrowing from other languages.[60]

Borrowed words are those that cannot be taken back "to the earliest known stages of a language,"[61] which, in the case of Old English, was mainly the lexicon imported from West Germanic. The first main phase of borrowing occurred following the Norman invasion of 1066. This event inaugurated a new phase of language development—known as Middle English—as the conquerors brought French to the British Isles. The result was a temporary linguistic class division, with the upper echelons of society switching mainly to French while the lower classes continued to speak Old English.[62]

Eventually, English regained dominance, but with the addition of numerous French words. French itself had roots in, and borrowings from, Latin, Arabic, and other languages, just as these had their own influences, especially Greek.[63] Thus some of the French terms borrowed by English themselves derived from elsewhere, producing a chain of transmission. For instance, the word "idea" originates in Greek but traveled via Latin and then French before being adopted by English.[64]

Finally, Modern English borrowed directly from numerous languages, particularly Greek and Latin. And some neologisms, coined for new inventions or concepts, are in fact compounds of Greek and Latin. For instance, television combines the Greek stem *têle* with the Latin *vīsiō*, thereby conveying a meaning of "far seeing."[65]

As such, English is a veritable cornucopia of borrowed words (with cornucopia itself deriving from the Latin *cornu copiae*, a mythical "horn of plenty" that is a symbol of nourishment and abundance).[66] Of the more than 600,000 lexemes in the OED, between 32[67] and 41 percent[68] are thought to be borrowed. (These percentages are relatively high in comparison to other languages. Uri Tadmor estimates a borrowing range of 62 percent at the upper end—for Selice Romani, a dialect in Slovakia—to just 1.2 percent at the lower, namely for Mandarin.[69]) Anthony Grant finds that 25 percent of English lexemes were borrowed from French, 8 percent from Latin, 3.5 percent from Old Norse, 2 percent from Greek, and 1.3 percent from Dutch and Middle-Low German.[70] A further 3.5 percent come from various other languages, including "pepper" (from Sanskrit, via Greek and Latin), "zero" (Arabic, via Italian), "banana" (Wolof, via Spanish), "silk" (Mongolian, via Latin), "tea" (a Tibeto-Burman language, via Chinese, via Dutch), and "taboo" (Tongan). The prevalence of borrowed words has been studied with respect to a wide range of source languages, including Arabic, Japanese, and Spanish.[71]

Collectively, these borrowings are usually referred to as loanwords. However, more specific terminology recognizes that such words can be at different stages of the borrowing process. Appropriately enough, this terminology itself involves loanwords (from German), namely *Gastwörter* (guest-words), *Fremdwörter* (foreignisms), and *Lehnwörter* (loanwords proper).[72] These gradations allow linguists to describe varying degrees of assimilation. Least assimilated are *Gastwörter*, whose foreign status is still explicit. Using the language of immigration, the OED previously referred to these as "aliens"—in contrast to *Fremdwörter*, which were labeled "denizens," and *Lehnwörter*, deemed "naturals." *Gastwörter* usually retain the pronunciation, orthography, grammar, and meaning of their original language; are limited to specialist (e.g., academic) vocabularies; and are italicized in type. *Gastwörter* itself is a *Gastwort*, with its usage in English generally confined to linguists.

Fremdwörter are more fully assimilated. They have been welcomed into the host language as stable and widely used entries in the lexicon, but nevertheless still tend to be perceived as foreign words. A well-known example is *Schadenfreude*, which refers to the pleasure taken in another's misfortune. *Lehnwörter*, finally, are so well integrated into the host language that speakers do not regard, or even recognize, them as being of foreign origin. These words are basically indistinguishable from the rest of the lexicon and are amenable to normal rules of word use and formation. The latter is itself one such word, derived from the Latin *formationem*, via the Old French *formacion*.

In the act of borrowing, the loanword usually becomes an unanalyzable unit in the recipient language.[73] That is, the corresponding word source in the donating language can be complex or even phrasal, but this internal structure is generally lost when it enters the host language. Hence, when transferred to English-speaking contexts, the French notion of *joie de vivre* becomes an indivisible lexeme unto itself, its constituent elements undifferentiated in borrowed usage. That said, if sufficient numbers of semantically related complex words enter a language, it may be possible for speakers to reconstitute and appreciate their morphological structure. This is often the case with neoclassical compounds using Greek or Latin. For instance, speakers may come to appreciate that words featuring the Greek root *ethno-* (e.g., ethnic, ethnography) all relate to nationhood in some way.

Besides loanwords per se, other varieties of borrowing exist. One is loan translations, or calques.[74] In these cases, only the word's meaning is borrowed, not its form. For instance, English includes two near-synonyms for God: omnipotent and almighty. Whereas omnipotent is a genuine *Lehnwort* (from the Latin *omnipotēns*), almighty borrows the meaning, but converts it into English via its component parts (*omni-* = all, *potēns* = mighty). Another variety is the loan blend, which occur when borrowed words are adapted using elements from the host language. For instance, Middle English featured the word *brownetta*, in which "brunette," borrowed from Italian, was combined with the native "brown." We also have semantic borrowing, which occurs when words take on new or additional meanings. Although English had borrowed the verb "to present" from Latin (via French) around the fourteenth century, the word acquired further meanings from French in the sixteenth century (e.g., to put on a show). Last, there is grammatical borrowing. English has assimilated numerous derivational morphemes—particularly from Latin (e.g., pre-) and Greek (e.g., anti-)—many of which can be used with stems of any origin.[75]

And then there exists a further world of words not *yet* borrowed. They could, and arguably should, become loanwords. I'd like to take the liberty of coining a new *Gastwort* to delineate such words: *Fremderwort*, "stranger word." As we'll see in the coming chapters, many such words might be of interest to us, bringing to mind the sentiment that a stranger is just a friend you haven't met.

This brings up a crucial question: Why are words borrowed? Essentially, what unites *Gast-*, *Fremd-*, *Lehn-*, and, *Fremderwörter* is that they often tend to be untranslatable. These words reveal "semantic gaps" in the languages lacking equivalent terms—languages that may then borrow these words to fill such gaps.

Semantic Gaps

Loanwords tend to start out as innovations in speech.[76] This kind of innovation might happen in several ways. Sometimes it arises through code-switching: a bilingual person using words from one language while speaking the other.[77] Sometimes speech innovations derive from socio-political changes, as with the Norman invasion.[78] Then there is the process of cultural influence or hegemony, as with the importation of American English terminology into other cultures over recent decades.[79]

But what makes a loanword stick? What does it do that makes it useful to a host language? To tackle this question, we must keep in mind the distinction between core and cultural borrowings.[80] Core borrowings occur when a new loanword replicates a word that already exists in the host language. The words may coexist; the loanword could replace the native word, which might have already fallen into disuse; or the loanword may augment the native word by introducing previously absent nuances of meaning. Core borrowings often occur for sociolinguistic reasons, whereby foreign words can convey intellectual prestige and cultural capital.[81] While the historical flow of core borrowings is a fascinating topic in itself, it is not of particular concern to us here, since these loanwords have English equivalents, and so are not untranslatable.

By contrast, the second category, cultural borrowing, is central to my purposes. Martin Haspelmath refers to these as "loanwords by necessity," for the recipient language lacks its own word for the referent in question.[82] This sort of borrowing might occur when a new invention, practice, or idea is introduced into a culture. In such cases, a loanword is used for pragmatic reasons: in the absence of an appropriate native word or coinage, the loanword is taken up because it *works*.[83] It is cognitively and socially useful, allowing speakers to articulate notions that they had previously struggled to.

In the terminology of Adrienne Lehrer—who drew on earlier work by Noam Chomsky—such words bridge "lexical gaps."[84] More specifically, they fill *semantic* gaps, which involve "the lack of a convenient word to express what [the speaker] wants to speak about," as Lehrer puts it.[85] This feature of loanwords is clear in Tadmor's analysis of loanword adoption across multiple languages.[86] He observes that borrowing tends to supply words for activities susceptible to the introduction of novel ideas. These include religious practice (an estimated 41 percent of religious terms in most languages are loanwords) and clothing and grooming (39 percent). Aspects of life less susceptible to innovation are less likely to face semantic gaps and thus involve less borrowing. Thus, languages usually provide terms relating to the body (14 percent loanwords), spatial relations (14 percent), and sense perception (11 percent) without recourse to borrowing: these are so basic and immutable that languages rarely have to rely on each other in order to develop appropriate terminology.

One might say that a semantic gap refers to a region of state-space that has not been circumscribed and labeled by a given language. Semantic gaps persist for a variety of reasons. For instance, within the gap might be a phenomenon that speakers of a given language have not experienced in much depth or detail. To return to the example above, since snow is not a prominent part of cultures where English developed, the language has relatively little corresponding terminology.

It may also be that speakers are familiar with the region of state-space in question but carve it up differently than do speakers of other languages. For example, many emotion theorists—most prominently Paul Ekman[87]—contend that people the world over have comparable emotional experiences, that we navigate the same general spectrum of feelings. But languages may delineate this affective terrain in different ways, such as by describing a particular class of emotion in more granular ways. For example, linguists have observed that the English concept of love is "polysemous in the extreme."[88] That is, the term spans a great range of feelings, covering a large swathe of state-space. By contrast, other languages may have developed a more nuanced lexicon to denote various types of love. As I explore in chapter 3, Greek is especially prolific in this regard.[89]

It is semantic gaps that arguably make words untranslatable, and opportune for borrowing. That said, I recognize that the notion of untranslatability can be problematic, and is disliked by some linguists (while others regard it as perfectly acceptable[90]). On the one hand, it could be argued that *no* word is ever truly translatable. As we have seen, post-/structuralism holds that words are embedded within complex webs of meanings and traditions; therefore, something is always lost in the act of translation, some nuance or meaning is not carried over so that the process is always "inexact."[91] On the other hand, it may be that nothing is ever genuinely *un*translatable. As Pullum suggests, even if a term lacks an exact equivalent in another language, it is usually possible to convey a sense of its meaning in a few words, or at most a few sentences. For this reason, some scholars prefer the designation "unlexicalized" to untranslatable. However, I suggest for pragmatic reasons that we retain the notion of untranslatability for cases when there exists no exact match for a term used by speakers of other languages.

The notion of borrowing such words is also problematic. A particular issue is that they do not necessarily retain the meanings they had in their original language. As discussed above in relation to the network principle, every word is embedded within networks of other terms that endow it with meaning. Thus, it is hard to understand a word in isolation from other terms in a system and the ways it is deployed in context. If words are taken out of their donor language, and inserted into a host language, this rich network of associations is not necessarily retained. Indeed, some scholars who endorse strong linguistic determinism argue that unless a person is enmeshed within the culture that produced a given word, he would be unable to fully understand or experience the phenomenon to which the word refers. For instance, Charles Taylor argues there is no way out of the "hermeneutic circle": concepts can only be understood with reference to other concepts within the language to which they belong. As he puts it, "We can often experience what it is like to be on the outside [of the circle] when we encounter the feeling, action, and experiential meaning language of another civilization. Here there is no translation, no way of explaining in other, more accessible concepts."[92]

However, articulating a milder view, Wierzbicka contends that we *can* escape the hermeneutic circle and approximate a feel for the meanings of untranslatable words.[93] True, people not part of a given culture may not appreciate the full richness of a term. As Wierzbicka puts it, using Wittgenstein's revealing phrase, "Verbal explanations of [untranslatable] concepts cannot replace experiential familiarity with them and with their functioning in the local 'stream of life.'"[94] But, Wierzbicka argues, "It is not true that no verbal explanations illuminating to outsiders are possible at all." This is especially the case if one does have some experiential familiarity with the phenomenon in question, however vague, even if one previously lacked a word to signify it.

The word *karma*, for instance, transmits something of its essence even to users who do not understand its structural connection to its original language, Sanskrit. In that context, *karma* refers broadly to causality in ethics. Most English speakers who use this word probably do not know how it relates to other Sanskrit terms nor its wealth of meanings in Hindu and Buddhist teachings. Nevertheless, English speakers find the word useful and arguably deploy it in ways that are not completely discordant with its original meanings.[95] Moreover, in the process of borrowing, loanwords also organically form network connections with relevant concepts in the new host language. For example, English speakers may come to understand *karma* in relation to their own ideas surrounding sin and justice stemming from various Western religious and nonreligious traditions.

In summary, notwithstanding the caveats above about the notion of untranslatability and the nature of the borrowing process, the phenomenon of untranslatable words rests upon the concept of semantic gaps. Visual aids may help to illustrate how semantic gaps relate to the kind of untranslatability I have in mind. The following figures are intended to depict the *n*-dimensional state-space of the experiential world, although it is only possible to portray this on the page as a two-dimensional projection of a three-dimensional area. In the figures, I use spheres to represent the region of state-space delineated by given words. Of course, as noted above, I recognize that words can be defined and deployed in different ways by different people, and, indeed, by the same person at different times. Thus, it is better to regard these circumscribed regions as a hazy cloud of possibilities rather than as a cleanly demarcated area.

As a reference point, figure 1.1 depicts a case in which a non-English word is regarded as having an approximate equivalent in English. I pair the English "love" with its German counterpart, and cognate, *Liebe*.* Because their cultural backgrounds ensure that "love" and *Liebe* have slightly different nuances and layers of meaning, I have represented these as nearly

---

*Liebe is the noun; the verb is *lieben*. Incidentally, in German, all nouns are capitalized in this way, whereas only "proper nouns" are in English. Other parts of speech (e.g., verbs) are uncapitalized.

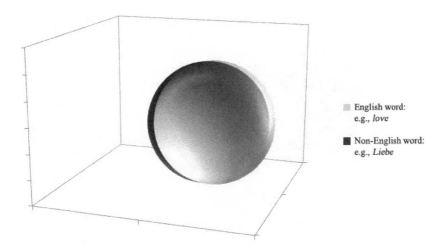

Figure 1.1
Nearly overlapping regions of state-space, representing a near-perfect equivalency between two words.

overlapping spheres—each is a close translation of the other, if not a perfect one.

By contrast, the next three figures represent the three main ways in which a word may be regarded as untranslatable. All three also take the English word "love" as their reference point. Figure 1.2 represents instances in which a non-English word occupies a region of state-space that has not been similarly delineated by any English word. In such cases, it is most likely that some English words capture aspects of the word in question, just as these English words in turn will have referents and meanings not included within the non-English word. I refer to this as "overlap-based" untranslatability, shown here by two somewhat overlapping spheres. The example uses the German term *Sehnsucht*, which roughly translates as "life-longings." *Sehnsucht* encompasses certain features of love, such as a deep appreciation and yearning for some object. However, as psychometric investigation by Susanne Scheibe and colleagues indicate, *Sehnsucht* also incorporates meanings not usually implied by the term love, including dissatisfaction with one's current state, and an appreciation of the ambivalent nature of life (i.e., the recognition that life is inevitably imperfect, and involves a blend of highs and lows).[96]

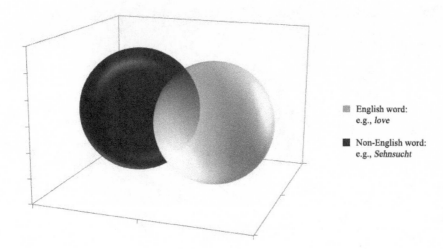

Figure 1.2
Somewhat-overlapping regions of state-space, representing overlap-based untranslatability.

The second and third forms of untranslatability reflect the network principle, particularly holarchy, whereby concepts can be encompassed by wider ones. These forms are also examples of the granularity principle, whereby one can zoom in and out of a given region of state-space. Thus, it is possible for a non-English word to be untranslatable because it encompasses a region of state-space *smaller* or *larger* than that encompassed by a comparable English word. That is, the meaning of the foreign word can be either more or less specific. In figure 1.3, I compare the English "love" to the narrower Greek *agápē*. Because *agápē* requires selflessness and charitability—which love can, but need not, incorporate—it occupies a smaller region of state-space. I call this "specificity-based" untranslatability.

Figure 1.4 inverts this condition: the non-English word occupies a larger region of state-space. Here, "love" is enfolded by the Chinese *Tao*, which could be regarded as the dynamic process of reality itself, encompassing everything in existence.[97] This is a case of "generality-based" untranslatability. Indeed, it is because some concepts, such as *Tao*, are all-encompassing that there are only three main kinds of untranslatability. It is not theoretically possible for a word to occupy a region of state-space that is unoccupied by another word, as all concepts could be enfolded by the *Tao* and similar notions, such as the Sanskrit *Brahman*.

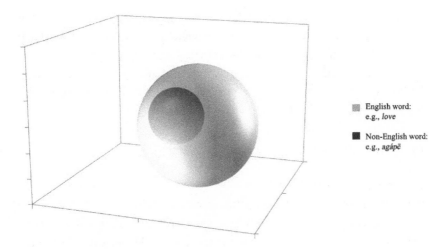

Figure 1.3
An English word encompassing a non-English word, representing specificity-based untranslatability.

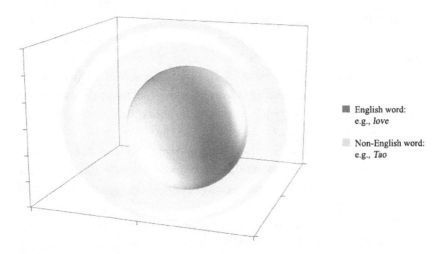

Figure 1.4
A non-English word encompassing an English word, representing generality-based untranslatability.

I've argued that the significance of untranslatable words is that they can augment or refine the maps provided by one's own language. Such words indicate the existence of phenomena—regions of experiential state-space—overlooked or undervalued by a given culture (in our case here, English-speaking cultures). These possibilities apply to all aspects of existence, not least of all well-being.

Exploring Well-Being

One could recognize the value of untranslatable words in all areas of life, but in this book I focus on well-being specifically. Although I do so because well-being is my field of scholarship—I am a lecturer and researcher in positive psychology—more fundamentally it is because I believe it to be a topic of great importance. It is also one that would benefit greatly from an exploration of untranslatable words, as academic understanding of well-being in fields such as positive psychology has thus far been rather Western-centric.

Western Perspectives on Well-Being

Positive psychology (PP) emerged in 1998, with Martin Seligman's inaugural address as president of the American Psychological Association.[98] Of course, many topics at the heart of PP—from the nature of happiness to the components of the good life—have been debated for millennia. And in the twentieth-century, scholars interested in humanistic psychology, such as the pioneering Abraham Maslow, further dove into these issues.[99] But the concerns of mainstream psychology generally lay elsewhere, until PP started capturing the attention of students and scholars in the late twentieth century (even if some regarded it skeptically as an eye-catching reworking of humanistic psychology).[100]

The field soon developed a body of empirical and theoretical work. For instance, drawing on historical ideas around happiness heavily debated by philosophers in ancient Greece, PP set about investigating the distinction between two main forms of well-being: hedonic (or "subjective")[101] and eudaimonic (or "psychological").[102] The latter represents a rare instance of psychology already having adopted an untranslatable word, *eudaimonia*, which was deployed by the likes of Aristotle to convey the notion of a virtuous and meaningful life.[103] Researchers then sought to elucidate the nature of these types of well-being, including identifying their subsidiary elements (in a good illustration of holarchical networks). Thus, today, subjective well-being is widely regarded as involving a cognitive component (judgments of life satisfaction) and an affective component (the ratio of positive to negative affect). Psychological well-being, on Carol Ryff's influential model, comprises six main dimensions: autonomy, self-acceptance, high-quality relationships, environmental mastery, meaning in life, and psychological development.[104]

As with any field—particularly one that has risen quickly to prominence—PP has received its fair share of criticism. Prominent among them is that it has developed and promulgated a somewhat culturally specific understanding of well-being, derived mainly from Western experience.[105] Much, though not all, of the empirical work in PP has relied on participants described by Joe Henrich and colleagues as WEIRD: they belong to societies that are Western, educated, industrialized, rich and democratic.[106]

Critics therefore charge that the field is biased toward Western ways of thinking and conceptualizing the world, and that its understanding of well-being is thus incomplete. For example, Dana Becker and Jeanne Marecek argue that PP has been influenced by a North American tradition of "expressive individualism,"[107] defined elsewhere as the "unmitigated reference to the value of the individual self."[108] As a result, the field has tended to view well-being primarily in individual psychological terms—that is, as a private mental state over which people retain control—while largely overlooking social factors that influence well-being, such as socioeconomic processes.[109]

A crucial aspect of PP's Western-centric bias is that its nomological network has mainly been structured in terms of the contours of the English language (with valuable exceptions, particularly *eudaimonia*). For instance, English has demarcated certain regions of state-space using constructs such as hope and optimism. Following this semantic structure, PP has set about identifying the properties of these regions by exploring what hope and optimism consist of.

While that kind of endeavor is valuable, what about regions of state-space that haven't been identified or labeled in English? There may be areas of real importance to well-being that have not figured into PP because they have not been represented in English. However, it is possible that these regions have been identified in other languages, resulting in an untranslatable word.

Exploring Untranslatable Words

In light of the critiques aired above, there has been a growing movement in PP toward cross-cultural scholarship, of which my project is a part. This movement partly represents Western scholars' response to these critiques, as in the pioneering efforts of the likes of Robert Biswas-Diener.[110] And it also reflects burgeoning interest in PP among scholars in non-Western countries such as China.[111]

Following the work of John Berry, I have isolated universalist and relativist trends in this emergent "positive cross-cultural psychology."[112] Universalism is more prevalent. This sort of research examines non-Western societies through the prism of Western psychological concepts, which are generally deemed universally applicable. Methods frequently include large-scale cross-cultural surveys. In Biswas-Diener's analysis of the Inughuit, Amish, and Maasai, for instance, people are assessed on standardized measures developed in Western settings—specifically, subjective well-being.[113] These kinds of studies rarely dwell on the possibility that there may be meaningful cross-cultural differences in the way well-being itself is experienced or constructed. As the economist Lord Richard Layard put it, "Of course one could question whether the word for 'happy' (or 'satisfied') means the same thing in different languages. If it doesn't, we can learn nothing by comparing different countries. In fact it does."[114]

Not all researchers in the field are comfortable with this reassuring perspective, though. Relativists, myself included, believe it is essential to explore and account for variation in the way people of different cultures relate to well-being—including how they define, experience, and report it.[115]

It was in the interest of adding to this relativist cross-cultural sensitivity that I embarked on a project to explore untranslatable words relating to well-being. My initial work involved a quasi-systematic review of academic literature and online media (e.g., websites and blogs)—quasi in the sense that there was not enough source material in academic psychology journals to permit a formal systematic review. I began by examining the first twenty relevant websites Google returned for the string "untranslatable words." On these sites, I looked for any word pertaining to well-being broadly construed, a category including health, happiness, success, and spirituality. This generated 131 words.

I then searched Google one language at a time, restricting myself to the official language of each of the world's 194 recognized countries,[116] by entering the string "[language] concept of" and "well-being" into the search engine. Each time, I entered the name of a different language. I browsed the first ten pages of each search result for phenomena related to well-being presented as unique to particular cultures. This strategy generated a further seventy-seven words.

Finally, I canvassed staff and students at my university, as well as family, friends, and acquaintances. This yielded another 8 words, for a total of 216.

I checked these words and their descriptions for accuracy by consulting native speakers, online dictionaries, and peer-reviewed academic sources when available. I then analyzed the words using a variation of grounded theory, an inductive approach to analysis of qualitative data.[117] Grounded theory largely involves examining data to see what themes emerge from it, then categorizing these themes into concepts that may form the basis of a new theory. The process is commonly employed with conventional qualitative data, such as interview transcripts. However, the process is adaptable, with considerable heterogeneity among studies purporting to use it.[118]

Grounded theory proceeds in three main stages. In the first, open coding, the researcher examines the data for emergent themes. I looked for words that appeared to share a common conceptual basis and grouped these under that theme. The second stage is axial coding, or cross-comparison to establish clusters of related themes. I compared the themes and then grouped them into categories, again based on conceptual similarity. Finally, the categories themselves are interpreted according to an overarching theoretical construct—well-being, in my analysis—which encompasses the data as a whole. The product in my case was an overarching accounting of the dimensions of well-being and their interrelationships.

There is significance in analyzing words thematically in this way (as opposed to, for instance, focusing primarily on their cultural origin). If one believes, with the strong relativists, that words are relevant only in the communities that created them—since outsiders would not be able to understand or experience the phenomena in question[119]—one would likely analyze words by culture. One might draw conclusions about people on the basis of their lexical habits, but those conclusions would not be generalizable to outsiders. However, I am a mild relativist.[120] I have argued that words, including untranslatable ones, may have universal relevance. It is my contention that all people—regardless of their cultural background and context—might be able to experience and appreciate the phenomenon in question, at least to some degree. As such, I have approached the words thematically, exploring how they align with the current nomological network of constructs in PP. In that way, we can appreciate how these words may be able to augment English-speakers' maps of well-being (as well as the maps of those who speak other languages).

My grounded-theory analysis produced six main categories of untranslatable words: positive feelings, ambivalent feelings, love, prosociality, character, and spirituality. I aggregated these six into three meta-categories: feelings (positive and ambivalent), relationships (love and prosociality), and personal development (character and spirituality). Thus, a convenient acronym—something academics, myself included, cannot resist—for this emergent theory of well-being might be the FRD model of well-being: feelings, relationships, and development.

These are arguably the three fundamental domains of well-being, covering respectively the main ways in which it is experienced (felt), influenced (through relationships),* and cultivated (in personal development). In this book, I explore each of these meta-categories over three separate chapters, analyzing the untranslatable words comprising the meta-category and discussing the thematic connections among them.

Before I turn to these chapters, I should note two sorts of caveats, one related to the contents of the lexicography, the other to the limits of translation.

As to the lexicography, it has expanded significantly since the publication of the paper and now contains more than 900 words and counting. The growth of the lexicography has certain implications. First, from the new words I have derived new themes, which I have added to the existing

---

*Relationships are of course not the only factor that influences well-being. Others include health, income, employment, activities, and values. However, research suggests that relationships are the most significant factor—as detailed in chapter 4—hence being described here as the main way well-being is influenced. In any case, these factors are to an extent interwoven throughout the other meta-categories: for instance, health manifests in part as feelings (e.g., sensations), while activities and values are important dimensions of personal development. A similar point applies to personal development too, which is the main—but not the only—way in which well-being is cultivated; indeed, relationships themselves are a significant resource in that respect.

categories. There has been no need to modify the higher-level categories developed in the paper, though, which speaks to their robustness in accounting for the domains of well-being.

Second, while this book aims to give a comprehensive account of the lexicography, only about one-third of the accumulated words are discussed. Especially deep themes, containing many words, are treated selectively rather than exhaustively; I aim to give a good sense of the theme, not laboriously describe every term.

Third, and relatedly, the lexicography is surely incomplete. It currently includes words from only just under one hundred languages, but there are more than 7,000 languages currently in existence,[121] a figure that grows further when dialects and linguistic subcultures are taken into account. It would be far beyond the capacity of this book—and probably any one person in a lifetime—to identify all relevant words. That said, as I discuss in the concluding chapter, I hope that this book will provide the foundation for further collection and analysis of untranslatable words.

The second caveat comes back to the prima facie paradox of writing in English about untranslatable words. After all, their defining feature is that they evade translation. However, as noted above, untranslatability just means lack of an exact equivalent in another language (in our case, English); it is usually still possible to convey a basic sense of meaning in a few words or sentences. Alas, this is the most I can do in the context of this book. To explore deeply the nuances of a term—its etymology, patterns of usage, diverse interpretations, and so on—would require at least an academic paper. As noted, such papers have been written about *Sehnsucht*, and similarly the Portuguese term *saudade*, which likewise approximates to a feeling of longing.[122] In order to conduct a comparative assessment, I must be more restrained. My aim is to be accurate, if not comprehensive.

To at least "catch the spirit" of the original word[123]—if only in part—I have consulted dictionaries and scholarly sources for each and have checked my descriptions and interpretations with native speakers. But, even then, it is probably not possible to arrive at a depiction that would satisfy all speakers of the donor languages represented here. Moreover, the explanations in this book cannot avoid the imprint of my individual reading of the source material, influenced by my background, beliefs, and biases, which I discuss further in the final chapter.

To provide a sense of how we might begin to translate the untranslatable—
and to highlight some of the issues and complexities involved in doing so—
in the next chapter I discuss the Sanskrit term *smṛti* in some depth. While it
will not be possible to extensively analyze all of the words in this way, the
discussion of *smṛti* serves as a case study of the concerns outlined above,
which bear on the lexicography as a whole. With that in mind, let's turn to
the first of the three meta-categories, feelings.

2 Feelings

Introduction

The lexicography's untranslatable words fall into three meta-categories: feelings, relationships, and development. As outlined in the previous chapter, I propose that these can be regarded as the fundamental domains of well-being, which is primarily experienced as feelings, influenced by relationships, and cultivated through personal development. I explore these three domains in depth in this chapter and the next two, beginning here with feelings.

Feelings, Emotions, and Qualia

"Feelings" is a complex and contested term. In a narrow sense, it is a synonym of "emotion"; more broadly, it refers to qualia in general.[1] I'll briefly consider these uses, with special consideration of their descriptive definitions: how the terms are used in everyday life. Indeed, this is my focus throughout the book. Although I am also interested in prescriptive definitions—how terms are operationalized in academia[2]—my primary concern is with language as it is used across cultures and therefore with descriptive definitions.

The narrower sense of "feelings," whereby one might equally describe happiness as a feeling or an emotion,[3] is common in everyday usage and, as such, is a useful descriptive definition. Prescriptively however, scholars tend to differentiate between the two. For instance, Antonio Damasio defines emotion as "a patterned collection of chemical and neural responses that is produced by the brain when it detects the presence of an emotionally competent stimulus," and feelings as "the mental representation of the physiological changes that characterize emotions."[4] He further suggests that while emotions are "scientifically public"—that is, visible in the physiology of the neurological system—feelings are private, subjective experiences. But because my focus is on how people use words in daily life, it is appropriate that I consider a definition of feelings as synonymous with emotions. Therefore, under the label of feelings, I analyze mental states that many theorists would strictly label as emotion rather than feeling.

I am also interested in the broader usage of feelings in everyday discourse, which encompasses all the ways in which life is subjectively experienced: moods, sensations, perceptions, and so on. These are qualia—everything one could say in response to the question, *What does life feel like?*, or, to paraphrase Thomas Nagel, *What is it like to be* a given person?[5] The range of phenomena that fall within this broadest remit of feelings is nicely expressed by the philosopher Frank Jackson, who was pivotal in developing the concept of qualia.[6] Jackson argues against the idea that "physical information"—such as data on neurophysiological states—equates to human experiences: "Tell me everything physical there is to tell about what is going on in a living brain," he wrote. "You won't have told me about the hurtfulness of pains, the itchiness of itches, pangs of jealousy, or about the characteristic experience of tasting a lemon, smelling a rose, hearing a loud noise or seeing the sky."

Thus, in addition to emotions, per the narrow everyday use of "feelings," I am concerned with exploring the terrain of qualia in general, per the broad use. But before thinking about particular untranslatable words related to feelings in both of these senses, let's fill in some details on what is meant by important associated concepts such as emotion.

Theories of Feeling and Emotion

Broadly speaking, the psychological literature features two main perspectives on emotions: naturalistic and constructivist.[7] Naturalistic models tend to regard emotions in an essentialist way as "natural kinds"—universal affective responses that, together, constitute human nature as shared among people. Within this perspective are two dominant theories: James Russell's circumplex model of affect,[8] and the paradigm of basic emotions associated with Paul Ekman.[9] The circumplex model holds that all affective states are generated by the interaction of two independent neurophysiological systems, gauging valence (pleasant vs. unpleasant) and arousal (active vs. passive). Theories of basic emotions, by contrast, hold that a "discrete and independent neural system subserves every emotion," as Jonathan Posner and colleagues put it.[10] On the basis of extensive cross-cultural research, Ekman suggests that all people experience and recognize five basic emotions: anger, disgust, fear, sadness, and enjoyment.[11]

As one might expect, this claim that emotions constitute natural kinds has been challenged. Arrayed against naturalistic models are constructivist theories, which usually counter that emotions are not universally available inner states. Rather, they are products of social interaction and of the broader cultural context in which this interaction occurs.

In this vein, too, there are competing perspectives. In many ways, the debate among constructivists aligns with that concerning the Sapir-Whorf hypothesis. On one hand, there are strong constructivists who argue against cross-cultural commonalities in emotions.[12] A pioneer here is Rom Harré, who contends that emotions exist mainly "in the reciprocal exchanges of a social encounter."[13] Since such encounters are mostly discursive, emotions are regarded primarily as a creation of language. Given cultural-linguistic differences, there is thus great variation in the way emotions are experienced, interpreted, and understood. Anthropologists such as Catherine Lutz, Gary Palmer, and Rick Brown align with this perspective.[14]

Others advocate elements of both the naturalistic and constructivist positions. Like mild Sapir–Whorf proponents, they argue that human experiences can be simultaneously universal and shaped by sociocultural contexts. Using my cartographic terminology, such theories hold that people may all access the same essential state-space, but languages carve this space up in different ways, affecting how it is experienced. Consider David Matsumoto and Hyi Sung Hwang's idea of culturally driven emotion regulation.[15] Per naturalistic theories, they suggest that humans inherit "a set of biologically innate emotions that are produced by a core emotion system." However, they further contend that the experience of these emotions—how they are felt, interpreted, and reacted to—is culturally "calibrated." Similarly, Lisa Feldman Barrett's conceptual-act model holds that discrete emotions emerge from a conceptual analysis of a "momentary state of core affect."[16] Core affect is universal, but the specific emotion one processes this as depends on one's linguistic-conceptual schemas.

Barrett's view fits neatly with my own. The momentary state of core affect arguably denotes the event of encountering a particular region of experiential state-space. Conceptual analysis, then, is the process by which the encountering person—influenced by his cultural context—identifies the state-space using the boundaries provided by his native language(s). Barrett also contends that it is possible to refine one's process of conceptual analysis, thereby developing greater emotional granularity, in line with the principle I discussed in chapter 1.

Emotional Granularity

Barrett proposes that people differ in their levels of emotional granularity[17] (also referred to as emotional differentiation[18]). Person A, with low granularity, and person B, with high granularity, can access similar regions of state-space—for instance a region broadly identifiable as happiness. But person A is unable to zoom in on the specific region; he has limited linguistic resources with which to conceptualize this feeling and may stick with the generic "happiness." Person B however has learned to segment this broad region into finer-grained parts. She may be not just happy, but specifically content, tranquil, joyful, or blissful. As Barrett puts it, she "more precisely" experiences her subjectivity and articulates her feelings.[19] Not just emotions but also qualia generally may be detected and explained with greater or lesser granularity. Seger Breugelmans and colleagues have demonstrated as much with respect to bodily sensations.[20] Thus, we might speak more broadly of *affective* granularity, rather than just emotional granularity.

Crucially, individual capacity for affective granularity appears not to be a fixed trait; evidence suggests that it can be nurtured. Early language learning consists in just this: developing greater granularity in describing not only feelings but all phenomena. (Recall the example of a student being introduced to classical music.) New research is testing therapeutic practices that may help people cultivate affective granularity, with the goal of enhancing well-being.[21] For instance, schoolchildren have been trained to expand their knowledge and use of words that describe emotions. This greater emotional vocabulary has in turn been associated with improvements in behavior and academic performance.[22] Specifically, some argue that those possessing greater differentiation are more aware of their subjectivity and thereby find it easier to regulate their emotions.[23]

That granularity may be fostered, and that doing so is conducive to well-being, are core premises of my project. It is my contention that engaging with untranslatable words enables us to develop a greater understanding of experiential state-space, which is valuable intellectually and may improve our lives.

To that end, let us begin to explore the lexicography. We'll start with examples from two broad categories of feelings that surfaced from the collection. It turns out that terms relevant to well-being describe more than that which is subjectively pleasant or enjoyable. There are, to be sure, positive feelings. But well-being also calls upon expressions of ambivalence. We'll deal first though with the positive feelings.

Positive Feelings

I am not the first to propose drawing on other languages to introduce more granularity in our description of positively valenced feelings.[24] Consider Ekman's approach to differentiating his five basic emotions, and specifically enjoyment. In his Atlas of Emotions project[25]—which also deploys a cartographic metaphor—he suggests that enjoyment can be deconstructed along a spectrum of intensity. From least to most intense, he isolates sensory pleasure, rejoicing, compassion/joy, amusement, *Schadenfreude*, relief, pride, *fiero*, *naches*, wonder, excitement, and ecstasy.

Thus, Ekman includes three foreign terms. There is the aforementioned loanword *Schadenfreude*, the Italian *fiero* (defined by Ekman as "enjoyment felt when you have met a challenge that stretched your capabilities"), and the Yiddish *naches* ("pride in the accomplishments, or sometimes just the existence of, your actual offspring or mentored offspring").

My analysis introduces further detail to this area. Whereas Ekman identified 12 different markers of enjoyment along a spectrum of intensity, I have so far uncovered over 130 unique terms. I group these into seven main themes, ordered here—as per Ekman—on a spectrum of intensity, from least to most highly charged: peace and calm, contentment and satisfaction, coziness and hominess, savoring and appreciation, revelry and fun, joy and euphoria, and bliss and *nirvāṇa*. Two other important forms of positive feeling, love and compassion, will be discussed in the next chapter, which concerns relationships.

Peace/Calm

A wealth of terms charts the tranquil ground at the lower end of the arousal spectrum. Here I will start by exploring one of them in-depth, to introduce readers to the sort of hermeneutic issues that surround the selection and interpretation of all the untranslatable words in the lexicon.

The Sanskrit term *smṛti*, more commonly known by its Pāli cognate *sati*, has attracted considerable attention worldwide thanks to its foundational role in the practice of mindfulness, which has become increasingly prominent across many cultures, including those in the West.[26] In headline terms, *smṛti* could be interpreted as a calm awareness of the present moment.[27] However, arriving at this interpretation is not so simple.

To begin with, that the term has cognates highlights the complexities of language evolution, including the sharing or borrowing of lexemes among languages. In this case, the languages are Sanskrit and Pāli. Sanskrit is generally regarded as emerging around the second millennium BCE as Vedic-Sanskrit, one of the oldest branches of the Indo-European tree. It began crystallizing into classical form around the fourth century BCE.[28] Classical Sanskrit was used across the Indian subcontinent as a literary and liturgical language; *Sanskrit* itself means refined, consecrated, or sanctified.[29] Pāli emerged between the fifth and first centuries BCE, possibly as an adaptation of a Sanskrit dialect.[30] The significance of Pāli mainly derives from its centrality in Buddhism, the tradition that formed around the teachings of Siddhārtha Gautama, better known by the honorific *Buddha* or "awakened one."[31] Buddhism's early foundational texts are known as the Pāli Canon. As a result, words relating to Buddhism usually have both Sanskrit and Pāli variants. Many subsequently became loanwords—with various degrees of alteration—in other languages as Buddhism migrated to China, Japan, and elsewhere, including more recently Western societies.[32]

Many words in this book are like *smṛti* and *sati*: although a given word may lack an equivalent in English, it might still be shared across multiple languages. Moreover, given the complexities of language evolution, including the widespread borrowing of words, it is often difficult to determine which language is the original source of a word. It is beyond the scope of this book to offer detailed etymologies and histories of transmission. Thus, when discussing a word, I just state the language(s) in which I encountered it in my search procedures.*

---

*That said, where relevant, I shall occasionally give a sense of the transmission of a lexeme across different languages. For instance, related to *smṛti* is *dhyāna*, which is sometimes translated simply as meditation but which perhaps more accurately denotes forms of concentrated attention or absorption. In this case, it is interesting

Beyond the origin of *smṛti* is the even more vexed issue of its interpretation. Deployed across multiple cultural contexts and time periods, *smṛti* has accrued many meanings. Capturing any one of these is difficult, since it involves a process of retrospective hermeneutics—trying to determine how terms were used in other cultures at other times. For instance, it has been suggested that in classical Sanskrit, especially before the appearance of the Buddha, *smṛti* connoted remembrance and recollection.[33] However, these days, under the influence of Buddhism, *smṛti* usually refers to a mental state involving present-moment awareness. (That said, the prior meaning is preserved to the extent that *smṛti* involves focusing on "what is otherwise too easily forgotten: the present moment," as Anālayo puts it.[34]) Crucially, the Buddha celebrated the benefits of this form of awareness, and—in teachings like the *Satipaṭṭhāna sutta*, a seminal instructional text of the Pāli Canon—urged its cultivation through meditation.[35]

Another source of shifting meaning is recent English usage in the form of a calque. Rather than directly borrowing *smṛti*, the loan translation "mindfulness" has become popular among Western publics and scholars. Indeed, each of the past few years have, on average, produced more than 500 academic papers on the subject.[36] This process of adoption and study has generated some interesting debates. One concerns the adequacy of the English word selected as a translation. "Mindfulness" was coined by the Buddhist scholar T. W. Rhys Davids at the turn of the twentieth century. Before that, he experimented with other terms.[37] In his 1881 publication of Buddhist *suttas*, *smṛti* was rendered as "mental activity" and even simply "thought."[38] It was only in 1910 that Rhys Davids settled on "mindfulness."[39] Later scholars and clinicians, who sought to harness the practice of *smṛti* as articulated in the Pāli Canon and other sources, embraced the term.

Among the most significant of these successors is Jon Kabat-Zinn. In the late 1970s, he created a pioneering Mindfulness-Based Stress-Reduction intervention, which was successful in treating chronic pain.[40] This intervention—and subsequent adaptations, such as depression relapse prevention using Mindfulness-Based Cognitive Therapy[41]—has also been

---

to note that *dhyāna* became *chán* when Buddhism was transmitted to China, which in turn was then rendered as *Zen* in Japanese, which has now become a loanword in English.

effective in ameliorating mental health issues and promoting well-being more broadly.[42] In operationalizing *smṛti* as mindfulness, Kabat-Zinn defined it as "the awareness that arises through paying attention on purpose, in the present moment, and nonjudgmentally to the unfolding of experience moment by moment."[43] This definition aligns to some degree with Buddhist descriptions of *smṛti*.

Although mindfulness has proven its utility, scholars continue to critique the word itself. Shauna Shapiro, one of the foremost researchers in this area, has argued that "mindfulness" is too cognitive and cerebral, and misses the affective qualities, such as compassion, embedded in *smṛti*.[44] She also points out that some Eastern languages do not divide thought and emotion as English does. For instance, the Sanskrit *citta* is often translated as signifying heart and mind together,[45] as is the Chinese *xīn*. Shapiro therefore contends that "heart-mindfulness" might therefore be a better rendering of *smṛti*.

Given these concerns, some scholars favor leaving *smṛti* untranslated and using it—or *sati*—as a loanword,[46] much like *karma* and other Sanskrit or Pāli terms relating to Buddhism that have been adopted by the West. However, even then, extracting *smṛti* from its early Buddhist context and deploying it in the contemporary West is not without its issues. Recall the network principle and the derivation of meaning from complex associations among words. In its original Buddhist context, *smṛti* was embedded in a rich network of ideas and practices that together comprise the *dharma*, a complex term with connotations of truth, laws, and teachings, which refers to the Buddhist path as a whole.[47] This network may not be retained when *smṛti* is transplanted into another cultural context.

Indeed, Kabat-Zinn himself warned, "The rush to define mindfulness within Western psychology may wind up denaturing it in fundamental ways," with "the potential for something priceless to be lost."[48] For example, one aspect of *smṛti* that arguably is in danger of being lost in translation is an inherent moral sensibility. In its original Buddhist context, *smṛti* was connected to ethical precepts and ideals by virtue of being embedded within the broader context of the *dharma*.[49] Critics point out that this sensibility could be appraised as lacking where mindfulness is used in ways that some construe as unethical, such as enhancing the operational efficiency of military personnel.[50] (That said, historically, meditation has at times been an adjunct to combat, suggesting that Buddhism probably has harbored such debates for a long time.[51])

But even if mindfulness does not retain all the meanings of *smṛti* in its original Buddhist context, it can still be of value. Moreover, as English-speakers adopt "mindfulness," it develops its own web-like associations. For instance, in the context of Western psychology, mindfulness has begun to become associated with cognitive models of attention and affective models of relaxation.[52] It is in the latter context that I use *smṛti* here, denoting a calm and composed mental state.

As a final point, *smṛti*'s adoption in the West supports my argument that engaging with untranslatable words can be beneficial both for academic psychology and for people in general. In spite of its divergences from *smṛti* as classically conceived, mindfulness has proved powerful, giving rise to a wealth of mindfulness-based interventions found to enhance well-being in diverse populations.[53]

Although I cannot address the lexicon's full contents in such depth, I'll briefly touch upon a few other words from the Buddhist tradition that fall within the ambit of peace and calm. Indeed, Buddhism is replete with such terms, as reflected in the production of entire Buddhist dictionaries, from Monier Monier-Williams's classic text, to Damien Keown's more recent offering.[54] Zen Buddhism, for instance, emphasizes *zanshin* and *seijaku*. Cayetano Sanchez defines *zan* as "remnants" or "that which endures,"[55] while *shin* is the Japanese rendering of the Chinese *xīn*, defined above as "heart-mind." *Zanshin* can thus be interpreted as "remaining mind," conveying a state of relaxed mental alertness, especially in the face of danger or stress, which is particularly relevant in the context of martial arts.[56] Likewise evoking composure, *seijaku* combines *sei*, translatable as "quiet," and *jaku*, which can connote tranquility. Together they refer to a quality of silence, calm, serenity—especially in the midst of activity or chaos—which is similarly valued in Zen and other spiritual traditions.[57]

Of course, Buddhism does not have a monopoly on peace and calm. For example, in classical Greece, *ataraxia* described a robust and lucid kind of tranquility. According to Darrin McMahon, this quality was particularly valued by Stoics, who regarded well-being as, in part, a function of the will, attainable by eradicating desire.[58] As Epictetus wrote, "The man who rids his mind of desire and avers things only within his sphere of choice has virtue and an untroubled mind."[59] *Ataraxia* has parallels with *smṛti* in that both imply decentering—a form of detachment David Fresco and colleagues define as "the ability to observe one's thoughts and feelings as temporary, objective events in the mind, as opposed to reflections of the self that are necessarily true."[60]

Other valuable words do not depict states of peace and calm directly but allude to actions or processes that engender them. Some of these are contemplative practices, which I discuss in depth in chapter 4. Aside from these, many calming words originate in temperate regions and may be interpreted as reflecting or recommending the avoidance of physical or mental exhaustion in hot climates. For instance, the Italian verb *meriggiare* and Spanish noun *siesta* refer to resting around noon, ideally in the shade.[61] Or pertaining to action, the Greek adverb *siga siga*, which literally means "slowly, slowly," conveys a positive sense of being unhurried.[62] Such words reinforce the idea of close intersection between climate, culture, and language, as discussed previously with respect to Eskimos.

Contentment/Satisfaction

Closely related to peace and calm are feelings that fall under the banner of contentment and satisfaction. In my cartographic terminology, these regions, and terms falling within them, could be said to overlap. For instance, *ataraxia* was viewed by Stoic thinkers as definitive of contentment.[63] This perspective accords with some in modern psychology, such as Charles Carver and Michael Scheier's model of self-regulatory coping, in which acceptance of circumstances is broadly regarded as constituting contentment.[64]

However, contentment and satisfaction also differ from peace and calm in nuanced ways. In particular, the former have somewhat more positive connotations and are subjectively warmer.

An interesting term in this context is the Mandarin Chinese *xìng fú*, which is often simply translated as "happiness." Another Mandarin word, *kuài lè*, is usually translated similarly, yet there are nuanced differences between the two, which suggests the inadequacy of rendering both with the same English term. Through agglutination, *kuài*, meaning fast or quick, joins *lè*, which refers to the condition of being joyful or cheerful. *Kuài lè* therefore appears to articulate a more hedonic form of pleasure.[65] By contrast, *xìng fú* combines *xìng*, referring to luck or fortune, and *fú*, denoting blessing or reward, suggesting a deeper form of contentment. In an online language forum devoted to Chinese, one speaker wrote, "You can use 'xing fu' when you think 'I'll ask for no more.' For example, you will feel 'xing fu' when you can get in a heated room in a blizzard. For someone with insomnia, he/she will feel very 'xing fu' when he/she can finally get a good night's sleep. Many people will feel 'xing fu' when they can marry someone they really love."[66]

One could argue that the two terms cover terrain similar to that of the two foundational forms of well-being identified in PP: *xìng fú* is perhaps comparable to eudaimonic "psychological" well-being, and *kuài lè* to hedonic, "subjective" well-being.[67] However, neither "eudaimonic well-being" nor "contentment" is an ideal translation for *xìng fú*, since these English (or anglicized) terms eschew its connotation of luck and fortune. That said, "happiness" did originally denote a comparable implication of fate, deriving as it does from the Middle English and Old Norse root *happ*, which refers to "chance, fortune, what happens in the world."[68] However, over the centuries, such meanings have come to be disassociated or disentangled from the notion of happiness. By contrast, scholars have suggested that Eastern concepts of happiness retain a degree of fatalism.[69] Potential explanations for this endurance include the continuing influence of beliefs in processes such as *karma*; a cultural premium placed on self-effacement, whereby people are encouraged to attribute success to external factors; and greater deference to authority, with a concomitant relative lack of autonomy.[70]

Further dimensions to contentment and satisfaction are revealed by a nexus of Northern European words that speak to a sense of security and intimacy. These include the now-well-known Danish notion of *hygge*, together with its near equivalents, the Norwegian *kos* and Dutch *gezellig*.* Such terms all convey—among other qualities—being safe, protected, and cared for. Moreover, these are depicted as archetypal examples of untranslatability, representing states of being regarded as characteristically Danish, Norwegian, and Dutch—at the heart of their way of life. Indeed, in 2016 alone, no fewer than nine popular books about *hygge* were published in English.[71] These tended to portray *hygge* as the "secret" to reported high

---

Hygge is also used in Norwegian, as well as *kos*. Both *hygge* and *kos* are nouns, but can be rendered as adjectives through a suffix, namely *hyggelig* and *koselig*; *gezellig* is already an adjective, derived from the noun *gezel*, meaning companion or friend.

levels of happiness in Denmark, alongside factors such as egalitarianism, progressive taxation, and state welfare policies.[72]

Hygge is thought to derive from the Old Norse *hugga*, which can mean "to comfort" and which may be the basis of the English "hug."[73] *Hygge*, *kos*, and *gezellig* can also be used to express feelings of coziness and hominess (and thus pertain to the next theme too).* However, speakers also use these words to describe the pleasures of enjoying a beer outside or cycling in the sunshine.[74] Perhaps, as one writer suggested, these words speak to feeling cozy "in one's heart," regardless of whether the material environment is itself cozy.[75] Whatever their exact boundaries, these words convey enjoyment of simple pleasures, an encompassing but modest form of contentment (i.e., one that does not rely on excess or extravagance).

In addition to *hygge*, Danish provides further detail to the state-space of contentment. For instance, the adjective *morgenfrisk* describes the satisfaction that arises from a good night's sleep.[76] Like its literal translation, the phonetically similar "morning-fresh," *morgenfrisk* has roots in the proto-Germanic *murgana* and *friskaz*, the latter of which also gives rise to the English "frisky."[77] Danish and other Nordic languages also feature *arbejds-glæde*, combining "work" (*arbejde*) and "happiness" or "gladness" (*glæde*) to denote the satisfaction gained from one's occupation[78] (with parallels to *fiero* in Ekman's Atlas of Emotions[79]).

Coziness/Hominess

As *hygge* and its relatives indicate, the state-space occupied by contentment and satisfaction overlaps with that associated with coziness and hominess. Besides *hygge* (which has been adequately covered above), a similarly relevant term is the Welsh *cwtch*. As a verb it means (transitively) to hug or cuddle and (intransitively) to "get cozy," and as a noun can refer to a hug or cuddle.[80] However, like *hygge*, it also describes places that engender these feelings. Commentators invariably describe such places as kinds of sanctuary, where one feels safe and welcome. A potential connotation is envelopment, as when the noun is used to describe a favored "cubby hole."[81]

---

*It could be argued that *hygge*, *kos*, and *gezellig* do not constitute feelings but rather judgments about phenomena that engender coziness or contentment. However, even if that is the case, they pertain to this chapter, since I am also interested here in words *related* to feelings.

A language which brings particular nuance to notions of coziness and hominess is German. There is *Geborgenheit*, which captures a sense of snugness but also feeling safe from harm. It derives from *geborgen*, a verb and adjective that can mean safe or sheltered as well as hidden.[82] Another term often translated as "cozy" is the adjective *gemütlich* (or abstract noun *Gemütlichkeit*). However, again, "cozy" is not quite right. Barbara Cassin identifies the root *Gemüt* as untranslatable, having been used by philosophers such as Emmanuel Kant to cover mind, mood, heart, and soul, yet without being reducible to any of these.[83] Further, Jakob von Uexküll suggests that German philosophers and mystics have used *Gemüt* to denote "the whole inner world of man."[84] *Gemütlich* also carries meanings of friendliness, soulfulness, and peace of mind, and therefore is often used to indicate a warm social atmosphere that inspires a sense of belonging.[85]

Another interesting example from German is *heimlich*, derived from the noun *Heim*—"home," in English—and the suffix *lich*, which indicates an adjectival form. *Heimlich* doesn't simply mean "homey," as one might expect; it alludes to that which is familiar and comfortable, and yet at the same time can also refer to secrecy, the clandestine, that which is or should be kept concealed from outsiders.[86] Moreover, according to Freud, in requiring secrecy in this way, the term can even allude to something being uncanny and frightening. Therefore, paradoxically, it can be interpreted as having meanings similar to those of its antonym, *unheimlich*.[87] This is possibly an esoteric interpretation, limited to select contexts such as psychoanalysis. But it speaks to the complex, even discordant, layers of meanings words can possess.

Savoring/Appreciation

Moving a notch further along the spectrum of intensity, the next theme is savoring and appreciation. These are sometimes treated as synonymous, or defined in terms of one another. For instance, Chia-Wu Lin defines savoring as "the appreciation of enjoyable life experiences."[88] However, as I understand it, savoring is more active, involving a conscious effort to be appreciative.[89] With that in mind, let's turn to foreign words in this realm. Some pertain mainly to the mental state of savoring or appreciation; others bring fascinating specificity to the phenomena that one might savor or appreciate.

Beginning with the mental state, a revealing term is the Icelandic adjective *hugfanginn*. This literally translates as "mind-captured" and refers to being enthralled, fascinated, or charmed by something. As its components suggest, it also implies that the condition of fascination may not be entirely voluntary. This comports with theories of attention holding that one's focus can be "captured" by phenomena that seem compelling or urgent.[90]

A more straightforwardly benign feeling is conveyed by the Swedish verb *njuta*, which denotes an especially deep form of appreciation. It suggests greater intensity than does the English "appreciate," which can sometimes, after all, indicate a merely superficial kind of valuation.[91] *Njuta* also gives rise to the noun *livsnjutare*, which parallels the French *joie de vivre* in referencing one who embodies a love of life.[92] Of similar potency to *njuta* is the Hawaiian noun and stative verb *mahalo*, which encompasses admiration, respect, esteem, and regard.[93] Its components (*ma, hâ*, and *alo*) convey a suggestion of divine presence, such that the term is used to express deep gratitude and spiritual blessing.[94] This is more refined territory than that of mere enjoyment.

Other words do not identify feelings of appreciation per se, but rather people who have them. An example is the Spanish loanword *aficionado*. Deriving from the transitive verb *aficionar*—to inspire affection or enthusiasm—*aficionado* entered English in the nineteenth century as a noun referring to someone who is especially passionate and knowledgeable about a phenomenon.[95] Interestingly, *aficionado* can also carry connotations of amateurism, but not in a disparaging sense: rather, an *aficionado* is to be celebrated because she does something for the love of it, rather than for extrinsic rewards like remuneration.

Finally, an array of words delineates specific forms of savoring and appreciation. Some of these pertain to engagement with one's surroundings, again reflecting the intersection of geography, culture and language. For instance, many temperate nations have words articulating the joys of strolling, including the French verb *flâner* (and the noun *flâneur*, denoting one who engages in the activity), and the Italian noun *passeggiata*. "Strolling" itself lacks the significance that these terms have in their respective cultures, where they refer to celebrated activities and indeed traditions, not merely a generic action. For instance, in her ethnography of an Italian village, Giovanna del Negro considers *passeggiata* a vital social ritual and "cultural performance."[96] Similarly, Walter Benjamin highlights the symbolism and importance of the *flâneur* in French culture, suggesting he came to prominence in the nineteenth century as a distinctive and often enviable type of person, such as a Romantic artist or "man of leisure."[97]

Japanese is particularly rich in terms conveying an appreciation of nature, which may reflect its extensive tradition of engaging with nature in art, as exemplified by the seventeenth-century poet Matsuo Bashō.[98] There is the evocative concept of *shinrin-yoku*—literally "forest-bathing"—which articulates the restorative feeling of soaking up the tranquility of natural environments. While Western scholars, particularly Wilbert Gesler in his work on therapeutic landscapes and healing places,[99] have explored the benefits of exposure to nature in general, Japanese scholars have studied the benefits of *shinrin-yoku* specifically, describing it as a form of "forest medicine."[100] A related term, *ohanami*, which means "flower-viewing," signifies the culturally valued activity of appreciating cherry blossoms in spring, and the gatherings (e.g., picnics) held in their graceful presence.[101]

Revelry/Fun

The final three themes in our first category—revelry/fun, joy/euphoria, and bliss/*nirvāṇa*—concern more strongly qualified positive feelings. These sections discuss varying degrees of pleasure; or, in the terms of academic psychology, the higher ranges of positive affect or hedonic tone.[102] However, the diversity and nuance of words in these sections again shows the limitations of generic terms such as "pleasure" and "positive affect" and highlights the value of granularity.

Revelry/fun covers especially sensual and lighthearted forms of pleasure. Or, to deploy a term that is approaching the status of a loanword—and indeed has been commodified as such[103]—the words in this section relate to the Gaelic noun *craic*, which captures a general sense of the experience of good times. Despite being a valued form of experience though, fun has attracted limited academic attention.[104]

Delving into this relatively unexplored area, we find many nuances in foreign terms related to pleasure, revelry, and fun. For instance, the Chinese verb *guò yǐn* conveys a sense of enjoying oneself to the fullest and of satisfying one's cravings.[105] This make sense etymologically; *guò* means to pass through or go across, and *yǐn* refers to addiction, craving, or habit. Thus *guò yǐn* incorporates shades of both compulsion and satisfaction, a combination not found in the English concepts typically used to translate it.

Satiety, in fact, is a common companion of forms of revelry. For example, the Dutch verb *uitbuiken*—"outbellying" or "to stomach out"—vividly describes the physical act of relaxing between courses or after a meal.[106] Relatedly, the Italian noun *abbiocco*—derived from the transitive verb *abbioccare*, meaning "to exhaust" or "tire"—articulates the usually pleasant drowsiness that often follows a large meal.

Moving toward the more spirited aspects of revelry, the Portuguese transitive verb *desbundar* can articulate a notion of abandon—the exceeding of one's limits, such as through disinhibited merrymaking. However, the term can also be deployed to explain more extreme behaviors, including the effects of "spirit possession."[107] Similarly, the Greek noun *kefi* conveys joyful enthusiasm but may also be applied to extremes of frenzy.[108] *Kefi* derives from the Arabic *kayf*, referring to pleasure and joy. However, exemplifying the tendency of borrowed words to shift in meaning, *kefi* signifies in Greek a culturally valued intense emotional state, usually one "heightened by alcohol," as Patricia Riak puts it,[109] and evoked by social occasions featuring music and dance.[110]

Overlapping with *kefi* are terms denoting the social occasions and activities that cultures have developed to enable revelry. For instance, the Balinese word *ramé* describes particularly festive parties and other lively social occasions.[111] For instance, the anthropologist Clifford Geertz argued that Bali's "crowded, noisy and active" cockfights epitomized the tumult of *ramé*.[112]

One could go on. Indeed, thousands of untranslatable words could be included within this theme of revelry and fun. For instance, there is a kaleidoscopic multitude of terms pertaining just to styles of music and dance, with hundreds generated within the Caribbean region alone (from reggae to rumba).[113] We will explore revelrous terms further in the next chapter, which attends directly to socializing and the feelings it generates.

Joy/Euphoria

Our penultimate section covers feelings related to the English loanwords joy, euphoria, and ecstasy. According to the circumplex model, these are emotional states at the high end of the valence spectrum (intensely pleasant), the arousal spectrum (highly charged), or both.

Throughout the centuries, joy has invariably been characterized as benign and even morally worthy. It entered English around the thirteenth century, from the French *joie*, meaning delight or even bliss, which itself derived from the Latin *gaudere*, "to rejoice."[114] In religious contexts specifically, joy described the just psychological rewards of faith and devotion.[115] These meanings have remained fairly consistent over the centuries. In contrast, euphoria and ecstasy have undergone processes of semantic change. Their malleability speaks to the shifting regions of state-space a given word might denote. And both can have complicated undertones of instability characteristic of this theme as a whole.

Euphoria combines *eû*, a prefix denoting "good," "well," or "beautiful," and *phérein*, a verb meaning "to bear" or "to carry."[116] In its original classical Greek context, euphoria usually referred to physical health, though it could also be deployed in a moral or developmental sense. For instance, Aristotle sometimes used it as a near synonym of *eudaimonia* and presented it as the outcome of a virtuous life.[117]

When euphoria entered English around the seventeenth century, it was still used primarily in a medical context, referring to the condition of feeling well and comfortable. It was particularly common in descriptions of patients made to feel better through medical intervention.[118] It may be this association with medically induced positive mental states that gave rise to modern uses of the term, which convey an intense feeling of well-being, often precipitated by an unusual or even extraordinary cause such as psychoactive substances.

"Ecstasy" likewise has evolved. Formed from *ek*, meaning outside or beyond, and *stasis*, which signified stature or standing, in its original Greek context it connoted a person standing outside herself in some fashion. One might thus be ecstatic in the sense of being astonished or entranced, insane or spiritually possessed.[119] When the word entered English in the fourteenth century, it was mainly used in reference to an exalted state of rapture or mystical union that could arise from contemplation of the divine.[120] Only later did ecstasy come to denote intense experiences of pleasure uncoupled from spiritual concerns. Now, in some contemporary usage, it can carry pejorative connotations; ecstasy, like euphoria, might be *too* intense, as well as artificial and/or socially inappropriate.[121] Thus, despite their strong positive valence, ecstasy and euphoria are not necessarily unqualified goods. Complex psychodynamics render the states they denote potentially unstable and difficult.

Other languages also incorporate terms blending intensity and instability, albeit in different ways, making them potentially instructive to speakers of English. Take for instance the French noun *jouissance*, derived from *jouissant*, meaning to enjoy or take pleasure in.[122] It can denote enjoyment or, more strongly, joy and delight.* However, more specifically, *jouissance* has come to be associated with sex, particularly orgasm.[123] Psychoanalytic theory, particularly in the work of Jacques Lacan, grasped this element of *jouissance*.[124] Lacan argues that people can bear only so much pleasure, possibly because at this limit arrives the painful realization of the inevitable comedown. For Lacan, *jouissance* represents the transgressing of this limit.[125]

Overlapping with *jouissance*, ecstasy, and euphoria are terms pertaining to ardor and passion. These are also ambiguous—intensely positively valenced, yet somehow excessive or unstable. For instance, the Russian noun *azart* describes excitement and fervor but is also associated with recklessness and risk-taking.[126] Similarly complex is the Spanish noun *duende*. In an artistic context, *duende* refers to a heightened state of emotion, spirit, and passion, particularly in the performance and appreciation of art forms such as flamenco.[127] The term derives from a magical elf-like creature in Spanish mythology, which suggests the nonrational and otherworldly nature of the mental state *duende* signfies.[128] The Arabic *tarab* describes a similar highly valued state of musically induced ecstasy or enchantment, as celebrated for instance by the Sufi tradition.[129]

Bliss/*Nirvāṇa*

Ecstasy tends to dissipate quickly. But some positively valenced feelings are more lasting, perhaps even relatively permanent.[130] These terms generally hail from religious contexts, implying that the feelings they describe usually are attained through spiritual practice.

*It is interesting to note how mild "enjoyment" is when compared to its stem, "joy." Etymologically, "enjoy" means "to give joy" or to "take joy in," and, in its original function as a loanword, it appears to have conveyed those meanings. However, its connotations of joy have eroded, and it now functions more as a synonym of "like." Indeed, sometimes "enjoy" implies no positive affect at all but can simply refer to the use or benefit of something. Using my cartographic terminology, one might say that while "joy" has continued over time to signify the same essential region of state-space, "enjoy" has gradually shifted to a slightly different area, one more muted in terms of intensity and valence.

Christianity has developed terms along these lines, such as "beatitude" and "grace," which perhaps parallel *eudaimonia*.[131] Beatitude was adapted from French in the fifteenth century and derives from the Latin *beatitudo*, which denotes blessedness and happiness. This type of positivity—conveying ultimate, supreme, or perfect happiness, and associated with religious or spiritual experience—is quite different from that of hedonism. Indeed, beatitude may not even be enjoyable as the term is usually understood. After all, as Christ said in the Sermon on the Mount, "Blessed [*beatitudo*] are those who are persecuted because of righteousness." Clearly, as McMahon argues, this is a rarified and exalted form of happiness.[132]

"Grace" has similar qualities. The word hails from the Greek *charis*, which in its original context conveyed a range of valued qualities such as kindness, charm, beauty, and nobility. In Greek mythology, these qualities were represented by goddesses known as charities.[133] The Latin equivalent *gratia*—meaning favor, mercy, or thanks—migrated to France in the twelfth century, in the form of *grâce*. Thereafter it was adapted in French and English to religious contexts, where it described divine blessing, favor, redemption, or support. Like beatitude, grace is thought to imply "true" happiness—deep, meaningful, and lasting.[134]

Eastern traditions such as Hinduism and Buddhism offer their own perspectives on the possibility of ultimate happiness, ones less familiar to speakers of English. One is the Sanskrit *ânanda*, frequently translated as bliss. However, in Hindu and Buddhist contexts, it is usually imbued with characteristics to which bliss need not pertain. For instance, the influential yoga teacher B. K. S. Iyengar discusses a "vast difference" between *ânanda* and another concept, *sukha*: the latter conveys ease, comfort, or pleasure, while the former has a "spiritual quality."[135] *Sukha* is usually regarded as conditional, dependent on a person's situation and therefore reflective of "worldly" happiness.[136] Conversely, *Ânanda* is seen more as unconditional and imperturbable. It is thought to arise when a person has developed sufficient "detachment," usually through spiritual practice.[137]

Ânanda may itself be superseded by a notion of which many in the West have heard, even if they are vague about its meaning: *nirvāṇa*. It would perhaps be easy to conflate the two. *Ânanda* describes an enduring state of well-being, and *nirvāṇa* a permanent cessation of suffering.[138] Within Buddhist psychology and metaphysics, however, it signifies something beyond the scope of *ânanda*. To achieve *nirvāṇa* is to exit the otherwise-endless cycle of *saṃsāra*—birth, death, and rebirth—pervaded by *duḥkha*, the antonym of *sukha*, denoting the suffering and dissatisfaction of daily life.[139] (One should note that this cycle can be interpreted according to various time-frames—from the succession of lives implied by theories of reincarnation, to the moment-to-moment way in which the self is continually brought into being.) This state is thought to be attained through reaching *bodhi*—awakening or enlightenment.[140] The sense of finality and liberation in *nirvāṇa* is reflected in the word's direct translation, "to blow out" or "extinguish." *Mokṣa*, largely associated with Hinduism, is similar, also referring to enlightenment and liberation from *saṃsāra*.

I explore these spiritual ideas in greater depth in chapter 4. But they are worth considering here, to draw attention to the outer bounds of the state-space of positive feelings. Such concepts show the far-reaching states of well-being humans might attain, greatly surpassing or superseding pleasure and satisfaction, and even euphoria and ecstasy.

Ambivalent Feelings

We have already encountered some complex concepts related to well-being. A few were not even wholly positively valenced, but included certain darker feelings among their psychodynamics. For instance, in denoting a heightened state of passion, *duende* features the potential for experiences which reflect passion's etymology, namely to suffer. But such concepts are not an aberration in our discussion here. The analysis uncovered a whole class of feelings that are entirely ambivalent,* involving a complex dialectical blend of light and dark elements.

These words are particularly important in the context of what my colleagues and I refer to as the "second wave" of PP.[141] This recent turn within

---

*Ambivalent emotions—also known as mixed emotions—can vary in their psychodynamics. For instance, in their Analogue Emotional Scale, Pilar Carrera and Luis Oceja differentiate between simultaneous and sequential ambivalent emotions. The former is an emotional state in which feelings of opposing valence are activated at the same time (a state also known as covalence). The latter is an emotional state in which a feeling of one valence is swiftly followed by one of the opposing valence. To this distinction one might also add a third category of variable ambivalent emotions, in which a given emotion might assume either a positive or negative valence, depending on the context. For instance, love might fall into this category, as discussed further below.

the field eschews the polarizing dichotomy between negatively valenced phenomena—conceptualized as undesirable and thus to be avoided—and positively valenced ones, understood as necessarily beneficial and thus to be sought. Increasingly, the field recognizes that well-being is a nuanced phenomenon, potentially involving qualities and processes that seem negative but actually serve people's best interests. Recall Ryff and Singer's conclusion that well-being involves an "inevitable dialectics between positive and negative aspects of living."[142]

We have identified several principles underpinning this dialectical conception of well-being.[143] First, the principle of appraisal reflects the idea that it can be hard to categorize phenomena as either positive or negative, since such appraisals are context-dependent. Though a state of mind is positive in valence, it may yet be negative in its utility, and vice versa. For instance, excessive optimism usually feels good, but it can lead to miscalculations of risk.[144] Conversely, defensive pessimism may feel unpleasant but also foster prudence, which facilitates well-being.[145]

A second principle, that of ambivalence, acknowledges that many desirable phenomena have positive and negative elements.[146] This is so even of love, arguably the most cherished of all experiences. As C. S. Lewis lamented, "To love at all is to be vulnerable. Love anything and your heart will be wrung and possibly broken."[147] Love contains the brightness of pleasure, joy, and bliss but inevitably harbors darker shades of worry, anxiety, and fear. Indeed, at times of particular concern or distress, it is possible for love to be wholly negatively valenced, thus rendering love an example of a variable ambivalent emotion.

Recognition of ambivalence leads inexorably to the third dialectical principle: complementarity. The light and dark of love—and other such complex feelings—are inseparable, complementary and co-creating sides of the same coin. Or, with C. S. Lewis, one might say the dysphoria inherent in love is not an aberration but rather its very condition (i.e., the "price" one must pay in order to also experience its great joys).

Before diving into the themes of this category, I will begin with an untranslatable concept that, although not a feeling per se, constitutes an overarching motif here: *yīn-yáng*.

Yīn-yáng

Yīn-yáng is central to Taoism, a philosophy and way of life indigenous to China. *Tao* is an all-encompassing concept—as noted in the previous chapter—and by its very nature indefinable and ineffable. Even so, it has been described as a "nameless, formless, all-pervasive power which brings all things into being and reverts them back into non-being in an eternal cycle."[148]

The origins of Taoism can be traced to the *I Ching*, or *Book of Changes*.* The purpose of the text, which in written form dates from circa 1150 BCE, was to guide a shamanic practice that had developed among the Zhou people, who would consult oracles for purposes of divination.[149] The *I Ching* helped practitioners interpret the sixty-four hexagrams on which the divination was based.[150] Importantly from our dialectical standpoint, the hexagrams represent not states of being but of becoming. The focal point of the hexagrams is always the moving lines—that is, any of the six regarded as dynamic or unstable.

Thus, the overarching concern of the *I Ching*, as its title suggests, is change—paradoxically, the one constant in the universe. As Hellmut Wilhelm explained in the introduction to his seminal translation of the text, "He who has perceived the meaning of change fixes his attention no longer on transitory individual things but on the eternal, immutable law at work in all change."[151] It is here we find the origin of Taoism, for this law is "the Tao, the course of things, the principle of the one in the many" (i.e., *Tao* is the constant that underlies the flux and multiplicity of the cosmos). Along with the ubiquity of change, the *I Ching* identifies the mechanism through which it occurs, namely, the dialectical interaction between oppositional qualities and processes. This dialectical philosophy is captured symbolically by the *yīn-yáng* construct.

Yīn means cloud, or cloudy, and *yáng* sun, or sunlit, and together they encapsulate various "tenets of duality."[152] Holistic duality—and its latter-day cousin, the principle of complementarity—holds that reality comprises opposites that depend on each other for their existence. Dynamic duality then holds that these opposites tend to transform into each other in a fluid process. As Yu-Lan Fung puts it, "When the sun has reached its meridian,

---

*The title *I Ching* is a romanization of the ideographs 易 and 經 using the Wade-Giles system. While very well-known terms, often proper nouns, continued to be rendered with Wade-Giles, the Pinyin system is more common for most uses these days. In Pinyin, the ideographs would be romanized as *Yì Jīng*. As a verb, *I/Yì* can mean "to change" and, as an adjective, "easy" or "simple." *Ching/Jīng* signifies "classic," in the sense of a canonical teaching or text.

it declines."[153] Thus, *yīn-yáng* does not refer to a pair of static opposites but to the ceaseless process of becoming. In the words of Li-Jun Ji and colleagues, "The pure yin is hidden in yang, and the pure yang is hidden in yin."[154]

Essentially, the overarching message of Taoism, expressed visually in the *yīn-yáng* symbol, is that a deep experiential understanding of the dialectics of the *Tao* is the path to psychospiritual liberation (a topic we shall explore further in chapter 4). In one way or another, most of the terms in this ambivalent-words category reflect principles of the kind associated with Taoism. With that in mind, let us turn to the words themselves, beginning with themes of hope and anticipation.

Hope/Anticipation

Hope is usually seen as a positive feeling. Pioneers of PP, such as Charles Snyder, have tended to agree, presenting hope in generally upbeat terms.[155]

Second-wave scholars such as Richard Lazarus have questioned this conventional view, arguing that hope is inherently covalenced.[156] We hope for an outcome only when it is uncertain, therefore hope inescapably involves a mix of confidence and anxiety. However, although hope is best described as ambivalent, it is obviously still pertinent to well-being, as are all the terms in this category.

Ambivalence of this sort is to be found in many non-English words concerning hope or anticipation, although each has interesting nuances. Some are highly optimistic and brightly toned. For instance, the German *Vorfreude*, literally "pre-pleasure," articulates the joy of looking forward to future gratifications. But usage of this term is fairly restricted to occasions when those gratifications are almost certain to arrive.[157] Then, a little less optimistic, and more shaded with negativity, are terms in which anticipation is mingled with impatience or frustration. The Inuit *iktsuarpok* is a fine example, purportedly applying to the activity of going outside frequently to check on the arrival of a person one can't wait to see.[158]

Hope of a different sort is found in terms expressing the sentiment that life will somehow unfold as it is supposed to. Consider the Icelandic *þetta reddast*, which *Iceland Magazine* called the country's motto.[159] Roughly translated as "It will all work out okay," the phrase is commonly used as a rallying cry when outcomes are not especially promising.[160] Many such terms leave the future in the hands of God or destiny. These include the

Arabic *In sha' Allah*, which translates as "may God wish it,"[161] or the Russian particle *avos*, which expresses faith placed in luck or fate.[162] Such terms do not convey assurance per se that a hoped-for event will occur. Rather, they assert that outcomes are predetermined, so there may be little point in worrying about them. Indeed, one might decide that any result is for the best, regardless of appearances—that events necessarily reflect some benevolent or at least unfathomable plan. Such beliefs can be a powerful resource, as Nada Eltaiba and Maria Harries observed in patients struggling with mental health conditions.[163]

Finally, there are more wistful words, tilted toward pessimism but not entirely bereft of hope. One example is the Italian adverb and interjection *magari*. The term can imply equivocation—as in, "I might be there"—but also longing: "If only I could ..."[164] Considerably more melancholic and even dark is the Korean *han*, which Heather Willoughby describes as a "Korean ethos of pain and suffering."[165] The term conveys a sense of sorrow essential to identification with the historic struggles of the Korean people. Yet Korean speakers have attested that the term contains flickers of hope, a quiet sense of waiting patiently for the end of an adversity.

Longing

In the previous section, we saw that hope, by virtue of its inherent ambivalence, can shade into longing. Let us explore the latter in more detail, for longing is a quintessential dialectical phenomenon—"a blend of the primary emotions of happiness and sadness."[166] Or, more poetically, "an emotional state suffused with a melancholic sweetness."[167]

You may recall from earlier the German noun *Sehnsucht*, a fascinating term rather evocatively translated as "life longings" and with roots in an "addiction" (*Sucht*) for "longing" or "pining" (*Sehn*). *Sehnsucht* thus speaks to longing as a state to which a person may be particularly drawn or may actively seek. Psychometric research led by Susanne Scheibe isolates six characteristics of the concept, whereby a person liable to moods of *Sehnsucht* would be likely to have:[168] (a) a belief that there exists an ideal path for one's life development; (b) a sense that his or her life is incomplete and imperfect; (c) a mental focus that spans past, present, and future; (d) ambivalent, bittersweet emotions; (e) deep reflection on life; and (f) a mental life rich in symbolism. The researchers conclude that *Sehnsucht* conveys "a constructive sense of the highs and lows, the gains and losses of life" in an emotional tone that "is fundamentally bittersweet, perhaps even closer to sweet-bitter."

This understanding of *Sehnsucht* clarifies something about longing: although it is ambivalent, it may also be important for well-being. The Welsh *hiraeth*, Portuguese *saudade*, and Russian *toska* convey other varieties of longing also perceived culturally as supportive of a good or complete life. These words convey a complex mix of nostalgia and yearning that are frequently tied to their respective cultures, to the point where a Brazilian unacquainted with *saudade*, say, or a Russian unfamiliar with *toska*, might be seen as lacking in some vital sensibility or cultural identity. For instance, Nikolas Coupland and colleagues define *hiraeth* as "a Welsh cultural longing for Wales" and cite a crisp example in tourist literature appealing to the Welsh diaspora.[169] "No one with a half drop of Welsh blood should fail to explore this land of *hiraeth*," one brochure reads.

Although Brazil or Portugal need not be the object of *saudade*, Brian Feldman describes it as "an emotional state that pervades Brazilian culture and thought" and Zuzanna Silva calls it a "key Portuguese emotion."[170] *Saudade* expresses longing for something gone missing, the particular emptiness that comes with the loss of something important, exciting, or enjoyable—desiderata that moreover may be irretrievable. This tragic irretrievability is similarly captured with respect to *hiraeth* by Robert MacFarlane, who defines it as an "acute longing for a home-place or time to which you cannot return & without which you are incomplete."[171] That said, such terms may also be directed at the unknown, such as hopes for a better future. Indeed, *saudade* gave rise to the *saudosismo* movement, which promulgated *saudade* as a Portuguese national value of transformative power.[172]

As for *toska*, Wierzbicka calls it "one of the leitmotifs of Russian literature and Russian conversation" and evidence against the universality of basic emotions.[173] The novelist Vladimir Nabokov said, "No single word in English renders all the shades of *toska*. At its deepest and most painful, it is a sensation of great spiritual anguish, often without any specific cause. At less morbid levels it is a dull ache of the soul, a longing with nothing to long for, a sick pining, a vague restlessness, mental throes, yearning. In particular cases it may be the desire for somebody of something specific, nostalgia, love-sickness. At the lowest level it grades into ennui, boredom."[174] Wierzbicka pairs *toska* with *duša* (soul, roughly) and *sud'ba* (fate, also roughly) as key terms defining Russian character and culture.

Not every form of yearning is culturally specific, of course. Some related words evoke freedom and adventure, longing for new places and experiences. There is the German *Wanderlust*, long-since borrowed by English, which suggests not just a desire to go hiking (its literal meaning), but also longing for a deeper sense of freedom, of being untethered.[175] German also features *Fernweh*, combining *Fern* (far, distant) with *Weh* (woe, pain) and articulating, in Barbara Gabriel's description, the tantalizing "call of faraway places."[176] This particularly applies to the unknown, conveying a strange sort of homesickness for places to which one has never been. English sources often characterize *Fernweh* as synonymous with *Wanderlust*, but *Fernweh* has a somewhat darker tone. Where *Wanderlust* often suggests a restless spirit of adventure, *Fernweh* is a counterpart to *Heimweh* (regular homesickness). Indeed, Rainer Diriwächter argues that many people, particularly the young, experience an oscillation between the two, simultaneously wishing to explore the world but also yearning for the safety of home.[177]

Although *Fernweh* and *Wanderlust* are ambivalent, at least expressing dissatisfaction with the status quo, they can be valuable in the pursuit of a good life. Both are frequently positioned as admirable qualities indicative of a romantic sensibility. Evidently, complex emotions are widely thought of as sources of depth and texture in life, reflective of good character.[178]

Pathos
A third category of ambivalent feelings can be grouped under the label pathos. Appropriately enough, that is itself a loanword, borrowed from Greek in the sixteenth century. In its original context, *páthos* denoted suffering and more generally emotion, or even simply experience.[179] In English though, it usually refers to the capacity of phenomena to evoke suffering— particularly sadness—in people.

One might wonder why sadness would arise in a book about well-being. Contemporary English-speaking cultures tend to regard sadness as an invidious and undesirable state, even to medicalize it as a mild form of depression.[180] But, as we have seen, negatively valenced emotions can potentially be valuable and adaptive. In that respect, Jean Decety suggests sadness can reflect moral sensitivity, specifically the admirable capacity to be compassionately moved by the suffering of others.[181] Similarly, studying the paradoxical "pleasures of sad music," Matthew Sachs analyzed sadness as a form of aesthetic sensitivity and refinement.[182] The capacity to be moved by art is not only considered an aspect of flourishing but also has been linked to well-being through a range of psychological processes, including regulating negative emotions (i.e., catharsis), retrieving valued memories, and inducing feelings of connectedness.[183]

Numerous terms capture and indeed even celebrate the capacity to be moved by life and art, to be sensitive, that is, to pathos. We have been introduced to *duende*, which can denote a heightened state of emotion and passion, particularly in response to art.[184] Notably, "passion" derives from the Latin *pati*, meaning to suffer or endure. When used in an artistic context, *duende* epitomizes passion's dialectical roots, reflecting openness to both the highs and lows of life. Thus the musician Nick Cave argues that love songs "must contain *duende*." As he puts it, "The love must resonate with the susurration of sorrow, the tintinnabulation of grief. The writer who refuses to explore the darker regions of the heart will never be able to write convincingly about the wonder, the magic and the joy of love."[185]

Such sentiments have a long pedigree, aligning with European Romantic sensibilities of the eighteenth century and since. Romanticism emphasizes the importance of emotion, including melancholic sensitivity to suffering. Indeed, that sensitivity is deemed the mark of a refined character. Some, such as Goethe in *The Sorrows of Young Werther*, even conjure a sensitivity too great to withstand the coarseness of the world.[186] Hence the Romantic valorization of experiences such as *Weltschmerz*, a German noun expressing world-weariness or hurt, and involving a nonspecific melancholy arising from the "pain of living."[187] Although *Weltschmerz* is not pleasurable, the bearer is often considered thoughtful, sympathetic, honest, and well meaning.

According to Robert Woolfolk, a melancholic aesthetic similar to romanticism came to be revered in Japan as well, particularly during the Tokugawa period (1603–1868).[188] This aesthetic was captured by the eighteenth century scholar Motoori Norinaga in the coinage *mono no aware*. Combining *aware*, which denotes sensitivity or sadness, and *mono*, which means "things," the term speaks to a capacity to be "touched or moved by the world," as Woolfolk puts it. However, where *Weltschmerz* connotes weightiness, *mono no aware* pertains more to the fleetingness of life and counsels a delicate appreciation of its ephemerality. This mood is reflected in earlier periods of Japanese literature, as well. Consider the opening lines of the fourteenth-century *Tale of the Heike*: "The sound of the *Gion shōja* bells echoes the impermanence of all things. ... The proud do not endure, they are like a dream on a spring night."[189]

The prevalence and importance of *mono no aware* in Japanese culture may be attributed in part to the influence of Zen, the branch of Buddhism that flowered in Japan from the twelfth century onward.[190] *Mono no aware* is an aesthetic approach to the cognizance of impermanence, which is central to Buddhist teaching. These teachings hold that life is defined by three *lakṣaṇas*, a Sanskrit term for qualities or attributes.[191] The first is *anātman*, roughly translatable as "no self," which reflects the idea that nothing has a fixed identity; instead, all things are brought into being as a result of their dynamic interconnections with everything else.[192] Following from this is *anitya*, often rendered as "impermanence," which holds that all phenomena are ephemeral and subject to change.[193] Failure to accept these principles leads to a third condition, the aforementioned *duḥkha*, referring to dissatisfaction or suffering. Buddhism teaches that people usually deny, or are ignorant of, the realities of *anitya* and *anātman*, and so allow themselves to become attached to things that inevitably change, producing *duḥkha*. Thus Buddhism counsels finding liberation from *duḥkha* through deep appreciation of *anitya* and *anātman*.

As such, recognition of impermanence is both sorrowful and yet subtly celebrated, a position of ambivalence. *Mono no aware* combines sadness with gratitude at the opportunity to witness life's beauty, however fugitively. Indeed, ephemerality is integral to its very beauty. As the fourteenth-century Buddhist monk Yoshida Kenkō explained, "If man were never to fade away like the dews of Adashino ... how things would lose their power to move us! The most precious thing in life is its uncertainty."[194] Or, as Lauren Prusinski puts it, "Beauty lies not in the object itself, but in the whole experience, transformation, and span of time in which the object is present and changing."[195]

Appreciation of Imperfection

Although Zen teaches that beauty is fleeting, it also suggests that a degree of beauty is retained amid change and decay. This insight is reflected in a class of Japanese words that speak to appreciation of what would typically be regarded as imperfection.

Preeminent in this respect is the well-known term, *wabi-sabi*, described by Alan Watts as one of the three main "perceptual-emotional moods" inculcated by Zen, along with *mono no aware* and *yūgen*, discussed below.[196] *Wabi-sabi* captures the charm of the aged and worn—"a crude or often faded beauty that correlates with a dark, desolate sublimity," Prusinski writes.[197] There is here a coherent aesthetic sense, characterized by austerity, imperfection, and awareness of the passage of time.[198] Jun'ichirō Tanizaki, in his classic 1933 exposition of Zen aesthetics *In Praise of Shadows*, wrote, "We love things that bear the marks of grime, soot, and weather, and we love the colors and the sheen that call to mind the past that made them." He describes preferring a "pensive luster to a shallow brilliance, a murky light that, whether in a stone or an artifact, bespeaks a sheen of antiquity."[199] Or, as the fourteenth-century monk Kenkō asked, "Are we to look at cherry blossoms only in full bloom, at the moon only when it is cloudless? ... Gardens strewn with faded flowers are worthier of our admiration."[200]

Each component of the term brings nuance to the whole. *Wabi* captures the importance of accepting the flaws of life, rather than engaging in a futile quest for perfection. As Dennis Hirota puts it, "*Wabi* means that even in straitened circumstances no thought of hardship arises. Even amid insufficiency, one is moved by no feeling of want. ... If you complain that things have been ill-disposed—this is not *wabi*."[201] Indeed, on this thinking we fail to understand the wonder and richness of life if we only value that which appears perfect or complete. This philosophy is prominent in the art of tea, a modality widely embraced by Zen and Japanese culture in general, wherein "flawed" utensils are more prized than ostensibly perfect ones. The seventeenth-century tea master Sen no Rikyū explained, "There are those who dislike a piece when it is even slightly damaged; such an attitude shows a complete lack of comprehension."[202] Hence Zen's revealing approach to ceramic repair, known as *kintsugi*, in which broken pieces are repaired using gold lacquer (*kin* means "golden," and *tsugi* "joinery").[203] The fault lines are neither hidden nor regarded as blemishes but rather accentuated, to relate the object's history and affirm the beauty in its flaws.

While *wabi* directs attention toward imperfection, *sabi* focuses on aging well—the way time, through wear, invests objects with gravitas and significance. As Horst Hammitzsch writes, *sabi* distils the notion of being "ripe with experience and insight" and evokes the sense of "deep solitude" that can accompany the passage of time.[204] A haiku by Bashō—widely considered the foremost proponent of the art[205]—captures the lonely beauty of *sabi*: "Solitary now—; Standing amid the blossoms; Is a cypress tree."[206] Zen suggests that our sorrow at impermanence and the passage of time might be transmuted if we could see it through the eyes of a contemplative such as Bashō.

Other Zen aesthetic principles do similar work, inducing us toward an emotional state of "heightened spirituality."[207] These include *koko*, which has been translated as "weathered beauty" or "austere sublimity," and *fukin-sei*, which roughly refers to asymmetry or irregularity.[208] Heightened spirituality is likewise embodied by *yūgen*, our last word for this chapter.

Sensitivity to Mystery

Yūgen is perhaps the epitome of an ambivalent feeling. Graham Parkes calls it the most ineffable of aesthetic concepts, though he tentatively renders it as "profound grace."[209] As the influential Zen scholar D. T. Suzuki elucidates, in philosophical texts *yūgen* tends to mean "dark," but in the metaphorical sense of mysteriousness. The term conveys unknowability, impenetrability, and obscurity. David Kaula sees in *yūgen* the "mysterious quiescence beneath all things"[210]—and the fundamental inability of the human mind to comprehend these depths.

However, *yūgen* holds within it the germ of possibility. Although the mystery of existence is beyond rational understanding, its deepest truths nevertheless can be sensed in some inchoate, intuitive way.[211] As Suzuki writes, the essence of life is "hidden behind the clouds, but not entirely out of sight, for we feel its presence, its secret message being transmitted through the darkness however impenetrable to the intellect."[212] *Yūgen* also suggests that one might be deeply moved by these mysteries, without quite knowing why. The thirteenth-century writer Kamo no Chōmei offers the following experience as an example of *yūgen*: "It is like an autumn evening under a colorless expanse of silent sky. Somehow, as if for some reason that we should be able to recall, tears well uncontrollably."[213]

Shini'chi Hisamatsu argues that much of Zen art endeavors to capture this sensibility.[214] As with *mono no aware* and *wabi-sabi*, art is seen as a more effective vehicle than discursive modes of representation, which are intrinsically unsuited to representing the ineffable. As Kaula explains, such art attempts to evoke a "muted, tranquil world in which nothing remains immutably fixed, a world of mist, rain, and wind, of snow and withering flowers."[215] The depths of such a world are "too fragile and elusive ... to be rationally understood or deliberately controlled" but can nevertheless be alluded to by the skillful artist, and perceived by the sensitive observer.

One might argue that Western cultures have identified opaque but moving experiences similar to *yūgen*. For instance, there is the state Abraham Maslow describes as one of "peak experience."[216] Such moments are hard to put in words, but they engender profound feelings of self-transcendence.[217] And classical Greek includes *aphaíresis*, which describes a process of abstracting or taking away. This notion has been deployed in contexts such as apophatic mystical theology, which holds that the nature of God cannot be stated directly but only alluded to through negative statements such as, "God is not *x*." Michael Sells describes *aphaíresis* in terms of "mystical languages of unsaying."[218]

But *yūgen* appears different in that it is evoked by seemingly ordinary phenomena. One need not contemplate the divine or the transcendent in order to discern profound depth. For instance, Allan Watts describes the following haiku by Bashō as the ultimate expression of *yūgen* in Japanese poetry: "On a withered branch; A crow is perched; In the autumn evening."[219] Western conceptions of peak experiences tend to assume some literal or metaphorical summiting, such as the achievement of a developmental milestone. *Yūgen*, by contrast, reveals the extraordinary in the ordinary and counsels receptiveness to it.

Summary

In this chapter, I have charted a range of entries in our first category of well-being: feelings (and associated phenomena). The untranslatable nature of these terms thereby furthers our understanding of this vital expanse. These include positively valenced feelings, covering seven broad, overlapping regions of state-space: peace/calm, contentment/satisfaction, coziness/hominess, savoring/appreciation, revelry/fun, joy/euphoria, and bliss/*nirvāṇa*. However, we also saw that well-being involves more than feeling good in the moment. A range of complex, ambivalent feelings can also be integral to flourishing. Among these are hope/anticipation, longing, pathos, appreciation of imperfection, and sensitivity to mystery.

The significance of these themes will be addressed further in the con-cluding chapter, and we will see other connections to these throughout the remainder of the book. In particular, many of the spiritual ideas alluded to here will be treated in more detail and with different goals in chapter 4, which focuses on personal development. For now, let us turn to the second meta-category of terms, those pertaining to relationships.

3 Relationships

Introduction

Recall our three overarching meta-categories, each of which traces a fundamental domain of well-being. In the previous chapter, we covered the first of these, feelings, through which we experience well-being. The second, and the subject of this chapter, is relationships, the principle source of influence over well-being. The final meta-category is personal development—the primary means through which well-being is cultivated.

Undoubtedly, there are resonances among these meta-categories, ways in which they overlap and are mutually reinforcing. The point here is not to demarcate rigid boundaries but to reflect on patterns in language use, and allow these to guide us toward ideas about well-being that might be overlooked if we were limited to the concepts available in English.

To that end, I turn to the language of relationships. It is no wonder that these form a large segment of the lexicography: relationships are as complex as they are essential to well-being. That complexity is captured in a profusion of words documenting the many nuanced forms of relation. Our languages would not be so prolific at developing these words if relationships were not so significant in our lives.

Relationships Promote Well-Being
One of the most comprehensive assessments of factors affecting well-being is the World Values Survey. Initiated in 1981, the survey asks nationally representative sample populations in nearly a hundred countries about their beliefs and values. Researchers have used the data collected to conduct ongoing time-series analyses of participant feedback. In the process, they have learned a lot about what people think is important.

John Helliwell and Richard Putnam have paid special attention to what survey respondents say about the good life.[1] They reviewed surveys spanning 1980 to 1997, covering over 87,000 people across 46 countries, to find the most prominent determinants of subjective well-being. Their top five factors, ranked in order of impact, were romantic and familial relationships, financial situation, work, community and friends, and health. Romance, Family, friends, and community are tightly bound up with concepts of relationship, as is work. There is no doubting that relationships constitute a backbone of lives well lived.

Why might this be? We can only speculate here, but many theorists draw on telic (i.e., goal-driven) models of need-satisfaction, in which well-being is dependent on what the environment provides. Ruut Veenhoven is influential on this score, arguing that well-being depends on livability (a congenial environment) and life-ability (one's ability to take advantage of this), each of which is enhanced by relationships.[2] Indeed, Robert Biswas-Diener suggests that relationships can "to some extent avert the psychological costs of material deprivation."[3] Siegwert Lindenberg and Bruno Frey's social production–function theory offers another spin on telic ideas. They propose that there are two ultimate goals—physical and social well-being—which are advanced by the pursuit of five instrumental ones: comfort, stimulation, status, behavioral confirmation, and affection.[4] Again, relationships have a clear role to play in furthering all of these goals.

Turning to Helliwell and Putnam's factors affecting well-being, the first is family, in particular the chosen family of a romantic relationship. Alongside the World Values Survey, numerous studies bear out the well-being benefits of such partnerships. For example, a survey of nearly 60,000 people across 42 countries found a consistent positive correlation between marital status and well-being.[5] Conversely, research shows strong negative correlation between well-being and relationship separation.[6]

The importance of romantic and family relationships can be accounted for in terms of the universalistic theories above, which look to the presumed essence of personhood to conceptualize what people usually need in life.[7] More prosaically, partnerships and families can also offer so-called protection effects beneficial to well-being. These include division of labor, and the emotional support of someone sharing goals and ideals similar to one's own.[8] Of course, many of these benefits are mediated by cultural context. For example, there may be greater social costs to unmarried life in certain cultures, boosting the well-being effects of marriage.[9] And the effect of widowhood on well-being is to a degree a consequence of the culturally variable status of widows.[10] In spite of these variations, though, across the great sweep of cultures, stable and loving partner and family relationships are widely regarded as the most significant predictor of well-being.

Helliwell and Putnam also emphasize the welfare benefits of broader social-support networks, from one's circle of friends to the wider community. Many social psychologists would explain the benefits of these networks in terms of what Pierre Bourdieu called social capital. This is "the sum total of the resources, actual or virtual, that accrue to an individual (or a group) by virtue of being enmeshed in a durable network of more or less institutionalized relationships of mutual acquaintance and recognition."[11]

Social capital is important in part because it is multidimensional.[12] Put differently, much of what matters in life can be articulated in terms of social capital. It may be a resource possessed individually, as in one's friends and other intimate contacts. It can be reflected in the community as a whole: a group that can more effectively pursue common goals is said to have greater social capital.[13] Social capital may manifest in attitudinal beliefs, such as trust in others.[14] It is also obtained through structured connections, such as those of a profession, institution, or organization.[15] And social capital might inhere in bonding and bridging—cohesion within groups and connection across them.[16]

Social capital's importance to well-being cannot be overstated. A striking example of its power—and thus, the power of relationships—comes from Finland. Researchers noticed that, in one coastal province, the Swedish-speaking minority lived longer active lives than the Finnish-speaking majority.[17] Although the two communities were similar in most respects—including genetic profile, socioeconomic status, education, and use of health services—there were remarkable disparities in morbidity, disability, and mortality. Swedish-speaking men lived 77.9 years on average, while Finnish-speaking men lived an average of only 69.2. The researchers suggest that these dramatic inequalities cannot be explained by conventional health-related risk factors. Instead, they point to indications of higher levels of social capital in the Swedish community, including more extensive voluntary associational activity, friendship networks, and religious involvement.

Neglecting Relationships

Unfortunately, although social relationships are good for us, prominent theorists such as Robert Putnam and Robert Bellah[18] have observed that Western societies are losing sight of their importance. An ethos of individualism is frequently invoked as an explanation for this trend, with Westerners being ever more prone to understand themselves primarily as individuals.[19] That is, as Geertz would have it, the Western subject is generally regarded as a "bounded, unique, more or less integrated motivational and cognitive universe."[20] Such individualism is partly defined in contrast to collectivism, supposedly the province of Eastern cultures. As Harry Triandis puts it, people in collectivist cultures are more likely to "define themselves as aspects of groups" and to "give priority to in-group goals."[21] Where individualism involves atomization, collectivism is steeped in relation.

That said, much like the troublesome East–West distinction itself, this individualist–collectivist binary homogenizes and obscures on its way to simplicity, disregarding strains of individualism and collectivism in all societies.[22] But it is nevertheless useful as a broad generalization, if only because people self-identify in this way, and not without consequences. Indeed, the individualist–collectivist distinction in self-identification has been corroborated across hundreds of empirical studies.[23] Moreover, the literature shows that self-identification of this kind may have consistent effects on outcomes like cognition, emotion, and motivation.[24] For instance, Richard Nisbett and colleagues report that East Asians are more likely to have "holistic" modes of cognition (i.e., attending to the entire field), and dialectical modes of reasoning, whereas Westerners are more prone to analytic modes of cognition (i.e., paying attention to a focal object), and use of formal logic.[25]

This individualistic sense of selfhood has also influenced the view of the person in Western academic psychology, which in turn affects how people perceive themselves. Mainstream psychology is mostly predicated on appraising and studying human beings as self-contained monads, and the field's individualism is reflected in myriad constructs, from self-determination to self-esteem, authenticity to autonomy.[26] The social, to the extent that it is recognized at all, tends to be constructed as an aggregation of individuals.[27]

Individualism permeates PP as well, leading theorists and practitioners to downplay the social context of well-being.[28] Notably, one of the most influential works in the field, Sonia Lyubomirsky and colleagues' analysis of factors contributing to variance in subjective well-being, holds that social circumstances are almost irrelevant.[29] Drawing on genetic studies of twins, the researchers proposed that only about 10 percent of the variance in subjective well-being is shaped by social circumstances, while 50 percent is determined by genetics, and 40 percent by "intentional activities," such as cultivating gratitude and practicing meditation.[30] This and related research has directed PP toward individually targeted interventions, such as developing aptitude for intentional activities.[31]

Such ideas are valuable, insofar as they constitute a broadly accurate analysis of factors contributing to well-being across a population. However, the statistics are often misconstrued. Assuming that the 10 percent figure is accurate across a population—a point which has been challenged, one should note[32]—it is not necessarily true of every person within that population. Commentators frequently make this error, known as an ecological fallacy. For people living in more challenging situations, the impact of their social circumstances upon their well-being is likely to be far higher than 10 percent. Consider that men in England's lowest socioeconomic class are almost three times more likely to have a common mental disorder than are those in the highest.[33] More broadly, a vast range of studies in social determinants of health demonstrates that, with respect to physical wellness alone, social conditions are deeply important.[34]

Engaging with Relationships

In sum, despite the many individualist currents pressing against Westerners, there really is no getting away from the importance of relationships to our well-being. Fortunately though, there also is no good reason to essentialize individualist traits; the West is neither inevitably nor intrinsically individualistic. As such, Western cultures may yet develop a greater appreciation of the value of relationships, perhaps simply by recognizing what has mattered all along.

I submit that this development process might involve engaging with unfamiliar concepts, such as those rendered in untranslatable words. Many cultures—including some Western ones, particularly Nordic[35]—have developed a nuanced vocabulary for describing relationships, covering the terrain in detail that English can often lack. For English speakers, reflection on these words may prove revealing.

I divide these terms into two broad categories: love and prosociality. Love refers to any relationship characterized by selectivity and closeness. Prosociality then describes all other social ties and networks. Each set of words will help us—academic psychologists, and people generally—refine our experiential maps and explore dimensions of social existence we had not previously attended to in detail.

Love

I may speak of love when describing my deep ardor and respect for my wife, the unshakable bond of care and loyalty I have with my family, the affection I feel toward my dog, my appreciation for the music of Tom Waits, even my occasional cravings for chocolate. All this is to say that, in English, "love" covers a lot of ground. It encompasses a multitude of feelings and attitudes; spans spectra of intensity, valence, and duration; and may be directed at all sorts of people, objects, and experiences. Indeed, Bernard Murstein describes love vividly as "an Austro-Hungarian Empire uniting all sorts of feelings, behaviors, and attitudes, sometimes having little in common."[36] Most words have multiple meanings, but love is "polysemous in the extreme."[37]

Recent scholars have attempted to delineate the many strands of love. One early and influential effort was by John Lee, who drew on classical Greek and Latin distinctions to identify six styles of loving.[38] He isolated three primary forms: romantic *érōs*, flirtatious, playful, but possibly manipulative *ludus*, and familial *storgē*. Pairing these generates three permutations. Combining *ludus* and *storgē* yields *prâgma*, a rational kind of love. From *érōs* and *ludus* arises *mania*—possessive and dependent. Finally, *érōs* plus *storgē* produces selfless *agápē*.

Another noted typology comes from Robert Sternberg.[39] His triangular theory holds that love emerges from the interaction of three principle components: intimacy, passion, and commitment. Alone and in combination, these give rise to seven types of love: liking (intimacy alone), infatuated love (passion), empty love (commitment), romantic love (intimacy and passion), companionate love (intimacy and commitment), fatuous love (passion and commitment), and consummate love (all three).

These models are largely concerned with love of other people, though they might be applied awkwardly to other phenomena. For instance,

Sternberg's triangle has been modified to explain consumers' brand loyalty on the basis of liking, yearning, and commitment.[40] Similarly, Yun-Oh Whang has argued that bikers genuinely feel *érōs*, *mania*, and *agápē* in relation to their motorcycle.[41]

What this suggests is that English subsumes a great deal under the category of love. Lee must have thought so, too, since he parsed love into more granular categories based on classical concepts. In doing so, he was essentially advocating a weak version of the Sapir–Whorf hypothesis, as I am. He chose terms from classical Greece and Latin precisely because they identified feelings familiar to, and understandable by, all people, but for which the English language lacked equivalents.

Lee helpfully expands our vocabulary with six pertinent words. Going further, I have located many more relevant terms, which enable us to achieve still greater granularity, including forms of love not aimed at people.* I group these into fourteen themes, each representing distinct forms of love. The first three are non-personal, directed toward experiences, non-human objects, and places. The remainder relate to people and are further grouped into three categories: caring, romantic, and transcendent love. In a spirit of poetic consistency, I label each of the fourteen forms using a relevant Greek term.

Nonpersonal Love

There is a Greek term, *meraki*, which could be loosely translated as "ardor," but specifically with respect to one's actions and creations. As Irene Sotiropoulou explains, *meraki* refers to "the care and love someone has for what he/she does."[42] I use it here to describe a passion for particular experiences and behaviors, which is the first form of nonpersonal love identified in the analysis. We shall not dwell on this form, since words pertaining to *meraki* can be found scattered throughout the book. These range from *aficionado* and *duende* in the previous chapter, to *ikigai*—a Japanese term relating to having purpose in life—in the next.

The second nonpersonal theme pertains to a love of objects. Here I mean "objects" in the widest possible sense, including not only physical things but also intangible phenomena, such as ideas. This latter usage is reflected

---

*However, over two-thirds include the Greek prefix *philo* or suffix *philia*, which inflates the number of terms, since one might use *philo* or *philia* to construct a neologism pertaining to any phenomenon.

in the loanword "philosophy," which derives from the Greek *philosophia* denoting love of knowledge and wisdom (*sophia*). Selecting an appropriate Greek label to represent love of objects is tricky, due to ambiguities and slippages in the meaning of terms over time and across contexts. In the end, I have chosen *érōs*, though not without reservations. My choice is based on its classical usage, where *érōs* denotes desire, but not necessarily sexual desire for people, as it often does in academic and popular literature today, and in the form "erotic." Rather, in the work of Plato and others, *érōs* more commonly describes appreciation of beauty, whereby one loves an object because it shares in the perfection of the divine forms. As Plato writes in *Phaedrus*, "He who loves the beautiful is called a lover because he partakes of it."[43] For sexual love specifically, I use *epithymía* instead, as explained below.

The third nonpersonal theme is the love of places, which I label *chōros*. As Eugene Walter argues, Ptolemy uses *chōros* to signify not the physical appearance of a place (*topos*) but its qualitative association, such as the affection and significance attached to it.[44] The related term *chōra* could also be used to denote a sacred place, and was deployed symbolically in philosophical texts to refer to a vital space, such as a metaphorical womb in which ideas gestate before being born.[45]

Many languages incorporate words that express a love of place, and not in the ambivalent, longing senses of *saudade* or *hiraeth*. One such word is the Māori noun *tūrangawaewae*, which literally means "a place to stand," describing land one would feel comfortable calling "mine" or "ours."[46] Relatedly, *mana whenua* delineates those who may exert moral authority and guardianship over a territory. This concept has had legal implications in New Zealand, where it has been incorporated into legislation that deals with guardianship and stewardship of natural resources.[47]

Similarly evocative of belonging is the Spanish noun *querencia*. Deriving from the verb *querer*, meaning to desire, it can refer to a place where one feels secure or from which one draws strength. As Ernest Hemingway famously explained in *Death in the Afternoon*, the term is commonly used in bullfighting to describe the bull's "preferred locality," where it "naturally wants to go in the ring."[48] In the case of people, Kirkpatrick Sale writes, *querencia* articulates the "deep sense of inner well-being that comes from knowing a particular place on the Earth; its daily and seasonal patterns, its fruits and scents, its soils and bird-songs. A place where, whenever you

return to it, your soul releases an inner sigh of recognition and realization."[49] The Welsh noun *cynefin* captures a similar sense of intimate relationship with the environment where one was born or raised, or to which
one feels "naturally acclimatized."[50]

Caring Love

Turning to love for people, I begin with care, which I distinguish from
romantic and transcendent love. I further delineate caring love into three
main forms.

The first is the love embodied in close friendship, which Plato called
philia.[51] So closely associated is Plato with *philia* that today love between
friends is often described as "platonic." In classical Greece, *philia* usually
referred to fondness, appreciation, and loyalty, in contrast to the desire
conveyed by *érōs*. Philia was bestowed not just on friends but also one's
family, community, and country.[52] In *Rhetoric*, Aristotle associates *philia*
with "doing kindnesses; doing them unasked; and not proclaiming the
fact when they are done."[53] Modern Greek also contains an interesting
derivation, *philotimo*. Sometimes rendered as "love of honor," this conveys
the culturally important ideal of respecting one's friends and the wider
community.[54]

Other terms describe acts of friendship pertaining to specific arenas,
such as spiritual practice. One example is the Hebrew noun *havruta*. Literally meaning "fellowship," it describes the practice of paired or shared
learning—particularly of religious texts, such as the Talmud—and the
bond that can result.[55] A similar concept is conveyed by the Sanskrit
kalyāṇa mitratā, which might be rendered as "spiritual friendship."[56] The
term derives from the adjective *kalyāṇa*, meaning "auspicious," "helpful,"
or "good," and the noun *maitrī*, which describes a form of compassionate
loving-kindness (as discussed further below). In a religious context, *kalyāṇa
mitratā* is deliberately, even formally, used to identify groups of people committed to helping one another along their spiritual and ethical paths.

A second form of caring love is directed at oneself. I refer to this with
the Greek *philautia*, which encompasses self-esteem, self-compassion, self-
regard, and self-respect. In classical Greece, *philautia* was recognized as a vital
component of a well-lived life. For example, Aristotle argued *philautia* was
the precondition for the other forms of love, and, if cultivated and deployed
skillfully, constituted a sound basis for ethics.[57] Contemporary psychologists

such as Kristen Neff also emphasize these self-valuing qualities.[58] Mind you, excessive self-regard can produce arrogance, egotism, and narcissism. Ideally though, the form I consider here does not come at the expense of others, who are equally respected and cherished. Thus, Aristotle's self-love is a reflective pursuit of virtue, a desire to cultivate one's character and thereby learn to extend affection and help to others.[59]

French has at least two forms of *philautia*, each of which can be admirable or problematic. The philosopher Jean Jacques Rousseau held *amour de soi*, which translates as "self-love," in high regard.[60] *Amour de soi* indicates a secure form of self-concern that is not contingent on others' validation. However, in this very security there is the potential for inconsiderateness.[61] Rousseau was more disparaging of *amour propre*, which also translates as "self-love" but carries connotations of vanity, and is seen as comparatively fragile and dependent on external validation.[62] Even so, because *amour propre* entails concern for others' opinions, it can lead to prosocial behaviors in hopes of currying approval.[63]

The third category in my typology of caring love is *storgē*, which readers will recall from Lee's theory, but which I use specifically to describe familial love. In classical Greece, *storgē* usually referred to care and affection of this sort.[64] Don Browning describes it in terms of the "deep and preferential investment by parents" in their children.[65] Admittedly, there is a fuzzy boundary between *storgē* and *philia*—as there is between many categories here—given that some close friends regard each other as family. Nevertheless, it is useful to differentiate between love of friends and the kind of unconditional, even instinctual, love that can exist between kin.[66]

One interesting term reflecting familial love is *kanyininpa*, from the Australian Aboriginal Pintupi language. Fred Myers describes this as "an intimate and active relationship between a 'holder' and that which is 'held,'" capturing the nurturance and protection parents usually provide children.[67] Built into *kanyininpa* are senses of unconditionality and responsibility that apply in family contexts, but usually not among friends (or at least not to the same degree).

The Yiddish *naches* (*nachat* in Hebrew)—which features in Ekman's Atlas of Emotion from the previous chapter[68]—articulates a more celebratory type of affection, in particular the pride felt in one's children, although possibly also unrelated mentees. A related Yiddish word is *kvell*, derived from a Germanic verb meaning to "well up." Where *naches* is a kind of pride, *kvell* refers to the overt expression of that pride.[69] What makes *naches* and *kvell* unique and difficult to translate is that they rarely refer to pride taken in others generally and instead are directed almost exclusively at people younger than oneself. By contrast, the Chinese *xiào*, often translated as "filial piety" or "family reverence,"[70] specifies respect for and devotion to one's elders and ancestors.

Romantic Love

Our inquiry now moves into the domain of romantic love, of which my analysis uncovered no fewer than five distinct forms. Any given partnership may involve any or all five types, in a mixture that may shift over time.

Much romantic love involves my first form, passionate love. This I label *epithymía*, which in classical Greek denoted desire and lust. The word has a revealing etymology, deriving from the Greek *thymós*, which connotes spiritedness and will. *Thymós* in turn is thought to derive from the Indo-European *dhu*, which evokes "the swirling of air in a vortex," and therefore in the context of passion implies a turbulent emotion that can be difficult to control.[71]

We have already broached the theme of sexual passion in the previous chapter with *jouissance*. Alluding more to the buildup to such a climax is *mamihlapinatapai*, from the Yagán language of Tierra del Fuego. Geoff Taylor defines this as "looking at each other hoping that either will offer to do something which both parties desire but are unwilling to do."[72] Thus, it can be used to describe a longing look between people that expresses unspoken mutual lust.[73]

Conveying more of the excitement of desire is the Tagalog *kilig*. This can simply mean to shake or tremble,[74] but it can also describe the "butterflies" in the stomach arising from an interaction with, or thoughts about, someone one desires or finds attractive. The term was added to the *Oxford English Dictionary* in 2016, where it is defined as "exhilaration or elation caused by an excitement or romantic experience."

The second form of romantic love involves playfulness, but potentially also manipulative "gamesmanship." Lee used the Latin *ludus* to describe these kinds of behavior; for consistency, I prefer the Greek equivalent *paixnidi*. Both can be translated as "game" or "play," and both are multifaceted, usable in positive or negative ways. But in their positive inflections—which are our primary concern here—they can refer to gestures of flirtation and coyness, and to seductive strategies such as playing hard to get.[75]

Although situated here as a variant of romance, *ludus* does not exclusively pertain to this category. The spirit of *ludus* can also infuse other forms of love, such as *philia* or *storgē*, as seen in forms of playful affection between friends or family members. An example of this is found in Tagalog, where *gigil* describes the "urge to pinch or squeeze something that is unbearably cute."[76] A similar note of playfulness is sounded in the French noun *frimousse*, which has been translated as "sweet little face" and is used to describe a person whom one finds cute or otherwise endearing.[77]

A more elevated instance of *ludus* infiltrating non-romantic forms of love is with respect to transcendent love, as found in esoteric contemplative traditions. For instance, the mystic Henry Suso (1300–1366) is credited with developing the notion of *ludus amoris*, which literally means "game of love" and has been used to depict the divine play of God.[78] The phrase refers to the way God is experienced as enticing, eluding, and ultimately embracing the spiritual seeker.[79] Comparable concepts are found in other traditions, such as the Sanskrit noun *līlā*, which has been deployed in Hinduism to describe the cosmos as the creative play of a divine being or power.[80]

However, *paixnidi* and *ludus* can also have negative connotations, describing scheming and deception in relation to love. Many of the studies drawing on Lee's typology emphasize this aspect. For instance, David Sarwer defines *ludus* as "a manipulative, game-playing orientation toward intimate relationships" associated with coercion.[81]

Indeed, one of the advantages of using untranslatable words to delineate different forms of love is that we can allow the good and bad ingredients to separate, conceptually if not experientially. Thus we arrive at the third and darkest inflection of romance, which Lee and I both label using the Greek *mania*. Of course, this is already a loanword, generically denoting madness or frenzy, as it did in classical Greece; the *manaie* were spirits who personified insanity, possession, and death.[82] With respect to love specifically, this troubled emotion has echoes in the French notion of *amour fou*, which translates as "mad love."[83] In themselves, *mania* and *amour fou* are not associated with well-being, but I include these in order to more fully understand the complexities of love—which of course *is* central to well-being—including its often ambivalent and potentially problematic nature.[84]

Contrasting with the intensity and instability of *mania* is the fourth form of romantic love, which Lee and I identify as *prâgma*. In its original Greek context, *prâgma* denoted a deed, action, or "thing done," and as such is the root for the English "pragmatism."[85] This form of love has tenuous parallels with Sternberg's "empty" love, which involves commitment but not intimacy. However, the pejorative connotation of emptiness does a disservice. *Prâgma* captures the idea that, while romantic love may often be passionate, it can also be a long-term process of building a life in partnership and forging bonds that do not depend on the whims of desire.

This aspect of romance is often overlooked, or perhaps is not even regarded as love, as Sternberg suggests. However, its value has been recognized by theorists such as Erich Fromm, who argued in *The Art of Loving* that people place too much importance on falling in love, and not enough on learning how to "stand in love."[86] The reasonableness of *prâgma* is captured by the French verb *s'apprivoiser*, which literally means "to tame,"[87] but which, in the context of a relationship, can describe a mutual process of accommodation, whereby both sides slowly learn to trust and accept each other.

Finally, the last form of romantic love might be regarded as the deepest, most intense, but possibly also the most tragic. This refers to the kind of bond that can appear ordained by fate—either to succeed or fail. I label this sort of love *anánkē*, after the Greek goddess of necessity, compulsion, and inevitability. "Even the Gods don't fight against *Anánkē*," the poet Simonides wrote.[88]

This preordained sense of fate is captured by the Japanese term *koi no yokan*. Translated as a "premonition of love," it articulates the intuition on meeting someone that falling for them may be inevitable.[89] This is not so much love at first sight as the more vertiginous feeling of being *about* to fall for someone. It also is imbued with "echoes of melancholy and uncertainty," as Kevin Williams puts it, since there is no guarantee the path of love will run smooth.[90] This concern is common in literature, where fated love is frequently tragic in its course; *Romeo and Juliet* may be the most famous case in the West.[91] The English term "star-crossed" captures this negative sense of fatedness, but not the positive sense also contained in *koi no yokan*.

Transcendent Love

Finally, we have three types of love characterized by the transcendence of personal needs and desires.

The first is described by the Greek noun *koinōnía*, which denotes communion, fellowship, intimacy, joint participation, and so on. However, I do not have in mind the general sense of community that, say, members of a church may feel.[92] Rather, picture a sudden efflorescence of participatory consciousness and collective euphoria at a worship service, or alternatively a rock concert or football game. It is specifically this kind of fugitive yet intense shared connection that *koinōnía* encapsulates. One is swept out of one's habitual self-contained individuality, and instead is momentarily united with some larger intersubjective unit, experientially becoming "one" with the group.

The second form of transcendent love is *agápē*, which also features in Lee's typology. In classical Greece, it usually denoted selfless forms of love. In English it is thought of mostly in terms of charity,[93] but in Greek versions of the Bible it is used to describe God's unconditional love for humanity. Followers are urged to emulate *agápē* in their worldly relations, hence the exhortation to "love thy neighbor." The sense here is of a universal love, embracing all humanity. In the New Testament, *agápē* is preeminent among the theological virtues. In the words of Saint Paul, "So faith, hope, love [*agápē*] abide, these three; but the greatest of these is love."[94]

This type of benevolent love is encouraged in other spiritual contexts too. I have already mentioned the term *maitrī* in the context of spiritual friendships.[95] So esteemed is *maitrī* in Buddhism that it is regarded in the Therevada tradition as one of the four *brahmavihāras*, or "abodes of *Brahma*" (the God of creation in Hindu theology—not to be confused with *Brahman*, which is discussed in the next chapter). *Brahmavihāras* denote the four qualities people are encouraged to develop, thereby becoming "*Brahma*-like" (a divinity who is specifically regarded as being loving and free from hate). In addition to *maitrī*, these are *karuṇā* (compassion), *muditā* (sympathetic happiness), and *upekṣā* (equanimity). *Agápē* captures a comparable spirit to *maitrī*, as does the Hebrew *hésed*, which is significant in Judaism. Relatedly, *gemilut hasadim* refers to bestowal or acts of loving-kindness.[96] Similarly exalted in Nguni Bantu languages, particularly Zulu and Xhosa, is the notion of *ubuntu*. As Archbishop Desmond Tutu explains, *ubuntu* "speaks of the fact that my humanity is caught up and inextricably bound up in yours. I am human because I belong. It speaks about wholeness; it speaks about compassion."[97]

Some languages make the universal character of loving kindness explicit by emphasizing kindness toward strangers. For instance, the Pashtun of Afghanistan and Northwest Pakistan have made the practice of *melmastia* a central tenet of ethical life. This may be translated simply as "hospitality," but scholars note that the connotations of the term are more radical. *Melmastia* is generally deemed unconditional, such that one should grant asylum to anyone who seeks it, even an adversary.[98] Similarly, Rawiri Blundell argues that the Māori noun *manaakitanga*, which has been defined as "reciprocal hospitality and connectivity,"[99] is a "cornerstone" of that people's tradition. It speaks to both the host's responsibility to welcome the visitor, and the visitor's invitation to partake of the host's generosity. There is more at stake than even care for others, though; the concept encompasses the pursuit of "common ground upon which an affinity and sense of sharing can begin."[100] Similar ideals are expressed by the Greek *xenia*, "guest-friendship" and the Hebrew *hachnasat orchim*, "welcoming the stranger."[101]

Our final form of transcendent love could be regarded as the counterpart to *agápē*. Recall the biblical conception of *agápē* as God's unconditional paternal love for humanity. Just as *agápē* flows downward from God, *sébomai*—which also features in the New Testament—reaches upward, reflecting a submissive stance of reverence and devotion.[102] There is an element of awe here, as reflected in Søren Kierkegaard's "fear and trembling,"[103] and described by Dacher Keltner and Jonathan Haidt as being at "the upper reaches of pleasure and on the boundary of fear."[104]

Like *agápē*, *sébomai* is found across traditions. For instance, in Hinduism and Buddhism, the Sanskrit term *bhakti* describes devotion toward spiritual ideas and beings, and the sacred generally.[105] There are also words for persons—aside from Gods—that may be a focus of such adoration, such as the Sanskrit *guru*, which denotes a revered spiritual teacher.[106]

Prosociality

Intimate bonds with select others are essential to well-being. But as we saw in the Finnish study, so are relations with others in general. Indeed, Nordic countries on the whole offer clues about the importance of these broader social relations. As we have seen, these places are consistently ranked among the happiest nations on earth. They are affluent and politically stable, which certainly helps.[107] But comparably wealthy and stable countries such as the United States and United Kingdom do not share the same high levels of overall life satisfaction.[108] Many theorists believe this is because Nordic communities tend to enjoy high levels of social capital, which is both attributed to and reflected in their relatively low levels of inequality and their egalitarian social policies.[109]

To foster the socioeconomic dimensions of well-being, it helps to recognize that well-being itself is inherently a social phenomenon, not exclusively a private psychological state. This can be hard for more individualistic societies to grasp. We might do better by cultivating a sensibility Carolina Izquierdo locates among the Matsigenka of the Peruvian Amazon, who do not consider themselves personally well if their social group is damaged or suffering.[110] I submit that untranslatable words might help people develop a less individualistic stance by bringing greater nuance to notions of prosociality. I group these words into five broad themes: socializing and congregating, morals and ethics, compassion and kindness, interaction and communication, and communality.

Socializing/Congregating

Our tour of prosociality opens with a celebration of socializing and congregating. We encountered a range of positive feelings pertaining to fun and revelry in the previous chapter. Here I touch upon the myriad social practices cultures have developed to enable such experiences—practices more nuanced than is captured by the generic English term "party."

Some of these terms are familiar because English speakers have already adopted them, taking advantage of their granularity. These include, for instance, the French *soirée* (a relatively cultured evening party, often centered on music or conversation), *aperitif* (which technically refers to a drink taken before dinner, but also covers the occasion itself),[111] and *salon* (an intellectual gathering).[112] Spanish has similar words such as *tertulia*, which refers to a social gathering or conversation that has literary or artistic overtones. Less refined is a *botellón*, which literally means "big bottle," and signifies a public congregation of people drinking, possibly to excess.[113] Such examples could be multiplied, but the point has hopefully been made: language can chart the state-space of socializing with fine precision, allowing us to discern subtleties in the ways people get together for enjoyment and stimulation.

Congregation can also have deep cultural meaning and importance, such as in religious contexts. Although I focus on spirituality in the next chapter, the social aspects of religious life are relevant here. (Although the distinction between religion and spirituality is fraught, spirituality is often regarded as more personal and self-defined, largely free of the rules, regulations, and responsibilities associated with religion.[114]) Indeed, religion is so influential, touching many aspects of life, that it is often difficult to disentangle religious and social practices.[115] Accordingly, the world's languages feature many religiously oriented forms of socializing. It would be impossible to cover all of them, so by way of example I will focus on Judaism—a religion especially abundant in social customs—and in particular on two quite different traditions.*

First, on a more festive note is the annual celebration and holiday of Purim, commemorating the saving of the Jewish people from an oppressive figure named Haman, as recounted in the Book of Esther.[116] The name itself may be the plural of *pūr*, meaning "lot," an allusion to Haman's practice of drawing lots to determine the date on which he would commit his atrocities (although other etymologies have also been suggested).[117] Purim is a generally joyous occasion, marked by customs aimed at fostering a lively atmosphere and community of care. For instance, participants exchange treats called *mishloach manot*, which literally means "sending of portions."

The joyousness of *Purim* is contrasted with the solemn gravity of *Shiv'ah*, or *Shiva*, a specific form of wake or collective grieving. Here the Hebrew word meaning "seven" is used to denote the week-long period of mourning prescribed in Judaism.[118] While the family are engaged in this mourning period (often referred to as "sitting *shiva*"), friends, relatives, and members of the wider community visit to pay a "*shiva* call," providing solace, as well as supportive necessities. This practice of *Nichum aveilim*—"comforting the mourner"—is regarded as a great *mitzvah*.[119] *Mitzvah* in itself is an important

---

*These traditions are very culturally specific, pertaining to Jewish people in particular. Thus, not all terms in the lexicography are equally amenable to being engaged with or borrowed by people outside the culture that created them. That said, some of the ideas and behaviours encompassed by such traditions may yet be relevant to people more broadly.

term, meaning commandment or law. To perform a *mitzvah* is to enact a deed in accordance with Jewish ethics, i.e., to fulfil one of God's commandments (of which there are 613 according to tradition).[120] And many such deeds—though by no means all—pertain to prosociality, hence their relevance here. *Mitzvah* also connects to our next theme under consideration, morals and ethics.

Morals/Ethics

Many terms describing moral and ethical concepts are untranslatable. I also discuss this topic in the next chapter, but I wish to introduce it here because ethical systems are created via prosocial processes, and are also often designed to engender prosocial behavior.

Morals—from the Latin *mōres*, connoting norms, custom, and tradition—can be conceptualized as beliefs and practices about right and wrong that are "sanctioned by the conscience of the community."[121] Ethics—from the Greek *ethikos*, meaning habit, custom, or usage, but also character or bearing—is the explicit codification of these morals as a system of prescriptions and proscriptions.[122]

Morals and ethics cover many areas of life, not only those relating to sociality. For instance, many cultures have developed dietary prescriptions that conceivably promote public health, but which are also concerned with notions of sanctity that are mostly unrelated to social considerations. The closely related Jewish and Muslim ideas of *kashrut* and *halal* are good examples. However, many ethical guidelines are in fact concerned with how we ought to treat one other.

Different cultures have developed a variety of foundational theories about morality—why it matters and why people should adhere to it. By way of example, I will focus on Buddhism, which has a particularly rich and theoretically detailed moral lexicon.

One of the teachings at the center of Buddhism is a doctrine known in Sanskrit as *pratītya-samutpāda*, often translated as the law of "conditionality" or "dependent origination."[123] It articulates the Buddha's insight into the causal nature of the universe, the ordered relationships between conditions and their effects. In Buddhism, this is arguably the meta law that underpins all other laws, such as the pivotal four "Noble Truths," known in Sanskrit as *catvāri āryasatyāni*.[124] We have already encountered the first truth, *duḥkha*, referring to the suffering and dissatisfaction that pervade life. The second is *samudaya*, which refers to the causes of *duḥkha*, namely attachment and craving. The third is *nirodha*, cessation, the termination of *duḥkha* by eliminating attachment and craving. The fourth is *mārga*, the path by which one can cease such craving and attachment. Buddhism promotes, in particular, the *ashtangika mārga*, or eightfold path.[125]

Buddhists regard such teachings as the key to well-being and ultimately *nirvāṇa*. As Urgyen Sangharakshita and Dharmachari Subhuti put it, "Once we have understood and are fully convinced about the nature of reality as paṭicca-samuppāda"—the Pāli term for this doctrine of causation—"we align ourselves with those regularities or laws that lead us to liberation."[126] These laws have been expounded upon in various ways in Buddhist literature. One influential analysis is the identification of five levels of conditionality, known as the fivefold *niyāmas*.* *Niyāmas* can be defined as "laws, conditions or constraints that govern processes or phenomena."[127] These identify domains of life subject to causal law-like principles.

Utu niyāma refers to the "law of the seasons," that is, the regularity of environmental phenomena. From the perspective of contemporary scientific understanding, it can be seen as equivalent to physical laws as they relate to inorganic phenomena, such as gravity. *Bīja niyāma* denotes the "law of seeds"—patterns in the realm of organic phenomena, such as might be studied by a modern biochemist. *Citta niyāma*, the "law of the mind" covers psychological processes, such as causes of mental events. *Karma niyāma* encapsulates "the desirable and undesirable results following good and bad action."[128] Finally, *dharma niyāma* is the "law of nature," which refers to the "spiritual potential" inherent in the universe. From a Darwinian perspective, this potential is revealed in the emergence of life and the evolution of sentient human beings, who are able to make spiritual progress.[129]

Buddhism deploys this framework as a rationale for morality. Of particular relevance are the last two *niyāmas*, *karma* and *dharma*. In itself, *karma* simply means "action," but popular usage of *karma* as a loanword does capture the key insight of the concept: actions have consequences. This differs subtly from Christian ideas of virtue and sin, in that no supernatural agency administers justice. Rather, in the Buddhist conception, we are rewarded or punished *by* our actions, not *for* them. As Chris Kang explains,

*The Buddha himself is only recorded discussing the *niyāmas* individually. In the fifth century CE, Buddhaghosa synthesized them into a fivefold schema.

"Volitional action rooted in non-greed, non-hatred and non-delusion (or in positive terms: generosity, love/compassion, and wisdom) gives rise to virtuous or positive imprints in the mind that would subsequently result in experiences of happiness and pleasure."[130] Thus, we see a powerful rationale for acting morally: moral acts benefit not only the recipient and the broader community but also the actor. This motivation then blends into the final level of causality, the *dharma niyāma*. Essentially, Buddhism holds that if one pursues ethical action, the result may be more than happiness or pleasure—it may be *bodhi* and consequently *nirvāṇa*.

I will return to the possibility of psychospiritual development in the next chapter. For now, let us consider some of the specific moral precepts that may lead people along the path to that goal.

Buddhist moral guidance and practice is known in Sanskrit as *śīla*. Three aspects of the Noble Eightfold Path are devoted to it: *vācā* (speech), *karmānta* (action), and *ājīva* (livelihood).* Various precepts specify in detail what then constitutes right speech, action, and livelihood. The best known and most widely adhered to are the *pañcaśīlāni* or "five precepts," which usually take the form of identifying a proscribed action.

The first proscribed behavior is *pāṇātipātā*—harming or killing. This precept can also be formulated positively as a commitment to, for example, *maitrī* and *ahiṃsā* (nonviolence). The second precept is *adinnādānā*, an injunction not to "take the not-given" (*asteya*)—an idea that is rather more subtle than simply not stealing—and in favor of generosity (*dana*). The third is *kāmesu micchācāra*, misconduct or "unwholesome" behavior concerning sexual or sensual activity. This is represented positively as the cultivation of *saṃtoṣa*, or total contentment. The fourth is *musāvādā* (false speech), or phrased positively, the cultivation of *satya* (truthfulness). The final precept is *surāmerayamajja pamādaṭṭhānā*, which refers to abstention from unmindful states related to alcohol or drugs; in positive terms, it enjoins the cultivation of *smṛti*. Most of these precepts relate, directly or indirectly, to the treatment of others.

So, having set out an example of a general theory concerning morals and ethics—using Buddhism as a case study—let us consider the various prosocial behaviors encouraged across the world's cultures. Many such behaviors pertain to kindness and compassion.

*These are conventional English translations. All of these terms incorporate various nuances and meanings.

Compassion/Kindness

In the section above, I explored the issue of morals and ethics by examining theoretical principles that explain *why* these are important for well-being. In doing so, I mentioned Buddhism's five precepts, most of which pertain to kindness and compassion in some way. Ideas relating to these precepts can be found across the world's languages.

Indeed, compassion and kindness themselves have interesting etymologies. As noted above, compassion derives from the Latin stems *com* (with) and *pati* (to suffer), thus connoting "a sense of shared suffering."[131] In this respect, it has parallels with its kinship loanwords *empathy* and *sympathy*, both of which have their origins in Greek.* As discussed in the previous chapter, *pathos* can mean suffering, but also refers more broadly to emotion, or even simply experience.[132] The prefix *em-* then denotes "in," while *sym—sun* in the original Greek—means "with." Empathy and sympathy thus respectively describe sharing in or with another person's feelings. These kinds of valorized relational processes are reflected here in a range of words.

Some terms refer to empathic sharing of sorrows and pains. One example is the Hebrew *koev halev*, which translates as "the heart aches," thus constituting a particularly vivid evocation of empathy (which need not always be heart-rending in this way). Others pertain to vicarious embarrassment, somewhat like cringing. These include the German *Fremdschämen*, combining *Fremd*, meaning foreign or other, and *schämen*, to be ashamed or embarrassed.[133] Conveying a more general concern for others' plight is the Māori verb and noun *aroha*. Although sometimes rendered as "mutuality,"[134] this translation lacks the warmth implied by the original. Finally, the Japanese term *omoiyari*, which has been defined as "altruistic sensitivity," has more active connotations.[135] Like sympathy and empathy, *omoiyari* indicates intuitive awareness and understanding of others' subjectivity. But unlike those, *omoiyari* also conveys a commitment to altruistic action on the basis of this intuition.

Compassion, empathy, and sympathy all involve sensitivity to others' emotions—but usually their feelings of dysphoria in particular. But

*Despite their common Greek roots, sympathy and empathy took different routes to English. Sympathy arrived from Latin in the sixteenth century. Empathy did not appear until the twentieth century, when it was adopted on the model of the German neologism *Einfühlung*, literally "into feeling."

we might also recognize and share in each other's joys. We have already encountered two non-English terms of this type, the Sanskrit *muditā* and Yiddish noun *naches*. The Hebrew *firgun* similarly expresses open pride and happiness in another's success but in more reciprocal terms. The relationship is not paternalistic, and there is a sense of sharing the other's joy as he experiences it. Likewise, the Dutch verb *gunnen* connotes allowing, conceding, and granting, and has been translated as "to not begrudge."[136] But the term is more complex than that, articulating as well the conviction that the other person deserves something positive and that, furthermore, one will derive satisfaction from their attaining it.

Whether one is empathizing with others in distress or sharing in their joy, compassionate feelings are widely associated with kindness, another sensibility to which different languages are attuned in varying ways.

As is often the case, the etymology and history of "kindness" tell us much about its meaning. The word derives from the Old English *cynde*, an adjective referring to the innate character of phenomena, and related to "kin."[137] In its earliest senses, kindness indicated the affection and concern of that type shared by kin or others of the same kind, such as a particular community or cultural group.[138] Over time, the ambit of kindness expanded to people in general, making for a more modest and achievable version of *agápē*.

I noted above that, today, *agápē* is often associated with charity, an understanding that reflects this latter-day overlap between kindness and *agápē*. We see a similar sort of conceptual merger in translations of the Hebrew *tzedaka* and Arabic *sadaqah* as charity.[139] In fact, both incorporate a sense of moral obligation absent from the English charity, connoting righteousness, justice, and fairness.[140] Whereas charity is seen as voluntary and magnanimous, *tzedaka/sadaqah* is one's duty.[141] A widespread conception of charity in these terms might make for a social revolution in approaches to well-being.

Where *tzedaka/sadaqah* relies on a kind of legalism, the Chinese *guān xì*, sometimes described as "interpersonal connections,"[142] is more transactional. Tapping into notions of *karma*, it reflects the idea that one who does good deeds might reasonably expect goodwill in return.[143] Meanwhile, the beneficiary of good deeds experiences an intuition of moral indebtedness and resulting obligation, called *ēn*. This intuition may play a role in the notion of *xiào*, filial piety.[144]

Interaction/Communication

Social harmony demands not only kindness but, more generally, effective interaction and communication. Thus, many terms extol the virtues of interacting and communicating skillfully.

One that we have been introduced to is the Buddhist precept of eschewing *adinnādānā*, which I described as an injunction against stealing. It is that, but not only in a material sense. It also can be interpreted as a prohibition against theft of all manner of phenomena—including dignity, for example, thereby enjoining people from, say, gossiping. In my PhD research, meditators spoke of cultivating more harmonious relationships through attention to *adinnādānā*.[145]

Alongside respect, politeness and civility are widely thought of as an important facet of prosocial interaction. The Persian *ta'ârof* is sometimes translated simply as "politeness," but it is a more nuanced form of ritual courtesy, particularly in relation to receiving and offering hospitality and gifts.[146] Abdi Raifee likens it to a "verbal wrestling match" in which hosts encourage their guests to have more food and drink, and guests insistently refuse before finally relenting. The term nicely captures the condition of hospitality, in which the host is eager to welcome, yet the guest hopes to "minimise imposition upon, or inconvenience to" the host.[147]

If *ta'ârof* has about it an air of negotiation, the Arabic noun *taarradhin* has even more so. This describes a positive solution to a disagreement—no begrudging compromise, but rather a win-win. As Aaron Wolf elucidates, this concept is influential in many predominately Muslim countries, serving as a guide diplomatic interaction.[148]

Diplomacy is enhanced by civility, another concept to which non-English languages bring nuance. The Catalan verb *enraonar* is often translated simply as "to speak," but, Enric Trillas and Maria Navarro explain, it implies communicating in "the best possible manner."[149] It means speaking "with a certain order, precision, calm and with the help of minimal but sufficient reasons to explain oneself." The goal is both to "be understood as clearly as possible," and to strive to understand the interlocutor in return.

The Fijian verb *talanoa* emphasizes civil discourse in another way, and roughly means "to tell stories." In telling one's story, one affords others context that helps them understand one's perspective. And in listening to others' stories, one bestows respect. The kind of discourse denoted by *talanoa* has benefits for well-being and has been harnessed as such in contexts ranging from conflict management to qualitative inquiry.[150] More generally, communication is enhanced by the pleasure taken in conversation. This is reflected in the evocative Arabic verb *samar*, denoting the culturally significant and popular activity of sitting in conversation in the evening.[151]

Across cultures and time periods, salutations and interjections have also served important, prosocial communicative functions. Indeed, the English "hello" is comparatively lacking in expressiveness, serving purely as a greeting. Consider the Hebrew *shalom* and Arabic *salām*, forms of which are used in greeting and parting but which also refer to peace, harmony, wholeness, prosperity, and tranquility.[152] Hebrew also features the well-known expression *mazal tov*. Literally "good fortune," *mazal tov* is used as a congratulation and yet carries an additional sense of hoping for the addressee's health and happiness.[153] More playful is the Hebrew interjection *tithadesh*, which translates as "may it renew you," "get new" or even "renovate yourself." The idea is to commend someone who has acquired a new possession or a fortuitous change in circumstance.[154] Or take the Japanese *otsukaresama*, derived from the verb *tsukarea*, meaning "to be or get tired," which articulates gratitude for another's efforts.[155]

Some positive interjections are not merely agreeable expressions deployed to smooth the passage of social interaction. They can be representative of a valued way of being. Something of this nature is seen with the Hawaiian word *aloha*—cognate with the aforementioned Māori *aroha*—which can be translated as the "breath of presence."[156] Not only does it serve as an expressive salutation, it is portrayed as epitomizing the spirit of Hawaiian culture.[157]

Moreover, skillful interaction need not only involve treating *people* well. Many cultures have developed words to reflect the notion that human beings can—moreover should—be in respectful and sensitive communion with the natural world. Consider *dadirri*, used in various Australian Aboriginal languages. This term describes an act of reflective, respectful, even spiritual listening. As Miriam-Rose Ungunmerr-Baumann of the Ngangikurungkurr tribe explains, it denotes "inner, deep listening and quiet, still awareness. ... When I experience dadirri, I am made whole again. I can sit on the riverbank or walk through the trees; even if someone close to me has passed away, I can find my peace in this silent awareness."[158] *Dadirri* transcends the act of listening and signifies a contemplative way of life in which one is receptive to, and reverent toward, the world.[159]

The notion of living "in tune" with nature is similarly captured by *hózhǫ́*, a term portrayed as constituting the essence of the Diné (Navajo) people, reflecting their ideal of existing in balance, peace, and harmony with the world. As Michelle Kahn-John and Mary Koithan elucidate, it constitutes a "complex wellness philosophy and belief system ... comprised of principles that guide one's thoughts, actions, behaviors, and speech."[160] Conversely, the Hopi term *koyaanisqatsi* represents an absence of this kind of harmonious connection. This has been translated as "nature out of balance" or "time out of joint," denoting a dysfunctional way of living that calls for urgent change or renewal.[161] These ideas of harmony are reflected in the final section here, which articulates a broader sense of communality.

Communality

Our final theme, communality, is concerned not with particular relationships but rather the togetherness of groups more broadly. This is perhaps exemplified by the Spanish idea of *simpatía*, which Harry Triandis and colleagues describe as a Hispanic "cultural script" that encourages people to "strive for harmony" in interpersonal relations, thereby enabling a social group—of whatever size, from a family to a society—to be in agreement and accord.[162] This idealized notion of social synchrony is likewise reflected in the Javanese *tjotjog*, which has come to prominence in academia through Geertz's work. He suggests it means "to fit, as a key does in a lock," and constitutes a "metaphysical concept" at the heart of Javanese culture.[163] In his analysis, it describes a cherished harmony. It can apply between friends, to a well-matched couple, agreeable food, clothes fitting, and generally to any desired outcome. Most relevantly here, it also describes the internal coherence of a group.

This ideal of communality is also reflected in terms articulating "community spirit," such as the Arabic *asabiyyah*, which has been translated roughly as "solidarity." It conveys a sense of intersubjective group consciousness and/or identity. Although sometimes equated with tribal loyalty, *asabiyyah* can depict more intangible bonds, such as between people united by religious beliefs or spiritual experiences.[164] Likewise, solidarity is conveyed by the Swahili term *tuko pamoja*, which can be translated as "we are together" or "we are one."[165] The Danish adjective *folkelig*, which literally means "folkish," suggests a sense of a specifically national spirit.[166] On an even grander scale, the Russian noun *mir* translates as "peace," but also "world" or "community," thus articulating a vision of global togetherness. It also may be accompanied by the adjective *Russkiy*, thereby signifying the "Russian world" in particular—all people who identify with Russia or feel themselves to be Russian, not only those within Russia's geographic borders.[167]

Other words describe people working together for the common good, an essential element of prosocial interaction. Many such terms hail from Nordic languages, being further indicative of their egalitarian and collectivist cultural commitments. These include *talkoot* in Finnish and *dugnad* in Norwegian. As Isto Huvila elucidates, these describe "a short, intensive, collective effort with a tangible goal," such as when people voluntarily pitch in to help someone renovate their home.[168]

There is also the fascinatingly ambiguous neologism *Janteloven*, coined by the Danish-Norwegian author Aksel Sandemose to describe the ten laws of Jante, a fictional community in his critical 1933 novel. These laws proscribe individualism and encourage collectivism.[169] In one sense, they could be regarded as exemplifying Nordic egalitarianism. However, per Sandemose's intention, the term is used colloquially in Nordic countries to denote social pressure toward conformity, and to criticize the notion that people should aspire to fit in to a collectivist mold.[170]

Janteloven is therefore emblematic of a tension at the heart of the way selfhood is often conceived and experienced in contemporary society: the felt need both to fit in and to become one's "own person."[171] In this chapter, I have been concerned with the first aspect of this duality. The next chapter turns to the second—personal development.

Summary

This chapter elucidates the ways in which relationships can be conducive to well-being. We explored terms subsumed under the label "love," charting all manner of close, intimate bonds. There were three forms of nonpersonal love: for activities (*meraki*), objects (*érōs*), and places (*chōros*). Next we discussed three forms of caring love: for friends (*philia*), family (*storgē*), and oneself (*philautia*). We then encountered five forms of romantic love, denoting relationships that are passionate (*epithymía*), playful (*paixnidi*), possessive (*mania*), sensible (*prâgma*), and fated (*anánkē*). Finally, there were three forms of transcendent love, including communion with a group (*koinōnía*), compassionate (*agápē*), and reverential (*sébomai*). We then considered prosociality more broadly, addressing the importance of socializing and congregating, morals and ethics, compassion and kindness, interaction and communication, and communality. In a counterbalance to this chapter, the next outlines the importance of individual development.

4   Development

Introduction

We now reach the final meta-category: personal development, the primary means by which well-being is cultivated. Before turning to the relevant words, let's consider why development is important for human flourishing.

Synthesizing Individual and Collective

At the close of the last chapter, we encountered the tension between community-mindedness and individualism. A strong sense of community enhances well-being by enabling accretion of social capital, but at the risk of enforcing conformity. Indeed, some models of mental health suggest that well-being consists in being attuned to one's culture precisely in this way, that is, fitting in not only socially, but also ideologically.[1] Critical theorists have questioned this vision of well-being though. What if the culture itself is problematic?[2] As Jiddu Krishnamurti puts it, "It is no measure of health to be well adjusted to a profoundly sick society."[3]

Experience suggests it is probably best to dissolve this tension, rather than attempt to resolve it, by pursuing both communality and individuality: don't give up on community, but also pursue one's agency and resist excessive obedience in the face of social pressure. For just as there are many good reasons to promote communality, there are also sound reasons to be wary of groupthink. In *Being and Time*, Martin Heidegger attempted to square the circle through the concept of *Das Man*, often rendered as "they-self" or "the they."[4] On this view, common ideas and values help to make us human, but we should also not fail to live authentically—to make our own choices and take responsibility for them.[5]

David Bakan makes the case for two basic modes of being along these lines: agency and communion.[6] Relatedly, Ken Wilber's vision is of people as separate entities, with their own needs, thoughts, and wills, but nevertheless "nestled in systems of cultural and social networks" that sustain them.[7] Recall Arthur Koestler's "holon"—the idea that everything is simultaneously a whole and a part. A person is a whole being but also part of a family and wider community. If well-being involves both community and agency, then it also demands both social life and personal development.

Personal Development
The notion of personal—that is, psychological—development has some parallels with physical development, in that both occur through an age-dependent process of maturation. One difference, though, is that psychological development is more likely to continue throughout the lifespan, or through a greater portion of it. If you graphed physical development, it would look like an inverted U.[8] Physical capacities mature up to some peak and then gradually decline.[9] Psychological capacities can also decline due, for instance, to aging-related cortical thinning.[10] But qualities such as spirituality and wisdom may build unto death, possibly making up for what is lost physically. Indeed, some studies suggest that overall well-being, incorporating all of the physical and psychological factors that make people feel well, tends to fall in middle age before rising again as people enter old age.[11] It is a testament to the power and possibility of lifelong psychological development that subjective well-being may improve even as the body is diminished.

Although there are many theories of personal development—some argue that it happens in discrete, well-defined stages, others see more diversity in developmental pathways—virtually everyone in the field considers it essential to well-being.[12] In this chapter, we will use untranslatable words to get to know this area in more depth and detail. As before, the aim is twofold: to enhance our conceptual knowledge of this relatively poorly understood area, charting the contours of growth with greater granularity and specificity; and to enrich our own experiential maps. We may learn to better appraise where we stand developmentally, and furthermore to venture into new existential regions, to see potentialities we previously couldn't.

This meta-category comprises two categories: character and spirituality. The first collects ideas about personal qualities and the fulfillment of potential. The second involves more rarefied or esoteric territory, reflective of the widespread view that, to truly attain life's peaks, one must cultivate some mode of spirituality.

Character

Character receives considerable attention in PP. In particular, it is generally regarded as a form of eudaimonic well-being. Recall that PP, albeit with some dissenting voices,[13] distinguishes between two main forms of well-being: hedonic and eudaimonic. The former, also known as subjective well-being, is constituted by positive feelings and cognitive appraisals of life satisfaction. Eudaimonic, or psychological, well-being encompasses rather different territory, being more about phenomena like meaning, virtue, wisdom, and fulfilment, such that a person who possesses these qualities would be deemed to enjoy high levels of eudaimonic well-being.[14] These are the kinds of qualities we shall be concerned with in this first category.

One of the most influential models of psychological well-being (PWB) comes from Carol Ryff.[15] Ryff draws on Aristotle's conception of *eudaimonia* as the "activity of the soul in accordance with virtue,"[16] as well as modern developmental theory, to conceptualize PWB as a dynamic process of psychological growth.[17] On this view, achieving PWB means working toward purpose in life, autonomy, positive relations, environmental mastery, self-acceptance, and personal growth.[18]

Although there is much to learn from Ryff's model, I believe it could yet be even more comprehensive. As critics have noted, the model omits spirituality specifically[19]—even if aspects of spirituality are encompassed by the other six components—despite this being an important trajectory of life pursuit for billions of people. And, like many of the theories we have encountered, Ryff's was conceptualized in a Western context mainly on the basis of work of Western research participants. Cross-cultural inquiry and input might expand Western psychology's perspective on what PWB can be. And particularly with respect to our aims in this chapter, there is room to look into elements of character beyond PWB,* important though it is.

---

*I am treating character, psychological well-being, and *eudaimonia* as largely synonymous. Although these constructs can all be conceptualized in various ways, I mean to suggest that character, psychological well-being, and *eudaimonia* roughly cover the same broad region of state-space.

The "values-in-action" (VIA) framework perhaps represents a more culturally encompassing paradigm. VIA focuses on the cultivation of "character strengths," defined as "positive traits that a person owns, celebrates, and frequently uses."[20] Instead of asserting that there are a handful of strengths everyone should have, the theory holds that people are most likely to flourish when they use and develop their particular strengths.[21] This hypothesis has been borne out in numerous studies, some cross-cultural, leading to a comprehensive and inclusive taxonomy of strengths.[22]

The current taxonomy features twenty-four such strengths, aggregated into six broad "virtues": (1) wisdom and knowledge (comprising creativity, judgment, perspective, curiosity, and love of learning); (2) courage (bravery, perseverance, honesty, and zest); (3) humanity (love, kindness, and social intelligence); (4) justice (teamwork, fairness, and leadership); (5) temperance (forgiveness, humility, prudence, and self-regulation); and (6) transcendence (appreciation of beauty and excellence, gratitude, hope, humor, and spirituality). Although this taxonomy is interesting in its own right—even if it has been criticized for its presumptions of universality and of the accultural nature of character[23]—especially pertinent for us is the way it was created.

The genesis of VIA is in the study of qualities celebrated throughout history and across cultures. Researchers assembled their taxonomy by studying some of the world's foundational religious and philosophical texts,[24] such as the *Upaniṣads*, *Analects* of *Confucius*, *Tao Te Ching*, *Tanakh*, New Testament, *Quran*, and Plato's *Republic*. From the *Analects*, for instance, *rén* (roughly, humaneness, benevolence), *yì* (duty, justice), *lǐ* (etiquette, decorum), *zhì* (wisdom, perspicacity), and *xìn* (truthfulness, sincerity) all have their imprint on the VIA framework.

This chapter complements the VIA approach, hopefully filling in some of its gaps. For, VIA's priority is to appreciate what is shared across cultures. Mine is to explore precisely what has not been: those ideas unique to a particular culture that might nonetheless be fruitfully integrated into others. I follow VIA and the like in choosing broad organizing themes, of which five main ones were identified: virtue, considerateness, understanding, self-determination, and skill.

Virtue

It behooves us to begin with virtue, since to an extent this theme is interwoven throughout all the others in this category. By virtue I don't mean its different types, in the plural—such as the six identified in the VIA schema—but rather the notion of virtue in itself.

Virtue per se is often thought of in terms of moral uprightness. A pivotal concept here is the classical Greek *areté*, denoting excellence or quality. This not only pertained to human beings, but anything that excelled at its purpose; a fast or strong horse, say, might be said to possess *areté*.[25] Applied to men specifically, *areté* could refer to "manliness."[26] More generally though, it often indicated moral excellence in people. This speaks to a conviction central to our purposes in this chapter: that fulfilling one's potential—a key component of well-being—means, in part, living virtuously.

As to how a person might cultivate virtue, Aristotle recommends *mesos*, denoting the mean or middle.[27] Virtue is embodied in the middle path between opposing vices of excess and deficiency.[28] Courage represents the optimal point between rashness and cowardice, generosity the balance between profligacy and miserliness, and so on. This is not simply an appeal to moderation or an argument for splitting the difference, though. Aristotle did not advocate, say, being moderately truthful in order to occupy some middle ground between honesty and lies. Rather, he believed that the appropriateness of given actions was based on context and that virtue, therefore, was not a matter of behaving according to some rigid conception of right and wrong. Rather, the virtuous person would take stock of his internal state and of the social world in order to reach the best possible choices.[29]

Besides words pertaining to the nature and dynamics of virtue, this theme also includes descriptors used to commend people who are deemed virtuous in various ways. One well-known example is the Yiddish *mensch*, derived from the generic German term for "person" and denoting a "good human being in its fullest sense," as Sherry Blumberg puts it.[30] Related, but not identical, are terms that speak to overall good bearing but with some emphasis on particular, albeit broad, qualities belonging to people of good character. An example is the German adjective *fein*, which Goethe considered untranslatable. This conveys bearing and grace, and more specifically nobility, honor, tenderness, and uniqueness.[31]

Some descriptors identify people who have reached certain psychological or spiritual peaks (and hence who, correspondingly, are perceived as exemplars of virtue). For instance, in Buddhism, virtue is associated with *bodhi* or awakening, hence the honorific Buddha. The Buddha himself adopted the label *tathāgata-garbha*[32]—usually rendered as "Buddha nature"—deriving from *garbha*, meaning womb or embryo, and *tathāgata*, which translates as "one who has thus come/gone" (i.e., to enlightenment). A related appellation is *arhat*, which denotes a worthy or "perfected" person. As described in the *Dhammapada* (the collected sayings of the Buddha), an *arhat* is as "firm as a high pillar and as pure as a deep pool free from mud ... perfectly tranquil and wise."[33]

Finally, there is a range of usually well-intentioned and complimentary adjectives pertaining to virtue that can, under some circumstances, be ambiguous or even pejorative. Consider the German *brav*, sometimes translated as "well-behaved." The term is often used to commend pleasant, earnest, and rule-abiding children. However, it can take on a patronizing air if applied to adults.[34] Similarly double-edged is the Japanese *majime*, which acknowledges people who are reliable and responsible but can also imply a sense of excessive seriousness or formality.[35] The Latin *pius* and English "pious" offer parallels, implying upright, faithful, and conscientious behavior, but also a lack of conviviality and spontaneity.[36]

Different cultures celebrate virtue in different ways. Having considered some of them, let's turn to three essential questions about living virtuously, and fulfilling one's potential more broadly. First, why would a person be virtuous, and cultivate self-development generally? Second, how would she know what virtue and self-development consist of? Third, how can she maintain virtue, and commit to self-development, despite pressures to behave otherwise? Broadly speaking, the answers are considerateness, understanding, and self-determination—all concepts to which non-English languages bring nuance.

Considerateness
One could argue that to be virtuous—and to flourish as a human being—one must first be considerate. That is, a precondition of virtue and self-development is caring about the quality and impact of one's actions. Without this basic sense of care—whether it be intuitive and implicitly felt, or conscious and explicitly reasoned—virtue and excellence would not arise. One would not even begin to strive toward the good, since one would have the nihilistic or apathetic perception that one's actions do not matter. This precondition of virtue, and of flourishing more generally, is captured by the term "considerateness," which derives from the Latin *consîderâtus* and comprises two fundamental qualities: awareness and care. That is,

considerate people are mindful of the impact of their actions on other people and themselves, and they moreover care about this impact.

Regarding awareness, I have already touched upon once concept from which English speakers can learn a great deal, namely *smṛti*. *Apramāda*, another Sanskrit term relating to awareness, contains an even stronger moral dimension. Variously understood as earnestness, vigilant care, unremitting alertness, diligence, moral watchfulness, and "awareness ... with regard to the sphere of qualities of good conduct,"[37] *apramāda* describes an awareness that is inherently and explicitly imbued with an ethical sensibility.[38] This is in contrast to *smṛti*, which is more morally neutral, and carries no specific connotation of ethics.

As for care, one important general principle is the "golden rule," which articulates an ideal of reciprocity developed and exalted by many philosophical and religious traditions, from Confucianism to Judaism.[39] In the *Analects*, for instance, Confucius is asked whether there is a "single word that can serve as a guide to conduct throughout one's life?" He replies with *shù*, a noun and verb conveying mercy and forgiveness, which he defines as "Do not do to others what you would not want others to do to you."[40] Elsewhere he also describes this reciprocity as the essence of the aforementioned *rén* (humaneness). Similarly, Rabbi Hillel (ca. 30 BCE–10 CE) emphasized the importance of reciprocity. Tradition has it that, asked to teach the entire Torah while standing on one foot, Hillel said, "What is hateful to yourself, do not do unto your fellow man. That is the whole of the Torah and the remainder is but commentary."[41]

Implicit in the terms above is a sense of why one should be considerate in this way. *Rén* describes a moral sensibility in which other people are deemed inherently worthy of being treated well. For its part, *apramāda* embeds awareness of the dynamics of *karma*, whereby right actions are regarded as benefiting both recipient and actor. As Kang puts it, "Volitional action rooted in non-greed, non-hatred and non-delusion ... gives rise to virtuous or positive imprints in the mind that would subsequently result in experiences of happiness and pleasure."[42] A person with a well-developed sense of *apramāda* would not only recognize the importance of treating other people well for their own sake but also, from a perspective of enlightened self-interest, realize that he, too, stands to benefit.

So, considerateness helps explain why people might want to be virtuous. But how does one know how to act virtuously, and more generally—since this category is not *only* about virtue—to live well and fulfil one's potential? That requires understanding.

Understanding

Recall that Aristotle's golden mean requires skillfully judging the best course of action in a given context. How does one judge? Here we come to another vital concept from classical Greece, *phrónêsis*, which is usually thought of as "practical" wisdom—determining ends to be pursued and ascertaining the best means of attaining them.[43] Aristotle regarded *phrónê-sis* as one of two intellectual virtues,[44] along with *sophia*, which refers to a more abstract, theoretical, even "transcendent" wisdom.* Indeed, many terms in this arena arise from classical Greece—from *logos* to *prâxis*—which reflects that culture's pioneering role in forging new ways of understanding the nature and potential of human beings.

Of course, terms relating to wisdom—and understanding more broadly—are found across the world's cultures and languages, many with distinctive nuances. Another language particularly rich in this regard is German, whose philosophical tradition has developed a unique lexicon pertaining to the way in which people understand the world. Some of these terms were used in common discourse before taking on specialized scholarly meanings that themselves became widely adopted as loanwords. Take *Weltanschauung*, which refers to a worldview, outlook, or overarching philosophy of life.[45] Besides its more general usage, it has been deployed by scholars, most prominently the psychologist Wilhelm Dilthey in the late nineteenth century, to articulate the epistemological claim that people necessarily appraise the world from a particular standpoint—that there is no objective "view from nowhere," in Thomas Nagel's terminology.[46] *Weltanschauung* played a key role in the development of fields such as psychoanalysis, hermeneutics, and critical thought, and is now widely used in English.[47]

Similarly influential are *Gestalt* and *Ganzheit*, which further elucidate the dynamics of how people understand their world, and which have provided the foundation for entire fields and paradigms within psychology. The former literally means "form" or "shape" and was harnessed in a philosophical context by Christian von Ehrenfels, who used it to denote the overall

---

*Aristotle further distinguished forms of wisdom from forms of knowledge, such as *epistēmē*, which pertains to understanding (e.g., in a scientific sense), and *techné*, which concerns craftsmanship and practical expertise.

configuration of something and to convey a sense of the whole being greater than the sum of its parts.[48] He saw *Gestalt* processing as a fundamental feature of the mind, enabling people to grasp patterns. The concept has led to practices such as Fritz Perls's *Gestalt* psychotherapy—concerned with "the total existence of a person"—and to conceptual paradigms like *Gestalt* theories of perception.[49] Relatedly, *Ganzheit* connotes unity, an "integrated whole."[50] This concept undergirds the field of *Ganzheit* psychology, which is described as the "holistic study of human nature."[51] Indeed, students of Wilhelm Wundt, widely regarded as one of the first modern psychologists, often referred to his work specifically as *Ganzheit* psychology.[52]

More recently, Heidegger has added to this lexicon terms such as *Dasein* and *Geworfenheit*. For him, wisdom consists in understanding the reality of these concepts in our lives. *Dasein*, which literally means "being here/ there," is Heidegger's preferred nomenclature for human beings. Somewhat akin to the psychological understanding of *Weltanschauung*, this captures the idea that people always exist in, and interpret the world on the basis of, a pre-given context. Moreover we inevitably come to the world with a certain *mood* (*Stimmung* in German)—that is, a state of mind, with specific intentions, priorities, feelings, and so on—which shapes how this context is engaged with.[53] Furthermore, *Geworfenheit*, often translated as "thrownness," articulates the notion that we inevitably find ourselves "thrown" into situations and contexts that are not of our choosing, whether unexpected encounters or the time and place of our birth.[54]

Heidegger approaches the phenomenon of understanding directly with two more innovatively deployed terms, *Ereignis* and *Erschlossenheit*, both of which relate to truth. The former means event, unfolding, or "coming into view," and conveys the idea that truth is something that "happens" or is revealed to us.[55] This connects to *Erschlossenheit*, often rendered as "world disclosure."[56] Heidegger relates *Erschlossenheit* to the Greek *alétheia*, which can be translated as truth or truthfulness, but which likewise carries connotations of revelation or disclosure.[57] Thus, Heidegger used *Erschlossenheit* to describe the process by which life becomes intelligible, meaningful, and relevant to human beings.

One could expand at length on Heidegger, but even this brief sample shows the potential for finding and developing terms that add nuance to our appreciation of understanding.

With that, we can turn to our third theme with respect to the cultivation of virtue, and of character more broadly: self-determination—the capacity to realize one's goals. For the desire to be virtuous and to live well, and the understanding to know what these consist of, count for little if one cannot actually manage to put these into action.

Self-determination

The analysis so far suggests that considerateness and understanding may be necessary conditions for virtue and personal development more broadly. However, they are not sufficient. It is vital that one be *able* to live virtuously and fully.

This capacity, which I call self-determination, has been articulated in numerous studies and theories. Perhaps the best known is Richard Ryan and Edward Deci's model, which conceptualizes self-determination in terms of autonomy, relatedness (i.e., being connected to others), and competence.[58] Outside of psychology, self-determination is more commonly associated with autonomy and competence in particular, denoting the freedom and capacity to make and pursue one's own choices.

It is the autonomy-centered concept of self-determination that I am most concerned with here. I see underlying it two key factors, which complement each other: the *will* to be virtuous, that is, the motivation to do right; and the *self-control* to carry out one's will by restraining oneself from doing wrong and instead skillfully cleaving to a righteous path.

Will itself is a complicated idea; a number of related words shed light on its meaning. These words fall into three broad areas: energy, grit, and independence. Taking energy first, many terms convey nuanced conceptions of vitality. One of the earliest and most important is *thymós*, which we encountered in chapter 3 in relation to *epithymía*. Sometimes rendered as "spiritedness," in classical Greece it carried many important meanings, including soul, will, and courage and was described as "the principle of life."[59] Other terms speak to energy in relation to tasks that needs completing, such as the Swedish verb *orka*, defined as "to have enough energy to be able to."[60]

Some terms offer explanations as to the *source* of people's energy. For instance, rather than conceiving of energy as a purely internal phenomenon, generated to varying degrees by individuals themselves, some cultures depict it as having suprapersonal provenance. These notions include *orenda*, formulated by the Huron people indigenous to North America, and the aforementioned *mana*, found in Polynesian languages. Both ideas are rooted in the conviction that the cosmos is suffused with a spiritual energy that exists outside people—as a nonpersonal divine force—and yet can be harnessed by individuals (such as shamans).[61] We shall further explore spiritual themes in the second part of the chapter below.

In addition to energy, the will involves qualities of grit. Grit has attracted much attention in PP recently through the work of Angela Duckworth, who characterizes it as "perseverance and passion for long-term goals."[62] Numerous terms pertain to this idea. Some are culturally vital, viewed as integral to or characteristic of certain groups. For instance, Finnish celebrates *sisu*, which has been defined as an extraordinary "inner determination," particularly in the face of extreme adversity.[63] Going beyond mere perseverance or resilience—according to analyses by Emilia Lahti, the scholar whose work on this concept inspired this lexicographic project—*sisu* is often exalted as a nation-defining quality that has enabled the country to thrive in the face of adversity.[64] Somewhat similarly, the Arabic noun *sumud* describes a determined struggle to survive, involving qualities including self-preservation, dignity, persistence, and forbearance. As Hala Nassar explains, this quality is valued particularly amid recent geopolitical turmoil in the Middle East, communicating a resolute desire and commitment to continue living in a particular location or in a certain way.[65]

Related to grit are terms pertaining to patience and stubbornness. The New Testament provides some good examples. No fewer than three Greek words, each with different nuances, describe the legendary forbearance of Job: *hypomonē* (cheerful endurance, constancy, standing firm); *kartería* (stubbornness, toughness, perseverance); and *makrothumeó* (being long-suffering, slow to anger and avenge).[66] These nuances are reflected across other words, too. For example, there is the evocative Dutch noun *engelengeduld*, which translates as "angelic patience" and refers to great forbearance, even "infinite" patience.[67] With a similar emphasis on extraordinary levels of forbearance, Japanese *gaman* has been described as "enduring the seemingly unbearable with patience and dignity."[68] With roots in Zen Buddhism, it emphasizes poise, equanimity, self-restraint, and stoic self-denial in the face of events outside of one's control.[69]

Relatedly, the commonly used injunction *ganbaru*, which literally means to stand firm, exhorts others to do their best—and indeed to "exceed" their best, going beyond what they believe themselves to be capable of—and to stick with a task until it is finished.[70] Similarly, the descriptive German *Sitzfleisch* conveys a stoical willingness to persevere with tasks that are hard or even just boring. More specifically, literally meaning "sitting flesh," it refers to a person who is "good at sitting it out." Also known as "chair-glue," it particularly denotes tenacity with respect to tasks that require physical inactivity and self-restraint, such as studious endeavours.[71] For instance, it has been described as the difference between a writer and an aspiring writer.

Finally, in addition to energy and grit, the will involves autonomy and related concepts such as freedom and independence. These qualities are reflected in a range of words, some with more positive connotations than others. *Wanderlust*, which we have previously encountered, is a more benign, possibly even romantic, example. Another is the Latin *solivagant*, which denotes a lone wanderer—someone whose freedom consists in being untethered to other people—and as such is used in astronomy to describe free-floating planetary objects.[72]

Other terms walk a fine-line between admiration of autonomy and wariness toward excessive free-spiritedness. Consider for instance the Yiddish loanword *chutzpah*. Although typically used to chastise a person who has overstepped the bounds of acceptable behavior, *chutzpah* has evolved to mean something akin to audacity, an ambiguous idea. One might therefore potentially commend another's *chutzpah*—having the guts to do something which one would not personally dare.[73] Similarly, the German noun *Willkür* may convey free-spiritedness and following one's own priorities, yet can also carry a disparaging notion of capriciousness and the disregard for rules and conventions.[74]

Thus, many cultures do not view autonomy and independence as unqualified goods. There is recognition that these can be problematic, and may lead to a willfulness that can be unhelpful or even destructive. This suggests that adaptive self-determination demands not only will but also the restraining hand of self-control. This was in some ways the essence of the Freudian conception of the psyche, which posited a continual tension between the *id* (elemental, instinctual drives), *superego* (internalized cultural norms and rules), and *ego* (the self-construct that must navigate between these).

Theories such as Freud's therefore identify the importance of restraining our more harmful impulses. This recognition is found in other languages too, with various words celebrating self-control or lamenting its absence. In the latter vein, Aristotle suggested that immoral people above all suffer from *akrásia*, or weakness of the will, which prevents them from acting in their best interests and instead leads to indulgence of wayward impulses. More positively, Greek thinkers exalted the ideal of *sóphrosuné*, which is associated with self-restraining qualities such as temperance, prudence, and self-control.[75] Finally, covering similar ground, the adjective *aútexoúsios* describes "mastery of oneself," the ability to exercise agency independently of one's emotions.[76]

Skill

The foregoing discussion has considered a wealth of terms relating to character, spanning qualities of virtue, considerateness, understanding, and self-determination. Most of these are not considered within their cultures as static traits but rather skills that can and should be cultivated. Naturally, there is some variation in this regard. Although Greek thinkers tended to depict admirable qualities as amenable to development, in some cases that possibility was limited to men of particular social standing, reflecting wider cultural prejudices of the time.[77] By contrast, it has been suggested that other traditions—such as Buddhism—offer paths of psychospiritual development that are more accessible, if not perfectly so.[78]

A wealth of words celebrates the skill needed to achieve personal development. To structure the discussion, I will draw on a trio of French nouns based around the verb *savoir*, meaning "to know"—that is, in the sense of know-how, not familiarity with some object. These are *savoir-faire*, *savoir-être*, and *savoir-vivre*.

Each of these compound terms traces different nuances of skillfulness. Perhaps best-known is *savoir-faire*, already a loanword. This describes knowing how to behave in a given situation, understanding how to speak and act appropriately.[79] As such, it is often described using terms such as diplomacy, finesse, poise, accomplishment, and adroitness (itself a loanword adapted from the French *adroit*, meaning "according to right"). *Savoir-faire* can also refer to the possession of practical, technical, or problem-solving abilities.

The quality of skillful problem-solving in *savoir-faire* is reflected in other languages, too. For example, the Portuguese notion of *desenrascanço*, roughly translatable as disentanglement, describes an imaginative resourcefulness in the face of new or unexpected situations—thus enabling one to extricate oneself from a tricky entanglement—particularly if one lacks the tools or techniques usually used in such cases.[80] Portuguese also features *jeito*, which can imply finding a way by any means, often circumventing rules or social conventions.[81] Similarly, the Italian verb *arrangiarsi*—which is often prefixed by *l'arte di* (the art of)—means to resourcefully make do, get by, or get along, though it may potentially also indicate that something is being achieved through underhanded methods.[82]

The second term involving *savoir* is *savoir-être*, which appends the verb "to be," implying a quality of knowing how to carry oneself. It has connotations similar to those of *savoir-faire*, but, where *savoir-faire* emphasizes practical skills, *savoir-être* celebrates social ones.[83] It can also convey grace, charm, and elegance, articulating the notion of a beautiful character, as opposed to simply physical beauty. The Greek concept of *eunoia*—created from *eû* (good, well, beautiful), and *noia* (mind, thinking)—is closely related, referring to goodwill, empathy, and the tendency to bestow approval on others. It also describes the capacity to evoke these qualities in others: one possessed of *eunoia* encourages similar benevolence in return.[84] Good interpersonal skills are likewise conveyed by the German term *Konfliktfähigkeit*, which denotes an ability to manage interpersonal conflict constructively, for instance, without becoming personally embroiled or affected.[85]

Relatedly, German also features the intriguing concept of *Fingerspitzengefühl*. Translatable as "fingertip feeling," it describes an overarching situational awareness, including an instinct for knowing how to act with tact and skill in a given situation. A Japanese variant of *savoir-être* is captured in the term *kokusaijin*. Literally meaning an "international person," *kokusaijin* describes someone who is cosmopolitan, usually well-traveled, and generally adept and comfortable at engaging with other cultures.[86]

The final French term is *savoir-vivre*, which refers to knowledge of how to *live* well.[87] France's reputation for good living is reflected in several terms that embody this ideal. These include *joie de vivre*, as mentioned in chapter 2, which articulates a zest for life, the "knack of knowing how to live."[88] This is no mere passing mood of positivity; it is a more general capacity to cultivate and savor the good things in life. It constitutes, as Susan Harrow and Timothy Unwin put it, "a Weltanschauung, a behavioral mode and form of practice. It is joy generalized, a result of many experiences, a sustained and boundless enjoyment of the here and now."[89]

Of course, the idea of savoring life is not limited to French culture, and expressions such as *joie de vivre* have their near equivalents in other languages (such as *livsnjutare*, also included in chapter 2). Such sentiments are further reflected in sayings that encourage people to live fully and/or have a good time. Particularly well known in that respect is the Hebrew phrase *l'chaim*, which literally means "to life" and is often used in social functions as a toast to health and life.[90]

These general terms are augmented by more specific ones that articulate what flourishing actually entails, which, according to much literature in PP, includes meaning and purpose in life.[91] The Japanese *ikigai*, which can be translated as a "reason for being," appraises life as "good and meaningful."[92] The experience of *ikigai* has been linked to psychological well-being and physical health and longevity.[93] Japanese also features the notion of *genki*, articulating another dimension of flourishing. The term literally means "origins of *ki*," where *ki* denotes a type of energy or life force (discussed further below as *qi*, the Chinese cognate of *ki*).[94] *Genki* thus implies being healthy, energetic, and full of life.

Finally, articulating the vital possibility that one can *learn* to live well, the German noun *Bildung* encompasses education, cultivation, and development. This in turn gives rise to compound terms such as *Bildungsroman*, describing a genre of novel depicting this celebrated process of personal development, as for instance in the works of Herman Hesse.[95]

Hesse provides a neat bridge to the second main category, concerning spirituality. Perhaps his best-known novel is *Siddhartha*, a poetic account of a spiritual seeker set around the time and place of the historical *Siddhārtha Gautama*, the Buddha.[96] Indeed, the very name *Siddhārtha* describes a person who has successfully achieved a valued aim, which in the case of this novel is ultimate self-fulfillment and liberation. Hesse's work reflects the idea, upheld in many cultures, that it is only possible to reach the peaks of development if one cultivates a sense of spirituality.

Spirituality

The preceding chapters have touched upon numerous topics, such as wisdom and morality, associated with spiritual and religious traditions.

However, although such phenomena are associated with spirituality, they are not inherently spiritual.[97] As such, this final category goes to the heart of spirituality, to that which could be regarded as *intrinsically* spiritual. An important aspect of this section will be exploring just what spirituality is. As we shall see, it arguably hinges above all on the concept of the *sacred*. Before I examine this term, though, let's take a moment to differentiate spirituality and religion.

Throughout much of history, religion and spirituality have been inextricably intertwined, and often treated as synonymous.[98] Etymologically, spirituality derives from the Latin *spiritualis*, which in turn is an adaptation of the Greek *pneumatikós*, an adjective that conveys a sense of being with or of the spirit of God.[99] A spiritual person was thus one in whom this spirit dwelt, or who was receptive to it, and often referred to a particularly devout subset of the religious community such as clergy. The term "religion," by contrast, has been used to describe the social institutions that formed around revered spiritual exemplars and their followers.[100] The term entered English in the twelfth century, via French, as an adaptation of the Latin *religio*, which connotes obligation and reverence and may in turn derive from the verb *religare*, meaning to bind.[101] Initially, religion usually referred to monastic communities, and to the spiritual ideas and practices that emerged within these, before more generally describing traditions that could unite people across multiple locales.[102]

In the wake of centuries of secularizing trends, spirituality has become increasingly differentiated from religion and from theism. Even as many people eschew traditional religion, large numbers report being drawn to spirituality.[103] Thus, spirituality as widely conceived today does not necessarily involve religious traditions or depend on theistic beliefs. As Harold Koenig puts it, spirituality is "something individuals define for themselves that is largely free of the rules, regulations and responsibilities associated with religion."[104] And note the non-theistic way in which Westerners have embraced Buddhism. Although some cultures bring theistic elements to Buddhism—such as pantheons of deities in Tibet[105]—research on Western "converts" suggests that many do not regard or interpret Buddhism as theistic, but nevertheless see it as spiritual in some way.[106]

If spirituality is not necessarily religious or theistic, what is it? Perhaps the most common way to understand spirituality is in terms of the sacred. This word is thought to have entered English via French in the twelfth century, derived from the Latin *sacrare*, which encompasses consecration, anointment, dedication, immortalization, and making holy.[107] Following the pioneering work of Emile Durkheim, the sacred is often understood in contrast to the profane: the latter pertains to ordinary everyday life, the former to "things set apart and forbidden."[108] A similar distinction is made in Russian: *byt* denotes everyday, domestic life, and *bytie* implies a spiritual or "authentic" existence.[109]

Thus, the term "sacred" signifies phenomena regarded as qualitatively "other" and out of the ordinary. This can encompass deities, places of worship, and relics, as well as any nontheistic yet mystical, supernatural, or sublime phenomena.[110] Indeed, the sacred could be anything meaningful to a person, such as a precious possession, memory, or value.[111]

In various ways, all the terms in this category of spirituality pertain to the sacred. These fall into three broad themes: the sacred itself (phenomena regarded as sacred, and their properties); contemplative practices (enabling people to engage with the sacred); and transcendence (experiences of the sacred). By putting these three categories together, a possible definition of spirituality suggests itself—namely, engagement with the sacred, usually through contemplative practices, with the aim of self-transcendence.

The Sacred

The sacred has been conceptualized in diverse ways cross-culturally. The relevant terms appear to fall into two main types: external and internal. Some terms describe phenomena outside the person, others inside. External terms refer to sacred realms or forces, perhaps associated with deities. Internal terms, such as spirit and soul, refer to the spiritual dimension within. We'll consider these two types in turn.

One of the oldest recorded examples of a sacred realm or force is the aforementioned *Brahman*. Barbara Holdrege suggests the *Vedas*, the ancient Hindu scriptures, deploy *Brahman* in four main ways: as the spiritual power inherent in the words and sounds of the *Vedas*; as the knowledge contained in the teachings; as the collective body of practices; and perhaps most relevantly here, as the ongoing process of creation itself.[112]

It has been argued that the earliest *Vedic* teachings expressed a form of animistic polytheism, conceptualizing the elemental forces of the universe as a pantheon of deities.[113] However, there later emerged a movement toward identifying a unifying principle beneath the flux of multiplicity and change, which became referred to as *Brahman*, described by David Ho as the "ubiquitous, absolute, formless, immaterial, immutable" all-encompassing ground of everything that exists.[114] Although there are many ways to interpret *Brahman*, it is frequently conceived as both transcendent—the source of everything that is, existing beyond the universe—and immanent, being everything that is, existing as the universe.

Similar notions of a universal spiritual force creating and/or permeating existence can be found across many cultures. These ideas have different nuances depending on the traditions and worldviews in question. Some conceptualizations of the sacred are particularly detailed, such as the esoteric *Kabbalah* tradition within Judaism. Without us delving too far into its complexities here, it begins with the notion of *Ein Sof*, which means unending or infinite, and in this context refers to God in its pure, transcendent essence, prior to self-manifestation (i.e., before becoming instantiated as the cosmos).[115] The tradition then identifies ten *Sefirot* (emanations), which constitute the way *Ein Sof* "reveals Himself," thereby creating the various spiritual and physical realms.[116] These are: (1) *Keter* (crown), which can be interpreted in this context as the initial impulse to become manifest in/ as the cosmos; (2) *Chokmah* (wisdom), the primary force in the process of creation; (3) *Binah* (understanding), which gives form to creation; (4) *Hésed* (loving-kindness), the love of creation; (5) *Gevurah* (power, judgment), the enactment of justice in creation; (6) *Tiferet* (beauty, balance), integrating *Hésed* and *Gevurah*; (7) *Netzach* (endurance, fortitude, triumph), the maintenance of the act of creation; (8) *Hod* (majesty, splendor), the glory of creation; (9) *Yesod* (foundation), the actual creation of reality, based on the preceding *Sefirot*; and (10) *Malchut* (realm), the product of the manifest cosmos itself.

In many cultures, divine powers and forces are frequently conceived of theistically. It is common, particularly in older contexts, to find polytheistic belief systems, with multiple deities that often personify certain phenomena. For example, Greek mythology tells a story about three "generations" of divine beings, elaborating upon their lineage and interactions.[117] First were the *Prōtógonos*, literally "first-born." In Hesiod's *Theogony* (ca. 700 BCE), these included *Kháos* (the void preceding the birth of the cosmos), *Gaia* (primordial Mother Earth), and *Ouranus* (sky or heaven).[118] *Gaia* and *Ouranus* created the second generation of twelve deities, known as the *Titânes*, who in turn begat the third generation, contemporary with the Greek people themselves. This cohort featured the twelve major Olympian Gods—who were also adopted in Roman mythology with alternate names—including *Zeus/Jupiter* (sky or thunder God, and supreme deity), *Poseidôn/Neptune* (the sea), *Háidēs/Pluto* (the underworld), and *Aphrodite/Venus* (love and beauty). There were also various lesser figures, such as *Érōs/Cupid* (desire) and *Dēmētēr/Ceres* (grain).

In some cultures, polytheistic systems developed into monotheistic frameworks. That said, the distinction between polytheism and monotheism is not always clear. The panoply of deities in Hinduism, for instance, are sometimes regarded as aspects or incarnations of a monotheistic *Brahman*.[119] Christianity has developed the complex concept of the Trinity, conceived as "one God in three Divine Persons." As elucidated by the Lateran Council IV, "It is the Father who generates, the Son who is begotten, and the Holy Spirit who proceeds."[120] Judaism is strictly monotheistic, and yet in the *Tanakh*, *Elohim* refers not only to God but also to other divine entities, often labeled "angels" in English.[121]

The foregoing discussion, while obviously not exhaustive, has shown the diverse ways in which the sacred has been conceptualized. I can now broach the second point above: many cultures view the sacred not only as suprapersonal, but also as inhering within people in some way as a spiritual dimension or aspect. In English, these ideas are captured by terms such as soul and spirit. The former is thought to come from the Old English *sawol*, which in turn derived from the Proto-Germanic *saiwala*. It has been speculated that *saiwala* means "of the sea," describing where spirits were believed to dwell before birth and after death, according to some Northern European mythologies.[122] Spirit is less culturally specific. It entered English in the thirteenth century, derived from the Latin *spiritus* (breath), and was used to denote the supposed animating principle or life force that endows beings with existence.[123]

This association of the spirit with the breath—and its conceptualization as a life force—is common across languages. Similar terms include *pneuma* in Greek, *qì* in Chinese (*ki* in Japanese), and *prāṇa* and *ātman* in Sanskrit. The latter features prominently in the Hindu philosophical school of *Védanta*, where—as in many other traditions—the spirit is regarded as partaking in, or being a manifestation of, the sacred. This notion is encapsulated in the phrase *Tat Tvam Asi*, which translates as "Thou Art That," conveying the idea that *ātman* is *Brahman*.[124] This philosophy is known as *Ádvaita*, a label often translated as "nondual," which expresses the idea that *ātman* and *Brahman* are not separate phenomena, but are ultimately one.[125] Liberation thus consists in experientially realizing this oneness.

Similar ideas are expressed in other traditions, albeit with slight differences. An interesting point of comparison in this regard is Buddhism. Living in a context suffused with *Vēdanta*, the Buddha agreed that liberation from suffering was possible. However, he disavowed the *Vēdanta* notion of *ātman*, an inner essence that would be the recipient of liberation. Instead, he taught the notion of *anātman*, or "no self."[126] As discussed in chapter 2, *anātman*—regarded in Buddhism as one of the three *lakṣanas*, that is, intrinsic qualities of existence—refers to the notion that all phenomena lack an intrinsic or fixed identity. Thus, the Buddha held that liberation would come through seeing all forms of selfhood as an illusion, leading to the ultimate and supreme state of *nirvāṇa*. Moreover, Richard Gombrich suggests that the Buddha extended his anti-essentialism to *nirvāṇa* itself, viewing it ultimately as also free from all limiting qualities.[127]

There are furthermore debates about the sacred *within* traditions, which tend to be heterogeneous. For instance, while Buddhism generally upholds the notion of *anātman*, this has led to complex doctrinal disputes concerning issues such as *karma* and reincarnation. If there is no self, then who or what is reincarnated?[128] Yet, despite these disagreements, Buddhist teachings generally all hold that the person in some way partakes in, or is a manifestation of, the sacred.

Moreover, Buddhism and many other traditions go further: this spiritual connection to the sacred is not simply an abstract philosophical idea that people are encouraged to believe in. More radically, practitioners are encouraged to cultivate a personal experience of this connection, primarily through contemplative practices, as the next section explores.

Contemplative Practices

Contemplative practices serve many purposes. From a sociological perspective, for example, such activities look like potent social bonding processes.[129] From the perspective of spiritual traditions themselves though, many such practices involve engaging with the sacred, however it is conceived. There is such a rich diversity of practices here—and thus of terms relating to these—that I cannot provide more than an indicative sample. However, our understanding of this terrain will be helped if, from a theoretical perspective, we conceptualize these varied practices as forms of meditation.

The term meditation itself derives from the Latin *meditatio*, meaning to engage in reflection. Originally used in the West to refer to all types of intellectual exercise, it eventually became more of a synonym for contemplation. For instance, in philosophy, it was common to speak of meditations on particular themes, such as Descartes' reflections on the human mind.[130] Similarly, meditation was used in religious contexts to describe reflection on aspects of the tradition, such as on "the sufferings of Christ on the Cross."[131]

In more recent years, meditation has been most commonly used in reference to Eastern practices. However, most cultures have developed activities that could be construed, in functional psychological terms, as forms of meditation. One helpful framework for conceptualizing these diverse forms comes from Robert Cardoso and colleagues, who argue that meditation practices can be differentiated according to four main parameters: (1) behaviors of mind (types of attention); (2) object (the focus of contemplation); (3) attitude (the emotional quality of the act); and (4) form (the physical nature of the activity).[132] I will use this framework here to guide our exploration of contemplative practices.

Per the first parameter, practices can differ in the way they deploy psychological resources. For instance, Buddhism incorporates two practices, *śamatha* and *vipaśyanā*, that are distinguished according to the behavior of mind they encourage. *Śamatha* is geared toward calming the mind through focused attention on a single stimulus or process, such as breathing.[133] By contrast, *vipaśyanā* refers to insight or "clear seeing," and is a practice of reflecting on the nature of reality.[134] In psychology, the latter has been operationalized as "open-monitoring," involving the "capacity to detect arising sensory, feeling and thought events within an unrestricted 'background' of awareness, without a grasping of these events in an explicitly selected foreground or focus."[135] Mindfulness practices based on *smṛti* are often cited as examples of *vipaśyanā*. However, such practices often incorporate elements of *śamatha* as well. For instance, the practitioner may begin with a period of focused attention on the breath to stabilize her awareness, before proceeding into the more expansive phase of open monitoring.[136]

The second parameter, object, turns our attention to the varied phenomena on which meditation might focus. One might reflect on bodily processes, such as breathing. One could dwell on ideas. Indeed, there is not much upon which one cannot meditate. As His Holiness the Dalai Lama puts it, meditation is "a deliberate mental activity that involves cultivating familiarity, be it with a chosen object, a fact, a theme, a habit, an outlook or a way of being."[137] For example, one cross-cultural topic of contemplation is death, known as *memento mori* in Latin, or *maraṇa smṛti* in Buddhism.[138] People may also focus on meaningful phrases or sounds, known in Sanskrit as a *mantra*, a loanword that translates as "mind tool."[139] And of course, people can reflect on phenomena directly associated with the sacred.[140] Often such practices are aided by physical objects such as religions icons.

The third parameter, attitude, relates to the emotions associated with contemplation. As noted, the Buddhist practice of *mettā bhāvana* is intended to engender *maitrī*, or loving-kindness.[141] Then there are practices that encourage reverence toward divine figures. This is particularly the case in monotheistic traditions. For instance, Judaism and Christianity both frequently invoke the term *Hallelujah*, Hebrew for "praise God"; when deployed in contemplative contexts (such as communal prayer or hymn), this not only exhorts believers to worship God, but to do so with an emotional spirit of gratitude, devotion, and rejoicing.[142] Reverential practices are also found in Buddhism, which encourages an array of deity meditations known as *iṣṭadevatā*, a compound of *iṣṭa* (liked, desired, revered) and *devatā* (divine being).[143]

The final parameter, form, concerns the various physical postures and actions involved in meditation. Yoga is one example. Derived from the Sanskrit *yuj*, meaning to bind or yoke, yoga is a system of practices originating in the Indian subcontinent during the third millennium BCE.[144] Yoga is designed to bring the different dimensions of the person—physical, psychological, spiritual—into union. There are many branches of yoga, each describing a particular spiritual path.[145] These include *karma* (selfless service to others), *jñāna* (knowledge and study), and *bhakti* (devotion and care). *Hatha*—the branch most commonly found in the West, where it is often mistaken as the only branch—refers to force or effort, and as a path of yoga centers on the practice of *āsana* (postures) and *vinyāsa* (dynamic transitions between postures).[146] It generally involves sequences of postures, the selection, duration, and speed of which vary by tradition, accompanied by meditative processes such as breathing and focusing techniques. Elsewhere, a wide variety of physically oriented contemplative traditions come from China. These include hundreds of techniques aggregated under the banner of *gong fū* (anglicized as kung fu), which literally means work, merit, or achievement, but which is used to refer generically to martial arts.[147] Some of these practices, such as *tài-jí* (tai chi),have become popular outside the sphere of martial arts per se.[148] Many practices center on *qì*, including the intricate body-mind techniques of *qì gong*.[149]

Despite their diversity, contemplative practices are unified in helping people to transcend conventional experience and thereby reach the peaks of development, according to numerous secular theories and spiritual traditions.

Transcendence

As alluded to above, cross-cultural surveys suggest that transcendence lies at the heart of most spiritual traditions.[150] Although this is a complex concept, a common theme is a shift away from the conventional sense of self—who one commonly perceives oneself to be, with a name, history, personality, occupation, and so on. This sense of self becomes seen in some way as illusory as one comes to identify with some larger experiential context (i.e., with a suprapersonal process or group).[151] Transcendence is not innately spiritual. For instance, analyses of crowd behavior at football matches, political rallies, and other events suggest that large groups have the power to subsume people's individual identities; they are "swept up" by the collective dynamic.[152] However, here we focus on transcendent experiences that are specifically spiritual.

Although transcendence does involve identification with some larger whole, it does not usually entail a disconnect from conventional identity. Sometimes this does happen: for instance, in trance states precipitated by psychoactive substances and rituals, a person may experience themselves in an entirely altered way, involving a "loss of self" as it is usually understood.[153] However, more commonly, spiritual self-transcendence involves a process whereby the conventional self is still acknowledged, yet "seen through."[154] For instance, in an advanced state or stage of psychospiritual development, one may view the self as a fiction even as one recognizes and takes care of this fiction. Hegel's formulation of transcendence using the complex verb *aufheben* (or noun *Aufhebung*)—rendered variously as to sublate, raise up, abolish, and at once to "negate and preserve"—captures this idea of seeing through.[155] As Wilber explains, what is negated is exclusive identification with a particular view of self.[156] The old sense of self is preserved but is now set within a more expansive experiential, possibly spiritual, framework.

Forms of transcendence are found across religions traditions. In Christianity, for instance, transcendence is reflected in evocations such as "I have been crucified with Christ; it is no longer I who live, but Christ who lives in me."[157] However, Buddhism has developed especially detailed theories of self-transcendence, as well as practices designed to inculcate it along several pathways, and so I shall focus in depth on this tradition.

One representative approach is that of the five *skandhas*. Translatable as "aggregates" or "heaps," this term refers to the corporeal elements of the person: substances such as flesh and bone, and processes such as circulation and respiration.[158] By reflecting on these elements in meditation, the practitioner may "deconstruct" her conventional notion of self. The idea is that one comes to appreciate that the Buddhist principles of *anātman* (no-self) and *anitya* (impermanence) apply to oneself, and so the immutable self is an illusion.[159] This is not to deny that people actually exist, nor to nihilistically claim that people do not matter, but rather to recognize that the self is an ephemeral mental construct. Similar ideas have been propounded by Western philosophers such as David Hume and William James, who understood the self as an aggregation of successive qualia or the "stream of consciousness."[160]

In practice, one reflects on the five *skandhas* in order to better understand how each, arising in sequence, generates the experience of self. The first *skandha*, *rūpa*, refers to matter or form—that is, the material body. Buddhist teachings suggest that *rūpa* is constructed from four *mahābhūta* (great elements or forces): *pṛthvī* (earth), *āp* (water), *tejas* (fire), and *vāyu* (air). Each refers to some aspect of the body:[161] *pṛthvī* encompasses that which is solid or hard, such as bones; *āp* that which is fluid, such as blood; *tejas* sensations of hot and cold; and *vāyu* that which is insubstantial and in motion, such as breath.

The second *skandha* is *vedanā*—affect and sensation.[162] When something is sensed in the experiential world, it is always already experienced as pleasant, unpleasant, or neutral. That is, when one's *rūpa* detects a stimulus, a feeling arises immediately. This generates the push and pull of aversion (to phenomena that evoke *duḥkha vedanā,* unpleasantness) and attachment (to phenomena that evoke *sukha vedanā,* pleasure).

The activation of *vedanā* gives rise to the third *skandha, saṃjñā,* which translates as perception and cognition.[163] *Saṃjñā* encompasses the higher-order cognitive mechanisms by which one processes and identifies stimuli.

These mechanisms then generate the fourth *skandha, saṃskāra,* a complex term rendered variously as "mental formations," "volition," and "karmic activities."[164] This *skandha* refers to psychological processes, such as trains of thought, activated by a stimulus. It also describes the way these processes generate urges to act in response to the stimulating phenomenon. These actions produce *karma,* with skillful and unskillful actions contributing to positive and negative future outcomes, respectively.[165]

All this occurs within fractions of a second, leading to the last *skandha, vijñāna,* which translates as consciousness or discernment. Only after a stimulus has been sensed and processed, and only after it has generated volitional impulses upon which one acts, does one truly become conscious of it.

Deep appreciation of the *skandhas* enables one to see through one's self-construct and consequently be liberated. This outcome relies on a perception and realization of what is called *śūnyatā.* Although often translated as "emptiness," *śūnyatā* captures the subtler idea that all phenomena, including the self, are conditional, dependent on conditions, and subject to change. As the Heart Sutra memorably puts it, "Form is emptiness and the very emptiness is form."[166] A person who attains a deep understanding and appreciation of *śūnyatā* attains enlightenment.[167]

As a final point, some have suggested that *śūnyatā* would be better translated as openness, boundlessness, or boundarylessness.[168] These terms reflect the notion that human beings tend to perceive, categorize, and experience the world by imposing boundaries on it. This is exactly what languages do, carving up existence into distinctive elements of experience. This book has made the case that our understanding of life can be enriched if we see how other languages have segmented the world. By doing so, we can refine our maps, adding finer-grained boundaries.

Yet, as these forays into Buddhist teachings suggest, we might do even more than refine our maps. By recognizing the constructed nature of our imposed boundaries, we may come to realize that they are useful illusions, that there are no absolute boundaries. This is the essence of *śūnyatā*: the promise that liberation comes from seeing through the very boundaries we have created.

Summary

Well-being is not only a matter of experiencing certain feelings or having nourishing relationships. Well-being is also developed through the cultivation of good character, comprising virtue, considerateness, understanding, self-determination, and skill. For many people, development is also premised on spiritual attainment. This often requires a conception of the sacred, a means of engaging with it through contemplative practice, and a resulting experience of self-transcendence.

5 A Map of Well-Being

This book has offered a unique overview of the state-space of well-being. I don't mean that as a boast but rather as a testament to the value of untranslatable words.

For all its lexical richness, the English language fails to address many aspects of life in detail, just as other languages may be lacking in some of the concepts in which English is strong. This is partly a function of the cultural contexts in which languages develop. One can therefore turn to languages other than one's own in order to fill these semantic gaps. This means borrowing other languages' *"Fremderwörter"*—"stranger-words," my term for potential loanwords that have not yet been embraced—thereby enriching one's lexicon.

I will substantiate and elaborate on this point in this concluding chapter. The first part summarizes the analysis so far and the cartographic theory of well-being based on it. This could be called the FRD framework of well-being, named for its three meta-categories: feelings, relationships, and development. This framework can enhance the current nomological network of constructs in fields such as PP, uncovering or emphasizing aspects of life that have been relatively overlooked.

The second part of the chapter turns from theory to practice, focusing on ways people can benefit from engaging with the words in the lexicography. I discuss approaches that might facilitate such engagement and sketch a research agenda for developing such an approach.

A Cartographic Theory of Well-Being

Throughout the book, I've mapped constructs pertaining to well-being that have so far not been explicitly identified in English. I've also tried to add signposts to this map using constructs that do exist in English, terms that serve as thematic and category labels.

As outlined in chapter 1, the way I created this map was through thematic analysis, specifically an adapted version of grounded theory. This method allows theory to emerge inductively from data,[1] in this case the untranslatable words themselves, along with their various renderings and interpretations.

I began by identifying themes in the data through a process of open coding. Next I grouped these themes into categories, and the categories into three meta-categories: feelings (positive and ambivalent), relationships (love and prosociality), and development (character and spirituality). These categories and meta-categories, together with their subsidiary themes, constitute the FRD framework of well-being, depicted in figure 5.1 below.

Each meta-category corresponds to a fundamental dimension of well-being, which is primarily—if not exclusively—experienced through feelings, influenced by relationships, and cultivated through personal development. Of course, the boundaries between the meta-categories are not always clean. Such coding dilemmas are common in qualitative analysis; themes frequently and legitimately fit into multiple categories, and the categories themselves do not have precisely delineated boundaries.[2] Even if the lines are fuzzy though, we can use the FRD schema to orient ourselves within the experiential state-space pertaining to well-being.

Before I turn to these three dimensions in turn, I will briefly summarize current PP theory on well-being. As noted in chapter 1, PP makes a foundational distinction between two main forms of well-being: hedonic, or subjective, and eudaimonic, or psychological.[3] Subjective well-being is

Figure 5.1
The three meta-categories of well-being, with their subsidiary categories and themes.

determined cognitively through judgments of life satisfaction, and through attention to affect (specifically, the ratio of positive to negative feelings). Psychological well-being is measured against more developmentally oriented criteria of autonomy, self-acceptance, relationship quality, environmental mastery, meaning in life, and psychological growth.[4] I should note that other multidimensional models of well-being have also been developed. For instance, there is Martin Seligman's PERMA model, which isolates five key domains of well-being: positive emotions, engagement, relationships, meaning, and accomplishment.[5] This model is increasingly substantiated by research;[6] however, the hedonic-eudaimonic distinction is better established and also continues to be tested and found useful.[7]

How do my categories map onto these models? There are some convergences, and some divergences. On a convergent note, my first category, positive feelings, roughly aligns with the affective component of subjective well-being, and with the positive-emotions domain of PERMA. However, my reading of positive feelings is broader, encompassing even numinous concepts well outside the scope of hedonic pleasure, such as *nirvāṇa*. In contrast, the second category, ambivalent feelings, does not sit easily within the above models. My third category, love, aligns broadly with Carol Ryff's model of psychological well-being, and specifically its dimension of relationships. However, my concept of relationships is arguably wider, extending to a fourth category of prosociality. Ryff's remaining five dimensions are then all encompassed by my fifth category of character. Finally, my sixth category, spirituality, is beyond the scope of these existing models.[8] The absence of ambivalent feelings, prosociality (to an extent), and spirituality from PP's most influential models of well-being speaks to the need for a more expansive framework of well-being. FRD aims to provide that.

Feelings

This first meta-category contains concepts that describe the way well-being is experienced. This includes not only emotions, but also qualia more broadly.[9] The meta-category comprises two categories, positive and ambivalent feelings.

As elucidated in chapter 2, my analysis of positively valenced feelings covered seven overlapping regions of state-space: peace and calm, contentment and satisfaction, coziness and homeness, savoring and appreciation, revelry and fun, joy and euphoria, and bliss and *nirvāṇa*. These seven themes are collected in figure 5.2, with sample words.

Per the granularity principle, each of these seven regions was deconstructed into smaller units through the analysis of relevant words. Many of these terms are instances of specificity-based untranslatability (see figure 1.3), in that they delineate a smaller and more precise region of state-space than that covered by the English thematic label. For instance, *jouissance* indicates not just joy, but often specifically the euphoria of sex. Other words are examples of overlap-based untranslatability (see figure 1.2): they and their corresponding English labels share regions of state-space (while also covering territory that is not shared). For instance, *hygge* arguably is not merely a type of contentment or satisfaction but an all-encompassing term that overlaps with these English constructs. Finally, in a few cases of generality-based untranslatability (see figure 1.4), the untranslatable word occupies a larger region of state-space than the English label. *Smṛti* is one example, encompassing a wealth of meanings, including but not limited to peace and calm.

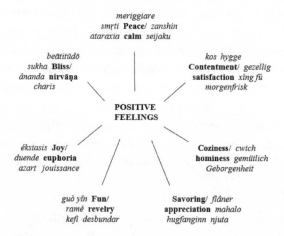

Figure 5.2
The seven main dimensions of positive feelings, with select words.

At this point, it is worth referring to the circumplex, basic, and constructivist theories of emotion introduced in chapter 1.[10] To an extent, my analysis is compatible with all of them. The positive feelings I isolate could fit within the two-dimensional state-space delineated by the circumplex model of affect, which holds that emotional states are generated by the interaction of two independent neurophysiological systems, valence and arousal.[11] All the terms within this category would be located toward the pleasant side of the circumplex grid, charting feelings from passive (e.g., peace/calm) to active (e.g., joy/euphoria). At the same time, the terms could arguably be situated within Ekman's naturalistic paradigm of basic emotions, specifically his broad spectrum of "enjoyment."[12] However, the words in this book bring greater granularity to this spectrum.

I lean toward a constructivist approach based on a milder version of the Sapir–Whorf hypothesis, which allows that there may be some universal human emotions, but that these are shaped by sociocultural contexts. Barrett's conceptual-act model clarifies my perspective. She argues that discrete emotions emerge from a conceptual analysis of a "momentary state of core affect."[13] Core affect may be hardwired into all people, but it is also mediated by a person's culturally influenced linguistic-conceptual schemas.

Translating Barrett's idea into my cartographic terminology, one encounters a region of experiential state-space, and then delineates and identifies this region using the boundaries provided by one's specific language(s). With Barrett, I contend that it is possible to refine this process of conceptual analysis and boundary-drawing and thereby develop greater emotional granularity.

Specifically, I suggest that we can so refine our conceptual analysis by engaging with untranslatable words. This is because such words delineate finer-grained regions of state-space than may be provided by the English language, and as such allow people to develop a more sensitive and detailed awareness and understanding of state-space. Later in the chapter, I will discuss potential research that might corroborate this claim.

We also encountered the category of ambivalent feelings. Perhaps contrary to expectation, well-being is not only a question of positively valenced feelings. A range of feelings blend light and dark yet are highly valued and indicative of a well-lived life. Flourishing is not always comfortable, as an emerging "second wave" of PP scholarship argues.[14] I grouped the words in

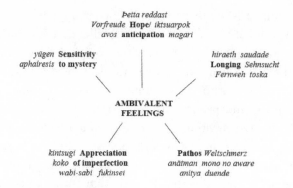

Figure 5.3
The five main dimensions of ambivalent feelings, with select words.

this category into five broad themes: hope/anticipation, longing, pathos, appreciation of imperfection, and sensitivity to mystery. These themes, and sample words, are outlined in figure 5.3 above.

Notably, many terms capturing ambivalent and dialectic states are found in Eastern cultures. For instance, the Chinese *yīn-yáng* encompasses numerous "tenets of duality."[15] Similarly, Zen artistic practices and aesthetic sensibilities can help people cultivate appreciation of dialectics. That said, I do not believe that these moods are accessible or comprehensible only to people from China or Japan. Just as people in the West increasingly engage with Buddhism,[16] they may also cultivate more dialectical modes of appreciation by engaging with the ideas and phenomena in this category.

Relationships

My second meta-category concerns relationships. Research suggests that relationships are the most significant factor affecting levels of happiness[17] and more generally are a major influence over well-being. This meta-category comprises two categories: love and prosociality—close bonds with select others, and networks of association among people in general.

My analysis identified fourteen distinct forms of love, which were grouped into four main types. This analysis extends previous theorizing on love by Lee and Sternberg.[18] As useful as these earlier models are, they are mainly restricted to love for people, and often in a romantic way specifically. They fail to account for many of the ways in which people use the term "love." In my analysis, first, there are three nonpersonal forms of love, for experiences (*meraki*), objects (*érōs*), and places (*chōros*). Second, there are three nonromantic, caring forms of love, specifically for friends (*philia*), family (*storgē*), and oneself (*philautia*). The third main form, romantic love, breaks down into five types, including passionate (*epithymia*), playful/game-playing (*paixnidi*), possessive (*mania*), sensible (*prâgma*), and fated (*anánkē*). Finally, we encountered three forms of transcendent love, group-based communion (*koinōnía*), compassionate (*agápē*) and reverential (*sébomai*). The four main forms, together with their various sub-forms, are detailed in figure 5.4 below.

When thinking about relationships, we also need to concern ourselves with more than close bonds. Prosociality, too, affects well-being. In understanding the importance of this category, I drew on Bakan's contention that people have two fundamental ontological modes of being: agency and communion.[19] Agency encompasses our existence as separate entities, while communion acknowledges that we are also inextricably situated within sociocultural networks.[20] Words in the prosociality category reflect the significance of communion and fell into five themes: socializing and congregating, morals and ethics, compassion and kindness, interaction and communication, and communality. These themes, and sample words, are detailed in figure 5.5.

This category is especially significant because community is widely thought to be overlooked in Western societies. The West—to the extent

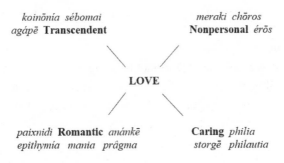

koinōnía sébomai
agápē **Transcendent**

meraki chōros
Nonpersonal *érōs*

LOVE

paixnidi **Romantic** *anánkē*
epithymia mania prâgma

Caring *philia*
storgē philautia

Figure 5.4
The four main forms of love, with select words.

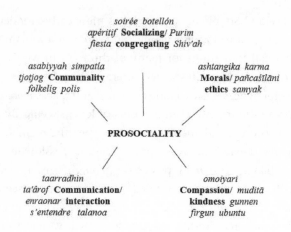

soirée botellón
apéritif **Socializing**/ *Purim*
fiesta **congregating** *Shiv'ah*

asabiyyah simpatía   *ashtangika karma*
tjotjog **Communality**   **Morals**/ *pañcaśīlāni*
folkelig polis   **ethics** *samyak*

PROSOCIALITY

taarradhin   *omoiyari*
ta'ārof **Communication**/   **Compassion**/ *muditā*
enraonar **interaction**   **kindness** *gunnen*
s'entendre talanoa   *firgun ubuntu*

Figure 5.5
The five main dimensions of prosociality, with select words.

that such a generalization makes sense—can be seen as broadly individu-alistic.[21] The individualist corners of the West might therefore learn from societies that show greater appreciation of the importance of social bonds, the importance of which to well-being has already been recognized by emerging paradigms such as positive social psychology.[22]

That said, for reasons we have examined, we do not want to be so invested in the importance of relationships that we lose sight of the value of individuality. The second meta-category is therefore balanced by the third, which addresses the significance of personal development.

Development

The third category of the FRD model is personal development—the culti-vation of well-being through the exercise of agency. It concerns the pos-sibility of fulfilling one's potential by bettering oneself. As with the other two meta-categories, development comprises two categories: character and spirituality.

I understand character to be the traits and elements of personality that cultures praise and encourage among their members. This aligns with usage in PP, most notably and pertinently the VIA paradigm of character strengths.[23] By analyzing foundational religious and philosophical texts, this initiative identified twenty-four qualities that different cultures have historically celebrated.[24] Following on VIA's inspiration, I sought to bring further detail to this area by focusing on concepts that are not shared—that may be unique to a particular culture. The lexicography currently features over 200 such terms, which I aggregate into five broad themes: virtue, considerateness, understanding, self-determination, and skill. These themes, and select key words, are detailed in figure 5.6.

Perhaps the most important difference between FRD and VIA is that the themes I isolate, and the constructs divided among them, are not just a typology of diverse individual strengths. My five character-related themes interrelate, in that collectively they constitute integral components in the process of character development. That is, virtue, considerateness, understanding, self-determination, and skill appear to be the mechanisms which enable the person to live well and fulfill their potential.

The first character theme is virtue. Virtue is central to Aristotle's conception of *eudaimonia*,[25] which has greatly influenced theories of personal development in PP. This theme does not so much concern specific behaviors regarded as virtuous. Rather, the focus is on the possibility of being virtuous per se. This is closely related to the second theme, considerateness, which pertains to the question of why, in the first place, one would want to be virtuous and of good character. Considerateness involves two essential

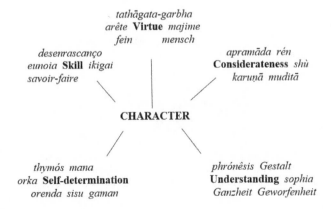

Figure 5.6
The five main dimensions of character, with select words.

qualities: *awareness* of the impact of one's actions, on others and oneself, and *care* for the consequences. The third theme, understanding, covers the knowledge required to be virtuous and to live well more broadly. An example is Aristotle's golden mean, discerned through wisdom.[26]

Yet, considerateness and understanding are not much use if one lacks the autonomy and capacity to make choices befitting a person of good character. Thus the fourth character theme is self-determination.[27] This is a matter of will and self-control, without which one cannot excel and fulfil one's potential. Skill, the final theme, recognizes that considerateness, understanding, and self-determination can be cultivated. They are not static traits but paths along which people may grow.

Skill is also vital to the second developmental category, spirituality. This area of psychological growth corresponds to the virtue of transcendence in the VIA framework. Crucially though, in my analysis, spirituality is not just one aspect of character. I place it in a separate category because, in many cultures, it is as necessary to development as character itself; reaching the peaks of flourishing requires spiritual cultivation. I organize terms related to spirituality under three main headings: the sacred, contemplative practices, and transcendence. These themes, and select key words, are illustrated in figure 5.7.

The sacred has been conceptualized in diverse ways cross-culturally. Across this diversity, relevant terms fall into two main types: words signifying phenomena outside the person, such as the notion of a sacred realm, force, or beings; and words denoting a spiritual dimension inside

Figure 5.7
The three main dimensions of spirituality, with select words.

the person, such as soul and spirit. The many traditions recognizing the idea of the sacred have also developed repertoires of contemplative practices to help people cultivate a sense of spirituality, including prayer and meditation.[28] The goal of such practices, and the spiritual sensibility they foster, is self-transcendence.[29] In this process, one's conventional sense of self is perceived as being illusory or partial. Instead, one feels a part of, or identifies with, some larger sacred context.[30]

As with feelings and relationships, the development meta-category is derived from untranslatable words and related English-language concepts. The extent to which the model can be operationalized and actually facilitate improvements in well-being is a matter for further research. Below, I will outline an agenda for that research. But first, I'd like to reflect on limitations of my analysis, to which the research agenda is in part a response.

Limitations

The most basic limitation is scope. The lexicography currently contains over 900 terms, but there are surely more among the some 7,000 languages in existence.[31] The list must therefore be regarded as a small sample, albeit one that may grow. A further constraint is that, in the context of this book, there is space to discuss only around a third of the words collected so far. Even then, my analysis of the included words cannot be comprehensive. That said, by keeping word-by-word analysis relatively brief, and necessarily partial, I am able to undertake a comparative inquiry.

Those analyses I am able to perform are inevitably influenced by my cultural background and personal characteristics. Any qualitative research will suffer from such drawbacks; the researcher inevitably supplies the "filter of salience through which data are sieved."[32] But while this cannot be avoided, it can at least be addressed through a commitment toward reflexivity—that is, through understanding and disclosure of one's situatedness.[33] My own attention is affected by my longstanding interest in Buddhism. It may be further relevant that I am a white, educated, British man, born in London to a loving middle-class family of working-class background. I therefore possess privileges that could influence my analysis.[34]

This situatedness is not necessarily a flaw, to be corrected. There is, after all, no unbiased epistemological "view from nowhere."[35] That another person might arrive at a different selection and interpretation of words, and thereby develop an alternative theoretical position, is not a problem.

Indeed, I hope that other researchers will do just this, bringing their own insights into well-being by analyzing the lexicography as their own perspectives allow.

At the same time, I do not wish to overemphasize my impact on the analysis. There are limits to reflexivity; even the lengthiest autobiographies fail to capture the near-infinity of stories and experiences that constitute a person. Indeed, as psychoanalytic theory has recognized, there is much about the person that is hidden to themselves.[36] To fully account for oneself is not possible.

What matters is to give the fairest possible account. In my case, that means deriving definitions and descriptions from peer-reviewed academic publications when possible and reviewing these derivations with an advisory group of bilingual speakers. These procedures help to ensure a degree of objectivity.[37] Moreover, the lexicography is a work in progress, with its contents being continually refined based on feedback.

With these limitations in mind, let us turn to the research agenda.

A Research Agenda

Further investigation will help to flesh out my proposed FRD model. I suggest a research agenda with two principal components: first, empirical data-gathering to strengthen the model; second, applied interventions to develop methods for operationalizing the model, and for harnessing the value of untranslatable words more broadly.

Data-gathering

The empirical side of the agenda aims to improve the lexicography and by extension the cartographic map of well-being based upon it.

For a start, the lexicography should be greatly expanded, and the map thereby enriched. Thus, a primary research goal would be to investigate the many languages not yet represented in the lexicography, while continuing to research the languages already included. This process could be aided by individual online contributors, such as those who have already helped compile the current lexicography through my website.

Data-gathering could also be done more systematically. One such approach, which could be ideal for a PhD candidate, would involve in-depth, semi-structured interviews with speakers of languages currently unrepresented in the lexicography. Participants would ideally, but not necessarily, be linguists, translators, or psychologists, and would also be bilingual in English.

The first purpose of the interview would be to identify words in the interviewee's language(s) of fluency that they deem be both untranslatable (in English) and pertinent to well-being. Interviewees would have advanced notice to think about potential words and ask others for suggestions. The researcher and participant would discuss these words in as much depth as feasible to better understand their etymology and cultural significance and to collect examples of use in context. Interviews would, as per my initial research, be analyzed using grounded theory.[38] Such a project could be carried out by multiple individuals on overlapping populations, building confidence in the comprehensiveness of the lexicography and the robustness of its definitions, derivations, and interpretations.

While we use qualitative research to expand the lexicography, we might also use factor analysis to quantitatively assess its contents. This would enhance our understanding of specific words, including their internal structure. We saw an example of this sort of research with Scheibe, who created a 28-item questionnaire to isolate six dimensions of *Sehnsucht*.[39] Such analyses can be used to develop psychometric scales pertaining to other untranslatable words, which would help to establish construct validity.[40] With more such scales, we will refine the FRD framework.

This research would help us ascertain the extent to which words truly are untranslatable. Consider *hygge*. Psychometric analyses would facilitate an understanding of where it sits within the nomological network of existing constructs within PP. For instance, we could determine the degree of overlap with related English constructs such as coziness and contentment. Doing so would refine the FRD map of well-being.

These various scales could also be subjected to cross-cultural testing (though translating the scales is of course no simple task).[41] Such testing would help us determine the extent to which people can understand and/or experience constructs that are not native to their cultures. Theorists have argued that languages borrow words in order to bridge semantic gaps; cross-cultural analyses would test this proposition. Moreover, such testing could validate my suggestion that people can cultivate an appreciation for untranslatable words and for the phenomena they refer to.

Another way to test the benefits of engagement with untranslatable words is through applied research with clinical and nonclinical populations (with an example of the latter being young people in educational settings). That is the second half of my research agenda: to design therapeutic interventions on the basis of untranslatable words.

Applied Interventions

A strong relativist might argue that an untranslatable word is truly understood only by members of the culture that created it, since outsiders would not be able fully to experience the phenomenon to which it refers.[42] But I am a moderate relativist. I contend that all people can access the experiences of other cultures to some useful degree and that, furthermore, all people can learn from descriptions of untranslatable words.

There is some evidence that people can adopt words from other cultures to their own benefit. Indeed, this process is integral to language development. Recall that as much as 41 percent of the English-language vocabulary is borrowed from other languages.[43] Indeed, even now, loanwords are everywhere in English and other languages, whether as a *Gastwort*, whose foreign provenance is explicit, a *Fremdwort*, which has been more thoroughly assimilated, or as a *Lehnwort*—a loanword proper, treated no differently than a native word.[44] Thus, I argue that English speakers—and indeed speakers of all languages—can benefit from engaging with the *Fremderwörter* in the lexicography (i.e., the words which have not yet been borrowed).

We can systematically foster this engagement using applied initiatives of the sort that have been used to enrich children's emotional vocabulary and granularity,[45] thereby improving their behavior, academic performance, and general well-being.[46] These initiatives are founded on the idea that emotional differentiation is associated with well-being. Studies suggest that people with greater differentiation are more aware of their subjectivity and so find it easier to regulate their attention and emotions, thus maintaining emotional equanimity.[47]

There is no reason comparable interventions could not be designed with respect to untranslatable words and offered to people of all ages. Indeed, this process has already happened with at least two words in the lexicography, *smṛti* and *maitrī*. Both have been harnessed in clinical and nonclinical settings to help people practice the qualities they denote: mindfulness and loving-kindness.[48]

These initiatives have implications for the debates above, particularly the issue of whether speakers can experience and understand phenomena signified by untranslatable words from other cultures. Critics have argued that the ways in which these Sanskrit terms have been conceptualized in contemporary psychology overlook some of their nuances. For instance, the calque "mindfulness" can be regarded as rather cerebral, understating *smṛti*'s compassionate qualities.[49] That said, the association of mindfulness with cognitive theories of attention is hardly outlandish when one considers the psychological nature of many Buddhist teachings on meditation.[50] For instance, the *Amitayus jhana sutta* instructs, "Cause your mind to be firmly fixed on [the object] so as to have an unwavering perception by the exclusive application of your mind."[51] Such language is not far removed from that of modern cognition-based interventions.

This process of adoption and adaptation speaks to another debate raised above: whether English speakers can be acquainted with a phenomenon signified by an untranslatable word.[52] Evidence suggests we can. Recall that the men I researched for my PhD reported a degree of familiarity with certain Buddhist concepts even upon first encountering them. This finding aligns with research on "trait" mindfulness, which observes that people who do not practice mindfulness, and who may even be unaware of the construct, nevertheless self-report experiences and states of mind that can be identified as mindful.[53]

Indeed, many scholars argue that mindfulness is not particular to Eastern cultures. For instance, in 1890 William James wrote, "The faculty of voluntarily bringing back a wandering attention, over and over again, is the very root of judgment, character, and will. An education which should improve this faculty would be *the* education *par excellence.*"[54]

What is special about Eastern cultures is that they have created practices to engender this quality, the kind of "education" James was referring to. Teachings such as the *Satipaṭṭhāna sutta* show that the Buddha realized that *smṛti* was something his followers needed to work on, even though they were presumably familiar with the concept itself.[55] The findings from my PhD research suggest people from diverse cultural contexts can also learn through this sort of practice. My research focused on the impact of masculinity norms—such as expectations that men be tough—on participants' mental health. Many reported previously experiencing restricted emotionality: they had been socialized to disconnect from their emotions to an extent. Research indicates that this is common among men and that it is associated with mental health difficulties.[56] But my interviewees explained that the cultivation of *smṛti* and *maitrī* in meditation had to a large extent empowered them to overcome their prior restricted emotionality, facilitating high-level emotional differentiation and intelligence.

Just as Kabat-Zinn and others have developed experiential and pedagogical tools to help people understand and cultivate *smṛti*, so too could researchers create programs to enable participants to experience and develop the qualities associated with other untranslatable terms.

This process would ideally follow standard protocol for creating behavioral interventions: a pilot study, followed by larger-scale empirical testing, randomized controlled trials, replication studies, and meta-analyses.[57] These studies could use psychometric scales—as discussed above—to assess the extent of improvement with respect to the outcome in question, and to well-being generally.

This book can provide the impetus for such research. But I believe that, even with just the lexicography as it stands, individuals can invest their experience and understanding of life with greater granularity and nuance. Hopefully I have made the case that we can always seek to improve our maps of existence and that untranslatable words offer a powerful means of doing so. By paying attention to such words as we proceed on our journeys, we may get to know the ground beneath us a little better. We will perhaps even be empowered to ascend to previously unknown heights of well-being, and to create the best lives we can.

Glossary

Here you'll find a handy list of the words from the lexicography that are included in the book. For each word, I have provided a brief working definition. As noted throughout the book, most of these words have multiple meanings, so the definitions here are necessarily partial. Because I haven't been able to include the full, and ever-expanding, lexicography, I hope readers will find the up-to-date version online: http://www.drtimlomas.com/lexicography.

To aid in pronunciation, I've rendered each word using the International Phonetic Alphabet (IPA), as well as "regular" English. Where possible, I've sourced IPA renderings from established dictionaries. In other cases, I have crafted an approximate IPA-style transliteration myself, based on audio recordings and/or pronunciation guides for the language in question. Given regional dialects and other sources of diversity in speech, there is rarely a single canonical way to pronounce a given word—nor, where applicable, to convert words to romanized script—so all the phonetic guides should be considered approximate.

Abbiocco. Italian / n. / abˈbjɔk.ko / ah-*byokk*-oh. The soporific and usually pleasant drowsiness that can follow a meal, especially a large one.

Adinnādānā (अदिननदाना). Sanskrit/Pāli / v., n. / ˈʌ.dɪ.naːdaːnaː / *uh*-dih-nah-dah-nah. Taking the not-given (refraining from which is the second of Buddhism's Five Precepts).

Ádvaita (अद्वैत). Sanskrit / n. / ʌd.vaɪ.tʌ / ud-vy-tuh. Nondualism; the notion that there is only one reality, such that, for instance, the person and the sacred are not separate.

Aficionado. Spanish / n. / ə.fɪs.jəˈnaːdəʊ / a-fis-yun-*ah*-doh. Someone who is knowledgeable and/or enthusiastic about something; can have connotations of being an amateur, in a benign sense. Lit. "to inspire affection."

Agápē (αγάπη). Greek / n. / ˌaˈgɑːpiː / ag-*ah*-pee.   Selfless, unconditional, devotional love.

Ahiṃsā/avihiṃsā (अहिंसा). Sanskrit/Pāli / n. / əˈhɪm.sɑː / uh-*him*-sah.   Nonharm; love.

Ājīva (आजीव). Sanskrit/Pāli / n. / ɑːdʒiːwʌ / ah-jee-vwuh.   Livelihood, work, mode of life; per *samyak-ājīva* (i.e., "right livelihood"), of the Noble Eightfold Path.

Akrásia (ακρασια). Greek / n. / ɑ.kræˈsi.a / ah-krah-*see*-ah.   Weakness of will; lack of self-control.

Alétheia (αλήθεια). Greek / n. / æ.leɪˈθi.a / ah-lay-*thee*-ah.   Truth, disclosure; "unclosedness," "unconcealedness."

Aloha. Hawaiian / int. / æˈləʊ.hæ / ah-*loh*-ha.   Hello and goodbye, with love and compassion; cognate with Māori *aroha*. Lit. the "breath of presence."

Amour de soi. French / n. / amuʀ də swʌ / a-moor-de-swuh.   Self-regard that is not contingent on others' judgment. Lit. "love of oneself."

Amour fou. French / n. / amuʀ fu / a-moor-foo.   Mad, crazy, foolish love.

Amour propre. French / n. / amuʀ ˈpʀɔ.pʀ / a-moor *prrop*-ruh.   Self-regard contingent on others' judgment. Lit. "self-love."

Ânanda (आनन्द). Sanskrit/Pāli / n. / ˈɑːnən.də / *ah*-nun-duh.   Bliss, lasting contentment; spiritual, "unconditional" happiness.

Anánkē (ανάγκη). Greek / n. / ɑˈnæŋ.kiː / ah-*nang*-kee.   Necessity, compulsion, inevitability, fate.

Anātman/anattā (अनात्मन्). Sanskrit/Pāli / n. / anˈɑːt.mən / an-*at*-mn.   Insubstantiality; lack of permanent self or soul.

Anitya/anicca (अनित्य). Sanskrit/Pāli / n. / æˈniːt.jə / a-*neet*-yuh.   Impermanence; the notion that existence is transient and evanescent.

Apéritif. French / n. / ap.eʀ.it.if / ah-per-ree-teef.   A drink taken before dinner (and the social occasion involving this).

Aphaíresis (αφαίρεσις). Greek / n. / ɑ.fəˈriːsɪs / aff-uh-*ree*-sis.   Abstractive negation; to withdraw or take away, thereby revealing the truth.

Aphrodíte (Αφροδίτη). Greek / pronoun / a.fro.di.tiː / ah-froh-dee-tee.   In Greek mythology, the Goddess of love (also beauty, sexuality, procreation); known as Venus in Roman mythology.

Apramāda/appamada (अप्रमाद). Sanskrit/Pāli / n. / ʌ.prʌˈmɑːdʌ / uh-pruh-*mah*-duh.   Earnestness, alertness, diligence, moral watchfulness.

Arbejdsglæde. Danish / n. / ˈɑːbaɪd̥ʰs͵glɪl / *ar*-bides-glil. Pleasure or satisfaction derived from work. Lit. "work gladness."

Areté (αρετή). Greek / n. / aˈre.tɛ̌ː / ah-*reh*-tay. Excellence, quality; virtue.

Arhat/arahant (अर्हत्). Sanskrit/Pāli / n. / ˈɑːhʌt / *aar*-hut. A worthy or perfected individual; one who has attained enlightenment.

Aroha. Māori / v., n. / æˈrəʊ.hæ / ah-*roh*-ha. To feel love, concern, compassion, empathy for someone; cognate with Hawaiian *aloha*.

Arrangiarsi. Italian / v. / a.ranˈdʒaːsi: / a-rran-*jar*-see. To make do, get by, get along.

Asabiyyah (عَصَبِيَّة). Arabic / n. / a.saːˈbiːja / ah-sah-*bee*-yah. Solidarity; group feeling or consciousness.

Āsana (आसन). Sanskrit/Pāli / n. / ʌːsə.nə / uh-suh-nuh. Yoga postures. Lit. "seat" or "sitting position."

Ashtangika/atthangika (अष्टांगिक). Sanskrit/Pāli / n. / ʌʃ.tʌŋ.gɪ.kʌ / ush-tung-gee-kuh. Eightfold, per Buddhism's Noble Eightfold Path.

Asteya (अस्तेय). Sanskrit/Pāli / v. / ʌ.steɪ.jʌ / uh-stay-uh. Refraining from taking or appropriating the "not-given." Lit. "non-stealing."

Ataraxia (αταραξία). Greek / n. / ɑ.təˈɹæk.siə / at-tuh-*rak*-sia. Robust and lucid tranquility; peace of mind; calmness.

Ātman/attā (आत्मन्). Sanskrit/Pāli / n. / ˈɑːt.mən / *uht*-mn. Soul, spirit; breath.

Aufheben. German / v. / ˈaʊf͵heːbən / *orf*-hee-bn. To sublimate; to raise up; to remove, suspend, repeal, set aside; to negate and yet also preserve.

Aútexoúsios (αὐτεξούσιος). Greek / adj. / ew.teˈxuːsi.os / ew-teh-*khoo*-see-oss. Mastery of oneself; exercising agency and free will.

Avos (авось). Russian / particle / ɐˈvosʲ / ah-*voss*. Maybe, what if; faith, trust, hope; serendipity, destiny, fate.

Azart (азарт). Russian / n. / ɐˈzɑːrt / ah-*zarrt*. Heat, excitement, ardor, fervor.

Bhakti/bhatti (भक्ति). Sanskrit/Pāli / n. / bʰʌɦk.tiː / bhahk-tee. Fondness, attachment, homage, reverence.

Bhāvana (भावन). Sanskrit/Pāli / n. / bʰɦɑːwnɑː / bh-*hav*-nah. Application, development, cultivation, practice, meditation.

Bīja (बीज). Sanskrit/Pāli / n. / biːdʒʌ / bee-juh. Seed(s); per *bīja-niyāma*, the "law of seeds," referring to causal patterns in the realm of organic phenomena.

Bildung. German / n. / ˈbɪl.dʊŋ / *bill*-doong.   Education, formation, accultura-tion, cultivation, development.

Bildungsroman. German / n. / ˈbɪl.dʊŋs ʁo.maːn / *bill*-doongs roe-mahn.   A coming-of-age story; a narrative of education or formation.

Binah (בּינה). Hebrew / n. / bɪˈnæ / bih-*nah*.   Understanding; the third *sephirot* in the Kabbalah tradition, denoting the process or quality giving form to creation.

Bodhi (बोधि). Sanskrit/Pāli / n. / ˈbaʊ.di / *boe*-dee.   Enlightenment, awakening.

Botellón. Spanish / n. / bɒ.teɪˈjɒnː / boh-tay-*yon*.   A public gathering in which people socialize and drink alcohol. Lit. "big bottle."

Brahman (ब्रह्मन्). Sanskrit / n. / ˈbrɑːˌmən / *brah*-mun.   The transcendent and immanent absolute reality; the supreme spirit that continually brings existence into being.

Brahmavihārā (ब्रह्मविहारा). Sanskrit/Pāli / n. / ˈbrɑːˌmə vɪˈhɑːrə / *brah*-muh vi-*har*-ruh.   Qualities Buddhist practitioners are encouraged to cultivate. Lit. "abode or dwelling of *Brahma*" (the God of creation in Hindu theology).

Brav. German / adj. / braːf / brraaf.   Pleasant, earnest, well-behaved.

Buddha (बुद्ध). Sanskrit/Pāli / n. / bʊˈdːhə / bd-*dha*.   An awakened, enlightened being.

Byt (быт). Russian / n. / bɪt / bweet.   Everyday, daily, domestic, and/or private life; quotidian existence; material culture.

Bytie (бытие). Russian / n. / bɪtʲɪˈje / bweet-ee-*yee*-ah.   Being; authentic and/or spiritual existence.

Catvāri āryasatyāni / cattāri ariyasaccāni (चत्वारि आर्यसत्यानी). Sanskrit/Pāli / n. / kʌtˈwɑːɹi ˌɑːjʌsʌtˈjɑːnɪ / cat-*vwah*-ree ah-yuh-suht-*yah*-nee.   Buddhism's four "Noble Truths." Lit. "truths of the noble ones."

Chán (禪). Chinese / n. / tʃæːn / chan.   Concentrated attention or absorption. The Chinese adaptation of *dhyāna*.

Charis (χαρις). Greek / n. / ˈkʰá.ris / *khah*-riss.   Grace, kindness, beauty, nobility.

Chokmah (הכמה). Hebrew / n. / xɒx.mæh / khokh-mah.   Wisdom; the second *sephirot* in the Kabbalah tradition, denoting the primary force in the process of cre-ation.

Chōros (χῶρος). Greek / n. / ˈkʰɔːrɒs / *khor*-ross.   A place; usually denotes the quality of the place.

Chutzpah. Yiddish / n. / ˈxʊts.pə / *khutz*-puh.   Insolence, cheek, audacity; nerve, effrontery, guts; may be used pejoratively.

Citta (चित्त). Sanskrit/Pāli / n. / tʃɪ.d̪æ / chih-dtha. Mind, consciousness, awareness; heart and mind combined.

Craic. Gaelic (Irish) / n. / kræk / crack. Fun, revelry, good times; "what's going on."

Cwtch. Welsh / v., n. / kʊtʃ / kutch. As verb: to hug or cuddle (transitive); to get cozy (intransitive). As noun: a hug or cuddle; a sanctuary; a safe, welcoming place.

Cynefin. Welsh / n. / ˈkʌ.nɨ.vɪn / *kun*-uh-vin. Haunt, habitat; a place where one feels one ought to live; the relationship one has with the place where one was born and/or feels at home.

Dadirri. Australian Aboriginal (Ngangiwumirr) / n. / dəˈdɪ.ri / duh-*dir*-rree. A deep, spiritual act of reflective and respectful listening.

Dāna (दान). Sanskrit/Pāli / n. / dɑːnʌ / dah-nuh. Generosity, giving; charity.

Dasein. German / v., n. / daːzaɪn / dah-zine. Martin Heidegger's term for a human being, capturing the view that people always exist in a context. Lit. "being here/there."

Das man. German / n. / das man / dass man. People, anyone; one. Lit. "they-self" or "the they."

Dēmētēr (Δημήτηρ). Greek / pronoun / dɪˈmiːtər / deh-*mee*-tuh. In Greek mythology, the goddess of grain, harvest, agriculture, fertility; known as Ceres in Roman mythology.

Desbundar. Portuguese / v. / dʒizbũˈdar / dez-bun-*dar*. Exceeding one's limits; shedding one's inhibitions (e.g., in having fun).

Desenrascanço. Portuguese / n. / ˌdɨ.zẽj.ʁɐʃˈkɐ̃.sʊ / *deh*-zen-hass-*can*-so. Artful disentanglement (e.g., from trouble); an improvised solution.

Dharma/dhamma (धर्म). Sanskrit/Pāli / n. / ˈd̪ʰɑːmə / *dhar*-ma. Law; what is established; principles of the universe; guidelines for action; teachings (often refers to the Buddha's teachings in particular).

Dhyāna/jhāna (ध्यान). Sanskrit/Pāli / n. / ˌgnˈjɑːnæ / gn-*yaa*-na. Intense, concentrated attention and absorption (e.g., regarding the nature of an object of meditation); cultivated and valorized states of mind (which can be ordered in a developmental sequence).

Duende. Spanish / n. / ˈdwɛn.d̪e̞ / de-*wen*-deh. A heightened state of emotion, spirit, and passion, often associated with visual art, music, and dance.

Dugnad. Norwegian / n. / duːɡ.nɑːd / doog-nard. A collectively undertaken task; voluntary community work.

Duḥkha/dukkha (ड़ु:ख). Sanskrit/Pāli / n. / ˈdʊ.kʰə / *duh*-kuh.   Dissatisfaction, discomfort, dis-ease; suffering.

Duša (душа). Russian / n. / dʊˈʂa / doo-*shah.*   Soul, spirit, heart.

Ego. Latin / n. / ˈɛ.gɔ / *eh*-go.   I, me, we; used by translators of Freud to represent the German *Ich*, referring to the construct of self.

Ein sof (אֵין סוֹף). Hebrew / n., adj. / ɛnˈsɒf / en-*soff.*   In the Kabbalah tradition, refers to the pure, transcendent essence of God, prior to manifestation in/as the cosmos. Lit. "unending or infinite."

Ekstasis (ἔκστασις). Greek / n. / ékˈstaːsis / ek-*stah*-sis.   The state of being or standing outside oneself; trance, displacement; ecstasy, rapture.

Elohim (אֱלֹהִים). Hebrew / n. / ɛl.ɔːˈhɪm / el-or-*him.*   God; deities, angels; sacred beings or messengers.

Ēn (恩). Chinese / n. / ɜːn / uhn.   Moral indebtedness; duty, obligation; repayment of a favor.

Engelengeduld. Dutch / n. / ˈɛŋ.gə.lən ˌɣə.dʊlt / *eng*-uhl-uhn-*kher*-dult.   Great patience. Lit. "angelic patience."

Enraonar. Catalan / v. / en.ra.oˈna / en-ra-oh-*nha.*   To discuss in a civilized, reasoned manner.

Enthousiasmos (ἐνθουσιασμός). Greek / n. / en.θu.si.asˈmos / en-thoo-sias-*mous.*   The state of being inspired, possessed, or driven by a divine being or force.

Epistēmē (ἐπιστήμη). Greek / n. / ɛ.pɪˈstiːmɪ / ep-e-*stee*-me.   Knowledge or understanding (e.g., in a scientific sense).

Epithymía (ἐπιθυμία). Greek / n. / e.pi.θyˈmi.a / ep-e-thy-*mee*-ah.   Desire; sexual passion.

Ereignis. German / n. / ɛɐ̯ˈ|aignɪs / err *ihg*-niss.   Something "coming into view"; the realm in which the "truth of being" is manifest.

Érōs (ἔρως). Greek / n., pronoun / ˈe.rɔːs / *eh*-ross.   Desire; passionate love; in Greek mythology, the God of desire (or love). Known as Cupid in Roman mythology.

Erschlossenheit. German / n. / ɛɐ̯ˈʃlɔsn.haɪt / err-*schloss*-un-hite.   World disclosure; the process by which things become intelligible, meaningful, and relevant to human beings.

Ethikos (ἠθικός). Greek / n. / i.θi.kós / ee-thhee-koss.   Habit, custom, usage; character, bearing.

Eudaimonia (ευδαιμονία). Greek / n. / juːdɪˈmoʊ.niə / yoo-de-*moe*-nee-uh. Being infused with divine grace; fulfilment, flourishing. Lit. "good spirit."

Eunoia (εὔνοια). Greek / n. / juːˈnɔɪ.ɑ / yoo-*noi*-ya. Good or beautiful thinking; a well mind.

Euphoría (εὐφορία). Greek / n. / ju.pʰo.ríːa / yoo-for-ree-ah. Intense excitement or joy. Lit. being of "good bearing."

Fein. German / adj. / fain / fine. Fine, tender; noble, honorable; unique.

Fernweh. German / n. / ˈfɪɜːn.veː / *fiern*-vay. Homesickness for the unknown; the "call of faraway places." Lit. "far pain."

Fiero. Italian / n. / ˈfjɛːɹo / fee-*yeah*-ro. Pride and satisfaction in one's achievements, usually with the implication that this satisfaction has been earned.

Fingerspitzengefühl. German / n. / ˈfɪŋ.ɐ.ʃpɪts.n̩.gə ˌfyːl / *fing*-ah-shpitz-en-gu-foo -eh. The ability to act with tact and sensitivity. Lit. "fingertip feeling."

Firgun (פירגון). Hebrew / n. / ˈfɪə.guːn / *feer*-goon. Ungrudging and overt pride and happiness at another person's success.

Flâner. French / v. / flɑ.ne / fla-nay. Leisurely strolling. *Flâneur* (noun): one who strolls.

Folkelig. Danish / adj. / fɒlˈkɪ.li / foll-*ki*-lee. Folkish; belonging to the people; democratic national spirit or sentiment; having broad popular appeal.

Fremdschämen. German / n. / ˈfʀɛmtˌʃɛːmən / *fremt*-shay-mn. Being embarrassed or ashamed for someone else; vicarious embarrassment; a cringing feeling.

Frimousse. French / n. / fʀi.mus / frree-moose. A sweet or cute little face.

Fukinsei (不均整). Japanese / n. / fuˈkɪn.seɪ / foo-*kin*-say. Natural and spontaneous asymmetry or irregularity.

Gaia (Γαῖα). Greek / n., pronoun / ˈɣɛ.a / *kheh*-uh. Earth; in Greek mythology, the primordial Mother Earth.

Gaman (我慢). Japanese / n. / gæ.mæɲ / gah-mahn. Patience; fortitude, endurance; self-control, restraint.

Ganbaru (頑張る). Japanese / v. / gãmˈbɑːɽɯᵝ / gam-*bar*-ou. To do one's best. Lit. "to stand firm."

Ganzheit. German / n. / ˈgænz.haɪt / *ganz*-hite. Unity; integrated whole; undivided completeness; total and complete.

Gemilut hasadim (גְּמִילוּת חֲסָדִים). Hebrew / n. / gɛ.miˈluːt ħæ.sæˈdiːm / geh-mee-*loot* hah-sah-*deem*. Acts of loving-kindness.

Geborgenheit. German / n. / ɡəˈbɔʁ.ɡn̩ˌhaɪ̯t / guh-*bor*-gn-hite.   Feeling protected and safe from harm.

Gemütlichkeit. German / n. / ɡəˈmyːt.lɪç.kaɪt / guh-*moot*-lish-kite.   A feeling of comfort, coziness, hominess. *Gemütlich* (adjective): cozy, homey, comfortable.

Genki (元気). Japanese / adj., n. / ˈɡɛŋ.kiː / *geng*-kee.   Being healthy, energetic, and full of life. Lit. the origin of *ki* (cognate with *qi*—see below).

Gestalt. German / n. / ɡəˈʃtalt / guh-*shtalt*.   An overall pattern or configuration; the notion that the whole is greater or other than the sum of its parts.

Gevurah (גבורה). Hebrew / n. / ɡə.vuːˈrə / guh-voo-*rruh*.   Power, might; judgment; the fifth *sephirot* in the Kabbalah tradition, denoting the enactment of justice.

Geworfenheit. German / n. / ɡəˈvɔːfən.haɪt / guh-*vor*-fuhn-hite.   "Thrownness"; the condition, characteristic of human existence, of being thrown into contexts not of one's choosing.

Gezellig. Dutch / adj. / ɣəˈzɛl.əɣ / khe-*zell*-ikh.   Cozy, warm, intimate; enjoyable; often a shared experience.

Gigil. Tagalog / n. / ˈɡʰiːˌɡɪl / *ghih*-gill.   The irresistible urge to pinch or squeeze someone because they are loved or cherished.

Gōng fu (功夫). Chinese / n. / ɡʊŋ.fuː / gong-foo.   Acquisition of a skill, particularly with investment of time and effort; more recent usage refers specifically to martial arts. Lit. "work" or "achievement."

Guān xì (關係). Chinese / n. / ɡwʊn.ɕiː / gwun-shee.   Cultivating relationships; reciprocal connections; networking; social karma.

Guò yǐn (過癮). Chinese / n. / ɡwɔ.jɪəɪn̩ / gwor-yiin.   Satisfaction of a craving; a pleasurable experience; to act to one's heart's content.

Gunnen. Dutch / v. / ˈɣʌn.ən / *khun*-un.   To think that someone deserves something good; to feel happy for others when they are deservedly rewarded.

Guru (गुरु). Sanskrit/Pāli / n. / ɡʊ.rʊ / goo-roo.   A religious or spiritual teacher, guide, master; a revered person.

Hachnasat orchim (הכנסת אורחים). Hebrew / n. / ħax.na.ʃat ɔːxɪm / hakh-nash-at orh-khim.   Welcoming or "bringing in guests"; offering hospitality and respect to strangers.

Han (한). Korean / n. / hæn / han.   Sorrow, resentment, regret; possibly with a sense of patiently waiting or hoping for amelioration.

Háidēs (Ἅδης). Greek / n., pronoun / haːɪ̯.dɛːs / har-dees.   The underworld; in Greek mythology, the God of the underworld, death, the dead, and riches. Known as Pluto in Roman mythology.

Halal (حلال). Arabic / n. / həˈlɑːl / huh-*lahl*. Allowed, permissible; in accordance with Islamic law, especially relating to food.

Hallelujah (הַלְלוּיָהּ). Hebrew / v., n., int. / ˌhæ.liˈluːjə / ha-leh-*loo*-yuh. "God be praised"; an expression of worship or rejoicing.

Hatha (हठ). Sanskrit / n., adj. / hʌ.θə / huh-thuh. A branch of yoga focusing on the practice of *āsana* (postures) and *vinyāsa* (dynamic transitions). Lit. "force, effort, exertion."

Havruta (חַבְרוּתָא). Hebrew / n. / χavˈʁu.ta / khav-*roo*-tah. The practice of paired or shared learning, usually of religious texts, and the bond that may develop as a result. Lit. "fellowship."

Hod (הוֹד). Hebrew / n. / hʊd / hoewd. Majesty, splendor; the eighth *sephirot* in the Kabbalah tradition, denoting the glory of creation.

Hózhǫ́. Navaho / n. / hɔ̃.ʒɔ̃ / hoh-zho. Peace, balance, beauty, harmony.

Heimlich. German / adj. / ˈhaɪm.lɪç / hime-lisch. Pertaining to the home; comfortable, familiar, known; secretive, clandestine.

Hésed (חֶסֶד). Hebrew / n. / ˈhɛ.sɛd / *khe*-sed. Loving-kindness, mercy; faithfulness, loyalty; goodness; salvation; the fourth *sephirot* in the Kabbalah tradition, denoting the love of creation.

Hiraeth. Welsh / n. / hira.ɪθ / heerr-ithe. Longing for one's homeland, with nostalgia and wistfulness.

Hugfanginn. Icelandic / adj. / ˈhuːfʌŋ.gɪn / *hoo*-fun-gin. To be charmed or fascinated by someone or something. Lit. "mind-captured."

Hygge. Danish/Norwegian / n. / ˈhʊːgə / *hhoo*-guh. A deep sense of place, warmth, friendship, contentment. *Hyggelig* (adjective): enjoyable, warm, friendly, pleasant.

Hypomonē (ὑπομονή). Greek / n. / i.po.moˈni / ee-poe-moe-*nee*. Patience; constancy; endurance; "standing firm."

Id. Latin / n. / ɪd / id. It or that; used by translators of Freud to represent the German *Es*, referring to instinctual drives.

Ikigai (生き甲斐). Japanese / n. / iːki:gɑi: / ee-kee-gaee. A "reason for being"; meaning, purpose in life. Lit. "life result, worth, use, or benefit."

Iktsuarpok. Inuit / n. / ɪk.ˈtsuɑːpɒk / ik-*tsua*-pok. Anticipation felt while waiting for another's arrival, often involving checking on their progress.

In sha' Allah (إِن شَاءَ اَللّٰهُ). Arabic / int. / ˌɪn.ʃˈɑ.lə / in-*shall*-ah. God willing; a hopeful wish. Lit. "may God wish it."

Iṣṭadevatā (इष्ट देवता). Sanskrit/Pāli / n. / ɪʃ.tʰʌ.deɪ.wʌ.tɑː / ish-tuh-day-vwuh-tar. Reverence of divine beings; deity meditation practice.

Janteloven. Danish/Norwegian / n. / ˈjan.dɜˌloʊʔən / yan-deh-low-ven. A set of rules discouraging individualism. Lit. "laws of Jante," from novelist Aksel Sandemose.

Jeito. Portuguese / n. / ˈʒej.tu / jay-too. Hack, solution; to find a way by any means, often circumventing rules or social conventions.

Joie de vivre. French / n. / ˌʒwɑː dɜ ˈviːvrɜ / jwa-de-vee-vruh. Zest for life; exuberance, ebullience; the knack of knowing how to live. Lit. "joy of living."

Jouissance. French / n. / ʒˈwi.sɑ̃s / szh-wee-sonse. Physical or intellectual pleasure; delight, ecstasy; an orgasm.

Kabbalah (קַבָּלָה). Hebrew / n. / ka.baˈla / kah-bah-lah. An esoteric spiritual tradition within Judaism. Lit. "received tradition."

Kalyāṇa-mitratā/mittatā (कल्याण मित्रता). Sanskrit/Pāli / n. / kælˈjɑːnɜ mɪt.rɜˈtɑː / kal-yah-nuh mit-ruh-tar. Spiritual friendship. Lit. "auspicious compassion."

Kāmesu micchācāra (कामेसुमिच्छाचारा). Sanskrit/Pāli / n. / kɑːmeɪ.sʊ mɪk.hɑːtʃɑːrʌ / kar-may-soo mik-har-char-uh. Misconduct or unwholesome behavior concerning sexual or sensual activity, refraining from which is the third of Buddhism's Five Precepts.

Kanyininpa. Pintupi / v. / ˌkæn.jɪnˈɪn.pɜ / kan-yin-in-puh. An intimate and active relationship between provider and recipient of care. Lit. "to hold."

Karma/kamma (कर्म). Sanskrit/Pāli / n. / ˈkɑːmɜ / kar-muh. A theory or principle of causality, particularly with respect to ethical behavior. Lit. "action, work, deed."

Karmānta/kammanta (कर्मान्त). Sanskrit/Pāli / n. / kʌ.mɑːn.tʌ / kuh-marn-tuh. Action, management; administration; per samyak-karmānta (i.e., "right action"), of the Noble Eightfold Path.

Kartería (καρτερία). Greek / n. / kɑ.tɛˈriːɜ / ka-teh-ree-uh. Stubbornness; toughness.

Karuṇā (करुणा). Sanskrit/Pāli / n. / kæ.rʉˈŋɑː / ka-roo-nar. Empathy, compassion; identifying with the others' suffering.

Kashrut (כַּשְׁרוּת). Hebrew / n. / kaʃ.ruːt / kash-root. Proper, legal, permissible; in accordance with Jewish law, especially relating to food.

Kefi (κέφι). Greek / n. / ˈkeɜ.fi / keh-fee. Joy, passion, enthusiasm; high spirits; frenzy.

Keter (כתר). Hebrew / n. / ˈkɛ.teɜ / keh-tair. The first sephirot in the Kabbalah tradition, denoting the initial impulse of Ein Sof to manifest in the world. Lit. "crown."

Khaos (χάος). Greek / n. / xáos / khah-oss. Chaos; in Greek mythology, the void preceding the birth of the cosmos.

Kilig. Tagalog / n. / kɪˈliːɡ / kih-*leeg*. The feeling of "butterflies" arising from interacting with someone one loves or finds attractive; exhilaration and elation, not necessarily romantic. Lit. "shaking" or "trembling."

Kintsugi (金継ぎ). Japanese / n. / kɪn.tsʊ.gi / kin-tsu-gi. The art of repairing broken pottery using gold; metaphorically, rendering flaws and fault-lines beautiful and strong. Lit. "golden joinery."

Koev halev (כואב לי הלב). Hebrew / v. / xəʊv xæ.lɛv / khoh-ev hah-lev. Empathy, compassion; identifying with the other's suffering. Lit. "the heart aches."

Koi no yokan (恋の予感). Japanese / n. / ˈkɔi.nɒ.jɒ.kæn / *ko*ee-nor-yo-kan. Premonition or presentiment of love; the feeling, on meeting someone, that falling in love is inevitable.

Koinōnía (κοινωνία). Greek / n. / kɔɪˈnəʊ.ni.ə / koy-*non*-ee-uh. Fellowship, communion; joint participation; connection, intimacy.

Koko (考古). Japanese / n. / kɒ.kɒ / ko-ko. Weathered beauty; austere sublimity.

Kokusaijin (国際人). Japanese / n. / kɒ.kuːsaiːdʒiːn / koh-koo-sah-ee-jeen. Someone who is cosmopolitan, flexible, and open-minded. Lit. "international person."

Konfliktfähigkeit. German / n. / kɒnˈflɪkt.feɪ.ɪç.haɪt / kon-*flict*-fay-ikh-hite. The ability to manage interpersonal conflict constructively, without becoming personally involved.

Kos. Norwegian / n. / ˈkɔːsʰa / *kor*-sa. Coziness, warmth, intimacy. *Koselig* (adjective): cozy, snug, warm, intimate, enjoyable.

Koyaanisqatsi. Hopi / n. / ˌkɔɪ.ɑːnɪsˈkɑːtsiː / koy-an-iss-*kah*-tsee. Nature out of balance; a dysfunctional state of affairs that calls for another way of living.

Kuài lè (快乐). Chinese / n. / ˌkwaɪˈlə: / kwy-*ler*. Pleasure, satisfaction; hedonic happiness. Lit. "quick joy."

Kvell. Yiddish / v. / kvɛl / kvell. To feel strong and overt (expressed) pride and joy in someone's success.

Lakṣaṇa/lakshana (लक्षण). Sanskrit/Pāli / n. / ˈlʊk.ʃʊn.ə / *look*-shn-uh. Symptom, sign; quality, attribute; "marks of conditioned existence."

L'chaim (לְחַיִּים). Hebrew / phrase / lᵊˈxaɪ.iːm / luh-*kha*-eem. A toast to another's well-being. Lit. "to life."

Lǐ (禮). Chinese / n. / liːi / lee-e. Etiquette, decorum; ceremony, custom.

Līlā (लीला). Sanskrit / n. / liːlə / lee-luh. In Hinduism, reality as the outcome of creative play by the divine. Lit. "game" or "play."

Livsnjutare. Swedish / n. / ˈliːf.sɘˌnjuːtɑ.reɪ / *leef*-suh-*nyoo*-ta-rey.   Bon vivant; someone who loves life and lives it to the fullest.

Logos (λόγος). Greek / n. / ˈlo.ɣos / *loh*-yoss.   Word, reason, plan; in theology, the principle of divine reason and creative order.

Ludus. Latin / n. / ˈɫuːdʊs / *loo*-dss.   Used to denote playful/game-playing forms of affection. Lit. "game" or "play."

Magari. Italian / adv. / maˈgɑːri / ma-*gah*-ree.   Maybe, possibly; hopeful wish, wistful regret; in my dreams, if only.

Mahābhūta (महाभूत). Sanskrit/Pāli / n. / mʌ.hɑːbʰuːtɘ / muh-har-bhoo-tuh.   Great elements or forces; the dimensions or components comprising the physical world: air, fire, water, and earth.

Mahalo. Hawaiian / n., v. / maˈha.lo / ma-*ha*-lor.   Thanks, gratitude; admiration, praise; respect.

Maitrī/mettā (मैत्री). Sanskrit/Pāli / n. / ˈmai.ʈɾi / *my*-tree.   Loving-kindness; benevolence.

Majime (真面目). Japanese / adj. / mɑːdʑ.mɛ / mah-jee-meh.   Reliable, responsible, diligent; serious, formal.

Makrothumeó (μακροθυμέω). Greek / n. / mæk.rɘʊ.θuːˈmeɪ.ɘʊ / mak-roth-oo-*mey*-oh.   Patience, forbearance; being long-suffering; slow to anger and avenge.

Malchut (מלכות). Hebrew / n. / mɒl.ʜuːt / mal-hoot.   Realm; the final *sephirot* in the Kabbalah tradition, denoting the "finished product" of the manifest cosmos itself.

Mamihlapinatapai. Yagán / n. / ˈmæ.mi.læ.pɪ.næ.tæˌpai / *mah*-me-lah-pee-nah -tah-*pie*.   A look between people expressing unspoken but mutual intent.

Mana. Polynesian languages / n. / ˈmɑ.nɘ / *ma*-nuh.   Spiritual energy or power; a sacred, impersonal force.

Mana whenua. Māori / n. / ˈmɑ.nɘ ˈfɛ.nʊ.ɘ / *ma*-nuh *fen*-oo-uh.   The *mana* held by people who have demonstrated moral authority and guardianship over a territory.

Manaakitanga. Māori / n. / ma.naːkɪ.tʌŋɘ / ma-*nah*-ki-tung-uh.   Hospitality, kindness, generosity, support; respect and care for others.

Mania (μανία). Greek / n. / ma.nía / mah-nee-ah.   Madness, frenzy, possession.

Mantra (मन्त्र). Sanskrit/Pāli / n. / mʌn.trʌ / mun-truh.   A meaningful word, phrase or sound serving as an object of focus in meditation. Lit. "mind tool."

Maraṇa smṛti/sati (मरण स्मृति). Sanskrit/Pāli / n. / mʌ.rʌ.nʌ smrɪ.tiː / muh-ruh-nuh smrih-tee.   Meditation on, or awareness of, death and mortality.

Mārga/magga (मार्ग). Sanskrit/Pāli / n. / ˈmʌɹːgʌ / *mur*-guh. A path, road, or way; can specifically denote a spiritual path.

Mazal tov (מזל טוב). Hebrew / int. / ˈmɑːzəl tɒf / *mah*-zul-toff. A blessing of health and happiness. Lit. "good fortune."

Melmastia (ميلمستيا). Pashto / n. / mɛlˈmæs.tiʌ / mel-*mass*-tiah. Hospitality; the moral obligation to offer sanctuary and respect to all visitors.

Memento mori. Latin / n. / məˌmen.təʊ ˈmɔːri / meh-men-toh *moor*-ee. An object or symbol that reminds or warns of death and mortality.

Mensch. Yiddish / n. / mɛntʃ / mentsh. A good human being in the fullest sense.

Meraki (μεράκι). Greek / n. / mɛˈræ.kiː / meh-*rrack*-ee. Ardor, especially for one's own actions and creations.

Meriggiare. Italian / v. / mɛ.rɪˈdʒeɑːrɪ / me-rri-*jah*-rri. To rest at noon, often in the shade.

Mésos (μέσος). Greek / n. / ˈme.sos / *meh*-soss. Mean; middle.

Mir (мир). Russian / n. / mir / meerr. Peace; world, community.

Mishloach manot (משלוח מנות). Hebrew / n. / miʃˈlo.aχ maˈnot / mish-*lo*-ah ma-*not*. Exchanging gifts of food and drink, specifically during the Purim holiday. Lit. "sending of portions."

Mitzvah (מִצְוָה). Hebrew / n. / ˈmɪts.və / *mitz*-vuh. Commandment; technically an action performed in fulfillment of religious duty, but also used colloquially in reference to good deeds generally.

Mokṣa/moksha (मोक्ष). Sanskrit/Pāli / n. / ˈmoːk.ʃə / *mohk*-shuh. Emancipation, liberation, release (particularly from *saṃsāra*).

Mono no aware (物の哀れ). Japanese / n. / mɒ.nɒ.nɒ.ɐ.wɐ.reɪ / mo-no-no-uh-wah-ray. Pathos; appreciating the transiency of the world and its beauty.

Morgenfrisk. Danish / adj. / ˈmɔːn.frɪsk / *morn*-frisk. Feeling rested after a good night's sleep. Lit. "morning-freshness."

Muditā (मुदिता). Sanskrit/Pāli / n. / mʊ.dɪˈtʰɑː / moo-de-*tar*. Sympathetic, vicarious happiness.

Musāvādā (मुसावादा). Sanskrit/Pāli / n. / mʊ.sɑːwɑːdɑː / moo-sah-vwah-dah. False speech, refraining from which is the fourth of Buddhism's Five Precepts.

Naches. Yiddish / n. / ˈnʌ.xəs / *nuh*-khuz. Joyful pride in the successes of another, often one's progeny or student.

Netzach (נצח). Hebrew / n. / neɪ.tsæx / nay-tsakh. Endurance, eternity; fortitude, triumph; the seventh *sephirot* in the Kabbalah tradition, denoting the endurance of *Ein Sof* in the act of creation.

Nirodha (निरोध). Sanskrit/Pāli / n. / nɪ.rəʊd.hʌ / ni-rode-huh.   Cessation; the third Noble Truth, holding that *duḥkha* can be addressed by overcoming craving and attachment.

Nirvāṇa/nibbāna (निर्वाण). Sanskrit/Pāli / n. / nɪəˈwɑːnə / nir-*vwah*-nuh.   Release from *saṃsāra*; "ultimate" happiness; total liberation from suffering. Lit. "extinguished" or "blown out," as a flame.

Niyama (नियम). Sanskrit/Pāli / n. / nɪˈjʌːmʌ / nee-*yuh*-muh.   Recommended habits or practices for right living. Lit. "observances, positive duties."

Njuta. Swedish / v. / njɵːta / nyoo-ta.   To enjoy deeply; to appreciate profoundly.

Ohanami (お花見). Japanese / n. / əʊ.hæ.næ.mi / oh-ha-na-me.   The culturally valued activity of gathering to appreciate flowers, particularly cherry blossoms. Lit. "flower viewing."

Omoiyari (思いやり). Japanese / n. / o.moi.jɑ.ri / oh-moy-yah-rih.   Altruistic sensitivity; an intuitive understanding of others' desires, feelings, and thoughts; action resulting from this understanding.

Orenda. Huron / n. / ɔˈɹɛn.də / oh-*ren*-duh.   Power, force; often with spiritual connotations.

Orka. Swedish / v. / ˈɔr̩ka / orr-kah.   To have energy for some task; being resilient, spirited, enthused.

Otsukaresama (お疲れ様). Japanese / int. / o.tsu.kɑ.rɛ.sa.mɑ / oh-tsoo-kah-reh-sah-mah.   Expression of thanks for another's work; gratitude and appreciation.

Ouranus (Οὐρανός). Greek / n., pronoun / oːra.nós / oo-rah-nohs.   Sky; heaven; in Greek mythology, the deity of the sky/heavens, son and/or husband of *Gaia*.

Paixnidi (Παιχνίδι). Greek / n. / pɛkʰˈniːdi / pekh-*nee*-dee.   Used to denote playful or game-playing forms of affection. Lit. "game" or "play."

Pāṇātipātā (पाणातिपाता). Sanskrit/Pāli / v. / pɑːnɑːtɪ.pɑːtɑː / pah-nah-ti-pah-tah.   Harming or killing living beings, refraining from which is the first of Buddhism's Five Precepts.

Pañcaśīlāni/pañcasīlāni (पञ्चशीलानि). Sanskrit/Pâli / n. / pʌn.tʃʌ.ʃiːˈlɑːnɪ / pun-suh-shee-*lah*-ni.   The five Precepts of Buddhism.

Passeggiata. Italian / n. / päs.sädˈjaːtä / pa-saj-*yah*-ta.   A leisurely stroll, turn, walk.

Philautia (φιλαυτία). Greek / n. / ɸɨˈlɔːtɪ.ə / fi-*law*-ti-uh.   Self-love, encompassing self-respect, self-compassion, and so on.

Philia (φιλία). Greek / n. / ɸiˈli.a / fi-*lee*-ya.   Friendship; platonic love.

Philotimo (φιλότιμο). Greek / n. / ɸɪlˈɔːtɪ.mɔ / fi-*loh*-tee-moh. The importance of respecting and honoring friends and family (and the wider community). Lit. "love of honor."

Phrónēsis (φρόνησις). Greek / n. / froʊˈniːsɪsː / froh-*nee*-siss. Practical wisdom; discernment; mental capacity to determine ends and means of attaining them.

Pneuma (πνευμα). Greek / n. / pnéu̯.ma / pnyoo-mah. Air, wind; breath; spirit, life-force.

Pneumatikós (πνευματικῶς). Greek / adj. / pnεβ.mɑ.tiˈkos / pnev-mah-tee-*kose*. Spiritual; pertaining to the spirit; being with or of the spirit of God.

Poseidôn (Ποσειδῶν). Greek / pronoun / po.see̯.dɔ̰ɲ / por-seh-dorn. In Greek mythology, God of the ocean, earthquakes, storms, and horses. Known as Neptune in Roman mythology.

Prâgma (πρᾶγμα). Greek / n. / ˈpraɣ.ma / *prayj*-mah. A deed, action, or "thing done"; used to denote rational, "sensible" love.

Prāṇa (प्राण). Sanskrit/Pāli / n. / prɑːnɑː / prah-nah. Air, wind; breath; spirit, life-force.

Pratītya-samutpāda / **paṭicca-samuppāda** (प्रतीत्यसमुत्पाद). Sanskrit/Pāli / n. / praˈtiːt.jʌ sʌ.mʊtˈpɑːdʌ / pruh-*teet*-yuh suh-muut-*pah*-duh. Dependent origination; the law of conditionality.

Prâxis (πρᾶξις). Greek / n. / prãːkʰ.sis / prakh-sis. Deed or action; the process by which a theory, lesson, or skill is enacted, embodied, or realized.

Prōtógonos (Πρωτογόνος). Greek / n. / proˈto.ɣo.nos / pror-*tor*-khor-nors. In Greek mythology, the first generation of deities. Lit. "first-born."

Purim (פּוּרִים). Hebrew / n. / ˈpʊərɪm / poor-rim. An annual celebration in Judaism (commemorating the saving of the Jewish people from a figure named Haman).

Qì (氣). Chinese / n. / tɕʰiː / chee. Air, wind; breath; spirit, life-force.

Qì gōng (氣功). Chinese / n. / tɕʰiː gʊŋ / chee-gong. A practice of developing mastery over body and mind. Lit. "breath work."

Querencia. Spanish / n. / kɛˈɹɛn.sɪ.ə / keh-*ren*-si-uh. A place where one feels secure and from which one draws strength.

Ramé. Balinese / n. / ɹɑːˈmeɪ / rah-*may*. A lively, boisterous social occasion.

Rén (仁). Chinese / n. / ɻɛn / ren. Humaneness, benevolence; the positive feeling attending altruistic behavior.

Rūpa (रूप). Sanskrit/Pāli / n. / ruːpə / roo-puh. Matter, body, material form; in Buddhism, the first *skandha*, referring to the material body.

Sabi (寂). Japanese / n. / sɑːbɪ / sah-bee.   Lonely, desolate, aged beauty.

Sadaqah (صدقة). Arabic / n. / sˤa.da.qa / suh-duh-kuh.   Generosity or charity, as mandated by justice; required righteous giving. Lit. "justice, righteousness."

Salām (سلام). Arabic / n., int. / saˈlaːm / sah-*lahm*.   Peace, harmony, wholeness, prosperity; welfare, tranquility; used also as a salutation.

Salon. French / n. / sa.lɔ̃ / sall-ohh.   Cultural events or groupings, usually devoted to literature and art, and often run by a female host. Lit. "lounge" or "sitting room."

Samar (سمر). Arabic / v. / ˈsa.mar / *sah*-mahrr.   To sit together in conversation in the evening.

Śamatha/samatha (शमथ). Sanskrit/Pāli / n. / ʃʌ.mʌ.θʌ / shuh-muh-thuh.   Slowing or calming down; one-pointed meditation (e.g., as a means to calm the mind). Lit. "pacification" or "rest."

Saṃgha/saṅgha (संघ). Sanskrit/Pāli / n. / ˈsə̃.gʌ / suhm-ghuh.   A Buddhist community. Lit. "assembly."

Saṃjñā/sañña (संज्ञा). Sanskrit/Pāli / n. / sə̃.gnjaː / suhm-gnyah.   Perception, cognition; in Buddhism, the third *skandha*.

Saṃsāra (संसार). Sanskrit/Pâli / n. / ˌsə̃ˈsɑːrə / suhm-*sah*-ruh.   Cyclic, circuitous change; a theory of rebirth; the nature of conventional existence. Lit. "wandering" or "world."

Saṃskāra (संस्कार). Sanskrit/Pāli / n. / sə̃ˈskɑːrʌ / suhm-*skar*-uh.   Mental volitional formations; karmic imprints; "conditioned things"; in Buddhism, the fourth *skandha*.

Saṃtoṣa/santosha (संतोष). Sanskrit/Pāli / n. / sə̃.təʊ.ʃʌ / suhm-toe-shuh.   Complete contentment and satisfaction.

Samudaya (समुदाय). Sanskrit/Pāli / n. / sʌ.mʊˈdaɪ.jʌ / suh-moo-*dye*-uh.   Origin, cause; Buddhism's second Noble Truth, specifying craving and attachment as the cause of *duḥkha*.

S'apprivoiser. French / v. / sˌapʀiˈvwa.ze / s-a-prre-*vwa*-zay.   In the context of a relationship, a mutual process of learning to trust and accept the other. Lit. "to tame."

Satya/sacca (सत्य). Sanskrit/Pāli / n. / sʌt.jʌ / sut-yuh.   Truth; truthfulness in speech, thought, and action; refraining from falsehoods or distortions.

Saudade. Portuguese / n. / sɐwˈða.ði / sow-*dha*-dh.   Melancholic longing; nostalgia; dreaming wistfulness.

Savoir-être. French / n. / sav.waʀˈɛtʀ / sav-wah-et-ruh.   Knowing how carry oneself; "soft" interpersonal skills. Lit. "knowing how to be."

Savoir-faire. French / n. / sav.waʀ.fɛʀ / sav-wah-fare.   The ability to behave in a correct and confident way across a variety of situations. Lit. "knowing how to do."

Savoir-vivre. French / n. / sav.waʀ.viv.ʀ / sav-wah-*veev*-ruh.   Familiarity with norms and customs; refinement. Lit. "knowing how to live."

Sehnsucht. German / n. / ˈzeɪnˌzuːxt / zeen-zukht.   Life longings; intense desire for alternative paths and states. Lit. an "addiction" to longing.

Sébomai (σέβομαι). Greek / v. / ˈsɛb.ɔm.ɑiː / *seb*-ohm-aaee.   To revere, honor; to be in awe of.

Seijaku (靜寂). Japanese / n. / ˌseɪˈdʒɐ.kə / say-*ja*-kuh.   Quiet tranquility; silence, calm, serenity, especially in the midst of activity or chaos.

Shalom (שָׁלוֹם). Hebrew / n., int. / ʃɔːˈlɔʊm / shor-*lome*.   Peace, harmony, wholeness, prosperity, welfare, tranquility; used also as a salutation.

Shinrin-yoku (森林浴). Japanese / n. / ʃɪn.ɹiːjɒk.ə / shin-ree-yok-uh.   Appreciating or "bathing" in the restorative power of nature. Lit. "bathing" in the forest.

Shiv'ah (שׁבעה). Hebrew / n. / ʃɪ.vʌʰ / shee-vuh.   The weeklong period of mourning prescribed in Judaism. Lit. "seven."

Siesta. Spanish / n. / sɪˈɛs.tə / see-*est*-uh.   A short nap, usually taken in the early afternoon.

Shù (恕). Chinese / n., v. / ʃuː / shoo.   Forgiveness/to forgive; mercy; reciprocity.

Siddhārtha/siddhattha (सिद्धार्थ). Sanskrit/Pāli / n., pronoun / sɪd.dɑːr.θʌ / siddar-thuh. One who has achieved an aim or object.

Siga siga (σιγά σιγά). Greek / adv. / siˈɣa siˈɣa / see-*yah* see-*yah*.   Being unhurried. Lit. "slowly, slowly."

Śīla/sīla (शील). Sanskrit/Pāli / n. / ʃiːlʌ / shee-luh.   Morality, ethics, virtue; custom, practice; conduct, disposition, nature, tendency.

Simpatía. Spanish / n. / sim.paˈti:æ / sim-pah-*tee*-ah.   Accord and harmony within relationships and society generally.

Sisu. Finnish / n. / ˈsi.su / *si*-soo.   Extraordinary determination and courage, especially in the face of adversity.

Sitzfleisch. German / n. / ˈzɪts̃.flaɪʃ / *zitz*-flysh.   The ability or willingness to persevere through tasks that are hard or boring. Lit. "sitting flesh."

Skandha(s)/khanda(s) (स्कन्ध). Sanskrit/Pāli / n. / ˈskʌn.dʌs / *skun*-duss.   Aggregate(s), heap(s), grouping(s); used to describe the five "elements" that constitute the human being.

Smṛti/sati (स्मृति). Sanskrit/Pāli / n. / smrɪ.ti: / smrih-tee. Mindfulness or awareness of the present moment. Lit. "recollection" or "remembrance."

Soirée. French / n. / swa.ʀe / swah-rray. A relatively cultured evening party, often centered on music or conversation.

Solivagant. Latin / n., adj. / sɔʊˈlɪ.və.gənt / so-*liv*-a-gnt. A lone wanderer; characterized by lone wandering.

Sophia (σοφία). Greek / n. / soˈfi.a / soh-*fee*-ya. Wisdom, knowledge.

Sóphrosuné (σωφροσύνη). Greek / n. / sɔːpʰroˈsý.nɛ / sor-phro-*sy*-neh. Excellence of character and soundness of mind; leads to other beneficial qualities, such as moderation and self-control.

Storgē (στοργή). Greek / n. / stoɹˈɣə / store-*geh*. Filial love; care and affection (e.g., between family members).

Sukha (सुख). Sanskrit/Pāli / n. / ˈsʊ.kʰə / *suh*-kuh. Pleasure; ease; satisfactoriness; antonym of *duḥkha*.

Sumud (صمود). Arabic / n. / səˈmuːd / suh-*mood*. Steadfastness, perseverance; a determined struggle to persist.

Śūnyatā/suññatā (शून्यता). Sanskrit/Pāli / n. / ʃʊn.jʌˈta: / shoon-yuh-*tah*. Emptiness; boundlessness, boundarylessness; the idea that all phenomena arise dependent on conditions, and have no intrinsic identity.

Superego. Latin (new) / n. / ˈsʊ.pɛr ˈɛ.gɔ / *su*-per *eh*-go. Used by translators of Freud to represent the German *Über-Ich*, referring to internalized societal norms and values. Lit. "above I."

Surāmerayamajja pamādaṭṭhānā (सुरामेरयमज्ज पमादट्ठाना). Sanskrit/Pāli / n. / sʊˈra:meɪ.rʌ.jʌ.mʌ.dʒʌ: pʌ.ma:dʌt.ha:na: / soo-*rah*-may-ruh-yuh-muh-juh puh-mah-dut-hah-nuh. Intoxicating and/or unmindful states resulting from consumption of alcohol or other drugs, refraining from which is the fifth of Buddhism's Five Precepts.

Taʻârof (تعارف). Persian / n. / tʰɒːˈrof / thar-*rof*. Politeness; social intelligence (e.g., in exchanging hospitality and gifts).

Taarradhin (تراض). Arabic / n. / ˈtæн.ræн.diːn / *takh*-rah-deen. A win-win; a solution or compromise in which both parties are satisfied.

Tài jí [Tai chi] (太極). Chinese / n. / taɪ tɕʰiː / ty-chee. A martial art involving slow, deliberate movements. Lit. "supreme" or "ultimate" force/energy.

Talanoa. Fijian / v. / tə.lə.noːə / tuh-luh-nor-uh. To tell stories; to chat or gossip in ways that can serve as a "social adhesive."

Talkoot. Finnish / n. / ˈtal.koːt / tahl-koort. A collectively undertaken task; voluntary community work.

Tao (道). Chinese / n. / tʰaʊ / t/d-ao. Omnipotent and all-pervasive creative/generative power; path or way; the unfolding process of reality itself.

Tarab (طرب). Arabic / n. / ˈtɑːrəb / tah-rrb. Singing, chanting; musically induced ecstasy or enchantment.

Tathāgatagarbha (तथागतगर्भ). Sanskrit/Pāli / tʌtˈhɑːgʌ.tʌ gɑːrb.hɑ / tuh-tar-guh-tuh garr-bha. Buddha nature. Lit. "one who has thus come/gone."

Tat Tvam Asi (तत्त्वमसि). Sanskrit / phrase / tʌt.twʌm.æsiː / tut-twum-ah-see. A central expression of Ádvaita philosophy, articulating the oneness of ātman and Brahman. Lit. "Thou Art That."

Techné (τέχνη). Greek / n. / ˈtékʰnɛː / tekh-nee. Craftsmanship; practical expertise.

Þetta reddast. Icelandic / phrase / ˈθæ.tæ ˈrɛtːast / tha-ta reht-ust. "It will all work out ok"; used especially when circumstances are not promising.

Tertulia. Spanish / n. / terˈtul.ja / terr-tool-ya. A social gathering or conversation, usually with literary or artistic overtones.

Thymós (θυμός). Greek / n. / θyˈmos / thoo-moss. Spiritedness; connotes flesh and blood.

Tiferet (תפארת). Hebrew / n. / tifˈʔeʁ.eθ / tif-air-eth. Beauty, balance; the sixth sephirot in the Kabbalah tradition, integrating Hésed and Gevurah.

Titânes (Τιτᾶνες). Greek / n. / ti.tanːɛs / tih-tah-ness. Titans; in Greek mythology, the second generation of deities.

Tithadesh (תתחדש). Hebrew / int. / tɪt.xa.dɛʃ / tit-kha-desh. Spoken to someone who has acquired a new possession or positive change in circumstances. Lit. "get new."

Tjotjog. Javanese / v. / tʃəʊ.tʃəʊg / choh-chog. To fit; harmony within relationships and society at large.

Toska (тоска). Russian / n. / tʌˈskaː / tuh-skah. Longing, often for one's homeland; nostalgia, wistfulness.

Tuko pamoja. Swahili / n. / tuːkə pæˈməʊ.dʒæ / too-kuh pah-moh-jah. Community togetherness. Lit. "we are one/together."

Tūrangawaewae. Māori / n. / təˌrʌŋ.gəˈwaɪ.waɪ / tur-rang-uh-why-why. A place where one feels rooted, empowered, and connected. Lit. "a place to stand."

Tzedaka (צדקה). Hebrew / n. / sˤə.ðaːqaː / su-tha-khaa. Generosity or charity mandated by justice; required righteous giving. Lit. "justice," "righteousness."

Ubuntu. Zulu/Xhosa / n. / ʊˈbuːn.tʊ / uu-*boon*-tuu. Being kind to others on account of one's common humanity.

Uitbuiken. Dutch / v. / ˈɔʊt.bɜːɣən / oat-ber-ghen. To relax satiated between courses or after a meal. Lit. "out-bellying."

Upaniṣads (उपनिषद्). Sanskrit / n. / ʊˈpə.ɳɪ.ʂəɖ̩/ oo-*puh*-nee-shuud. The foundational texts of what is now referred to as Hinduism; the concluding sections of the four *Védas*. Lit. "sitting down near."

Upekṣā/upekkhā (उपेक्षा). Sanskrit/Pāli / n. / u.pɛkʰˈʃɑː / oo-pek-*shah*. Equanimity, detachment; calmness, balance.

Utu (उतु). Sanskrit/Pāli / n. / ʊtʊ / uu-tuu. Seasons, per *utu-niyāma*, the "law of the seasons": the regularity of environmental phenomena.

Vācā (वाचा). Sanskrit/Pāli / n. / wɑːkə / vwah.kuh. Speech, voice; per *samyak-vāc* (i.e., "right speech"), of the Noble Eightfold Path.

Vedanā (वेदना). Sanskrit/Pāli / n. / veɪ.dʌ.nɑː / vwey-duh-nar. Feeling tone; valence of a sensory object (pleasant, unpleasant, or neutral); in Buddhism, the second *skandha*.

Vijñāna/viññāṇa (विज्ञान). Sanskrit/Pāli / n. / vɪg.njɑːnə / vwig-yah-nuh. Consciousness, mind; discernment; in Buddhism, the fifth *skandha*.

Vinyāsa (विन्यास). Sanskrit/Pāli / n. / vɪnˈjɑːsə / vwin-*yah*-suh. A form of yoga centered on dynamic movement between *āsana*. Lit. "to place in a special way."

Vipaśyanā/vipassanā (विपश्यना). Sanskrit/Pāli / n. / vɪ.pʌʃ.jʌ.nɑː / vwih-puhsh-yuh-nah. Insight; clear-seeing, seeing into; cultivating awareness (e.g., of the nature of reality).

Vorfreude. German / n. / ˈfoːɐ̯.fʁɔɪ̯də / *for*-fhroy-duh. Joyful anticipation derived from imagining future pleasures.

Wabi (侘) Japanese / n. / ɰɑːbɪ / wah-bee. Imperfect, rustic, remote, weathered beauty.

Wabi-sabi (侘寂): Japanese / n. / ɰɑːbɪ sɑːbɪ / wah-bee sah-bee. Imperfect and aged beauty; the aesthetics of impermanence and imperfection.

Wanderlust. German / n. / ˌvæn.dɛˈlʊst / *van*-deh-*loost*. Desire or predilection for travel and adventure. Lit. "desire to hike."

Weltanschauung. German / n. / ˈvel.tæn.ʃaʊʊŋ / *vell*-tan-shao-ung. An overarching worldview or philosophy of life.

Weltschmerz. German / n. / ˈvelt.ʃmeəts / *velt*-shmerts. World-weariness, world-hurt; causeless melancholy.

Willkür. German / n. / ˈvɪl.kyːɐ / *vill*-kuah.   Following or obeying the will; choosing to obey oneself; arbitrariness, capriciousness.

Xenia (ξενία). Greek / n. / x.sen.ía / kh-sen-ia.   Guest-friendship; the importance of offering hospitality and respect to strangers.

Xiào (孝). Chinese / n. / ɕi.aʊ / shee-aow.   Filial piety; family reverence.

Xīn (心). Chinese / n. / ɕɪn / shin.   Heart, mind, spirit.

Xìn (信). Chinese / n. / ɕɪn / shin.   Truth, truthfulness; sincerity; trust, trustworthiness.

Xìng fú (幸福) (Chinese, n. / ɕɪŋ.fʊː / *shing*-fuu.   Contentment; deep happiness. Lit. "fortunate blessing."

Yesod (יסוד). Hebrew / n. / jɪs.sɒd / yiss-sod.   Foundation; the ninth *sephirot* in the Kabbalah tradition, denoting the creation of the manifest world.

Yì (義). Chinese / n. / jiː / ee.   Duty; justice; a moral disposition toward goodness.

Yīn-yáng (陰陽). Chinese / n. / jiːn.jʌŋ / yin-yung.   Holistic duality; dialectical, co-dependent opposites. Lit. "cloudy sun."

Yoga (योग). Sanskrit / v., n. / jəʊ.gʌ / yoh-guh.   A psychophysical system of spiritual training and development. Lit. "to yoke, add, join, unite, attach."

Yūgen (幽玄). Japanese / n. / ˈjuːgən / *yoo*-gn.   Obscurity, cloudy impenetrability, unknowability, mystery.

Zanshin (残心). Japanese / n. / zãn.ɕɪn / zan-shin.   A state of relaxed mental alertness, especially in the face of danger or stress. Lit. "remaining or enduring heart-mind."

Zen (禪). Japanese / n. / zɛ̃N / zun.   Concentrated attention or absorption. The Japanese adaptation of *dhyāna*.

Zeus (Ζεύς). Greek / pronoun / zɛ.us / zeh-oos.   In Greek mythology, the God of sky, thunder, law, order, and justice; supreme deity of the Olympian Gods. Known as Jupiter in Roman mythology.

Zhì (智). Chinese / n. / tʂɚ̩ / jirr.   Wisdom, perspicacity, knowledge.

Notes

Preface

1. T. Lomas, "Towards a Positive Cross-Cultural Lexicography: Enriching Our Emotional Landscape through 216 'Untranslatable' Words Pertaining to Wellbeing," *Journal of Positive Psychology* 11, no. 5 (2016): 546–558.

2. E. W. Said, *Orientalism: Western Conceptions of the Orient* (London: Penguin, 1995).

3. E. Wenger, *Communities of Practice: Learning, Meaning and Identity* (Cambridge: Cambridge University Press, 1998).

4. T. Lomas, T. Cartwright, T. Edginton, and D. Ridge, "New Ways of Being a Man: 'Positive' Hegemonic Masculinity in Meditation-Based Communities of Practice," *Men and Masculinities* 19, no. 3 (2016): 289–310.

5. B. L. Fredrickson, M. A. Cohn, K. A. Coffey, J. Pek, and S. M. Finkel, "Open Hearts Build Lives: Positive Emotions, Induced through Loving-Kindness Meditation, Build Consequential Personal Resources," *Journal of Personality and Social Psychology* 95, no. 5 (2008): 1045–1062.

6. T. Lomas, K. Hefferon, and I. Ivtzan, "The LIFE Model: A Meta-Theoretical Conceptual Map for Applied Positive Psychology," *Journal of Happiness Studies* 16, no. 5 (2015): 1347–1364, 1347.

7. Lomas, "Towards a Positive Cross-Cultural Lexicography."

8. M. Dunn, S. J. Greenhill, S. C. Levinson, and R. D. Gray, "Evolved Structure of Language Shows Lineage-Specific Trends in Word-Order Universals," *Nature* 473, no. 7345 (2011): 79–82. See also http://ethnologue.com.

9. A. Lehrer, *Semantic Fields and Lexical Structures* (Amsterdam: North-Holland, 1974), 105.

10. L. J. Cronbach and P. E. Meehl, "Construct Validity in Psychological Tests," *Psychological Bulletin* 52, no. 4 (1955): 281–302.

Chapter 1: Mapping Well-Being

1. A. Korzybski, *Science and Sanity: An Introduction to Non-Aristotelian Systems and General Semantics*, 5th ed. (New York: Institute of General Semantics, 1933/1958), 58.

2. F. H. Rhodes, *Earth: A Tenant's Manual* (New York: Cornell University Press, 2012).

3. M. A. Rappenglück, "Palaeolithic Timekeepers Looking at the Golden Gate of the Ecliptic: The Lunar Cycle and the Pleiades in the Cave of La-Tete-Du-Lion (Ardéche, France)," *Earth, Moon, and Planets* 85 (1999): 391–404.

4. N. J. Thrower, *Maps and Civilization: Cartography in Culture and Society* (Chicago: University of Chicago Press, 2008).

5. A. Cecconi and M. Galanda, "Adaptive Zooming in Web Cartography," *Computer Graphics Forum* 21, no. 4 (2002): 787–799.

6. S. Bhatt, D. J. Weiss, E. Cameron, D. Bisanzio, B. Mappin, U. Dalrymple, K. E. Battle, et al., "The Effect of Malaria Control on Plasmodium Falciparum in Africa between 2000 and 2015," *Nature* 526, no. 7572 (2015): 207–211.

7. M. M. Van De Pitte, "Husserl's Solipsism," *Journal of the British Society for Phenomenology* 8, no. 2 (1977): 123–125.

8. J. Fell, "Identifying Neural Correlates of Consciousness: The State Space Approach," *Consciousness and Cognition* 13, no. 4 (2004): 709–729.

9. D. J. Chalmers, "Facing Up to the Problem of Consciousness," *Journal of Consciousness Studies* 2 (1995): 200–219.

10. F. Jackson, "Epiphenomenal Qualia," *Philosophical Quarterly* 32, no. 127 (1982): 127–136, 127.

11. V. Burr, *An Introduction to Social Construction* (New York: Routledge, 1995).

12. C. Brickell, "The Sociological Construction of Gender and Sexuality," *Sociological Review* 54, no. 1 (2006): 87–113.

13. W. O. Bockting, G. Knudson, and J. M. Goldberg, "Counseling and Mental Health Care for Transgender Adults and Loved Ones," *International Journal of Transgenderism* 9, nos. 3–4 (2006): 35–82.

14. F. de Saussure, *Course in General Linguistics* (New York: Philosophical Library, 1916).

15. J. Jenning, "Structuralism," in *The Edinburgh Encyclopedia of Continental Philosophy*, ed. S. Glendinning (Edinburgh: Fitzroy Dearborn Publishers, 1999).

16. C. Lévi-Strauss, *The Naked Man* (Chicago: University of Chicago Press, 1981), 786.

17. J. Derrida, *Margins of Philosophy* (Chicago: University of Chicago Press, 1982).

18. G. Rail, "Introduction," in *Sport and Postmodern Times*, ed. G. Rail (Albany: New York Press, 1998), xii.

19. A. McRobbie, *The Aftermath of Feminism: Gender, Culture and Social Change* (London: Sage, 2009).

20. J. A. Russell, J.-M. Fernández-Dols, A. S. Manstead, and J. C. Wellenkamp, *Everyday Conceptions of Emotion: An Introduction to the Psychology, Anthropology and Linguistics of Emotion* (New York: Springer Science & Business Media, 2013).

21. L. J. Cronbach and P. E. Meehl, "Construct Validity in Psychological Tests," *Psychological Bulletin* 52, no. 4 (1955): 281–302.

22. D. Meunier, R. Lambiotte, A. Fornito, K. D. Ersche, and E. T. Bullmore, "Hierarchical Modularity in Human Brain Functional Networks," *Frontiers in Neuroinformatics* 3 (2010): 15–26.

23. A. Koestler, *Janus: A Summing Up* (London: Hutchinson, 1978).

24. C. Y. Liu, A. P. Krishnan, L. Yan, R. X. Smith, E. Kilroy, J. R. Alger, J. M. Ringman, and D. J. J. Wang, "Complexity and Synchronicity of Resting State Blood Oxygenation Level-Dependent (BOLD) Functional MRI in Normal Aging and Cognitive Decline," *Journal of Magnetic Resonance Imaging* 38, no. 1 (2013): 36–45.

25. T. Kohonen, *Associative Memory: A System-Theoretical Approach* (London: Springer Science & Business Media, 2012).

26. B. B. Mandelbrot, *The Fractal Geometry of Nature* (New York: Macmillan, 1983).

27. R. P. Honeck, M. Firment, and T. J. Case, "Expertise and Categorization," *Bulletin of the Psychonomic Society* 25, no. 6 (1987): 431–434.

28. K. Honkalampi, J. Hintikka, A. Tanskanen, J. Lehtonen, and H. Viinamäki, "Depression Is Strongly Associated with Alexithymia in the General Population," *Journal of Psychosomatic Research* 48, no. 1 (2000): 99–104, 99.

29. R. L. Miller, *The Linguistic Relativity Principle and Humboldtian Ethnolinguistics: A History and Appraisal* (Berlin: Walter de Gruyter, 1968).

30. J. G. Herder, *Essay on the Origin of Language* (Chicago: University of Chicago Press, 1772/1966).

31. W. von Humboldt, *Prüfung der Untersuchungen über die Urbewohner Hispaniens Vermittelst der (Researches into the Early Inhabitants of Spain with the Help of the Basque Language)* (Hamburg: Richter, 1821).

32. E. Sapir, "The Status of Linguistics as a Science," *Language* (1929): 207–214.

33. B. L. Whorf, "Science and Linguistics," *Technology Review* 42, no. 6 (1940): 229–231, 247–248.

34. P. Kay and W. Kempton, "What Is the Sapir–Whorf Hypothesis?" *American Anthropologist* 86, no. 1 (1984): 65–79.

35. B. L, Whorf, *Language, Thought, and Reality: Selected Writings of Benjamin Lee Whorf*, ed. J. B. Carroll (Cambridge, MA: MIT Press, 1956), 213–214.

36. L. S. Vygotsky, *Thought and Language* (Cambridge, MA: MIT Press, 1962); V. Voloshinov, *Marxism and the Philosophy of Language* (Cambridge, MA: Harvard University Press, 1986), 26.

37. P. Lee, *The Whorf Theory Complex* (Amsterdam: John Benjamins, 1996), xiv.

38. S. Pinker, *The Language Instinct: The New Science of Language and Mind* (London: Penguin, 1995).

39. L. Perlovsky, "Language and Emotions: Emotional Sapir–Whorf Hypothesis," *Neural Networks* 22, nos. 5–6 (2009): 518–526.

40. S. T. Katz, *Mysticism and Religious Traditions* (Oxford: Oxford University Press, 1983).

41. A. Huxley, *Perennial Philosophy* (London: Chatto & Windus, 1947).

42. D. Evans, "Can Philosophers Limit What Mystics Can Do? A Critique of Steven Katz," *Religious Studies* 25, no. 01 (1989): 53–60; R. King, "Mysticism and Spirituality," in *The Routledge Companion to the Study of Religion*, ed. J. R. Hinnells (Routledge: London, 2005), 306–322, 317.

43. K. A. Lindquist, "Language Is Powerful," *Emotion Review* 1, no. 1 (2009): 16–18.

44. A. Wierzbicka, *Understanding Cultures through Their Key Words: English, Russian, Polish, German, and Japanese* (New York: Oxford University Press, 1997), 18.

45. M. McLaren, *Interpreting Cultural Differences: The Challenge of Intercultural Communication* (Dereham: Peter Francis, 1998), 14.

46. A. Wierzbicka, *Understanding Cultures through Their Key Words: English, Russian, Polish, German, and Japanese* (New York: Oxford University Press, 1997), 1.

47. G. K. Pullum, "The Great Eskimo Vocabulary Hoax," *Natural Language & Linguistic Theory* 7, no. 2 (1989): 275–281.

48. F. Boas, *Handbook of American Indian Languages* (Washington, DC: Smithsonian Institution, 1911).

49. L. Martin, "'Eskimo Words for Snow': A Case Study in the Genesis and Decay of an Anthropological Example," *American Anthropologist* 88, no. 2 (1986): 418–423.

50. Pullum, "The Great Eskimo Vocabulary Hoax."

51. O. H. Magga, "Diversity in Saami Terminology for Reindeer, Snow, and Ice," *International Social Science Journal* 58, no. 187 (2006): 25–34, 25.

52. H. Thorpe, "Embodied Boarders: Snowboarding, Status and Style," *Waikato Journal of Education* 10, no. 1 (2016): 181–202.

53. A. Wierzbicka, *Understanding Cultures through Their Key Words: English, Russian, Polish, German, and Japanese* (New York: Oxford University Press, 1997), 18.

54. A. P. Grant, "Loanwords in British English," in *Loanwords in the World's Languages: A Comparative Handbook*, ed. M. Haspelmath and U. Tadmor (Berlin: De Gruyter Martin, 2009), 360–383.

55. H. R. Loyn, *Anglo Saxon England and the Norman Conquest* (London: Routledge, 2014).

56. P. Durkin, *Borrowed Words: A History of Loanwords in English* (Oxford: Oxford University Press, 2014).

57. J. J. Smith, *Essentials of Early English: Old, Middle and Early Modern English* (London: Routledge, 2006).

58. L. J. Brinton and E. C. Traugott, *Lexicalization and Language Change* (Cambridge: Cambridge University Press, 2005).

59. C. Dickens, *Bleak House* (London: Bradbury and Evans, 1853).

60. H. Paul, *Principles of the History of Language*, trans. H. A. Strong (New York: MacMillan, 1889).

61. W. P. Lehmann, *Historical Linguistics: An Introduction* (New York: Holt, Rinehart & Winston, 1962), 212.

62. W. Rothwell, "Arrivals and Departures: The Adoption of French Terminology into Middle English," *English Studies* 72, no. 9 (1998): 144–165.

63. P. Rickard, *A History of the French Language* (London: Routledge, 2003).

64. A. P. Grant, "Loanwords in British English," in *Loanwords in the World's Languages*, 360–383.

65. T. M. Green, *The Greek and Latin Roots of English*, 5th ed. (New York: Rowman & Littlefield, 2014).

66. R. P. Oliver, "'New Fragments' of Latin Authors in Perotti's Cornucopiae," *Transactions and Proceedings of the American Philological Association* 78 (1947): 376–424.

67. P. Durkin, *Borrowed Words: A History of Loanwords in English* (Oxford: Oxford University Press, 2014).

68. U. Tadmor, "Loanwords in the World's Languages: Findings and Results," in *Loanwords in the World's Languages*, 55–75.

69. Ibid.

70. A. P. Grant, "Loanwords in British English," in *Loanwords in the World's Languages*, 360–383.

71. G. H. Cannon and A. S. Kaye, *The Arabic Contributions to the English Language: An Historical Dictionary* (Berlin: Otto Harrassowitz Verlag, 1994); G. Cannon, "Zero Plurals among the Japanese Loanwords in English," *American Speech* 59, no. 2 (1984): 149–158; J. Algeo, "Spanish Loanwords in English by 1900," in *Spanish Loanwords in the English Language*, ed. F. Gonzalez (Berlin: Mouton de Gruyter, 1996), 13–40.

72. G. H. Cannon and A. S. Kaye, *The Arabic Contributions to the English Language: An Historical Dictionary* (Berlin: Otto Harrassowitz Verlag, 1994).

73. M. Haspelmath, "Lexical Borrowing: Concepts and Issues," in *Loanwords in the World's Languages*, 35–55.

74. P. Durkin, *Borrowed Words: A History of Loanwords in English* (Oxford: Oxford University Press, 2014).

75. Y. Matras, "Utterance Modifiers and Universals of Grammatical Borrowing," *Linguistics* 36, no. 2 (1998): 281–331.

76. Haspelmath, "Lexical Borrowing."

77. C. W. Pfaff, "Constraints on Language Mixing: Intrasentential Code-Switching and Borrowing in Spanish/English," *Language* (1979): 291–318.

78. W. Rothwell, "Arrivals and Departures: The Adoption of French Terminology into Middle English," *English Studies* 72, no. 9 (1998): 144–165.

79. R. Phillipson, "English for Globalisation or for the World's People?" *International Review of Education* 47, no. 3 (2001): 185–200.

80. Haspelmath, "Lexical Borrowing."

81. A. Blank, "Why Do New Meanings Occur? A Cognitive Typology of the Motivations for Lexical Semantic Change," in *Historical Semantics and Cognition*, ed. A. Blank and P. Koch (Berlin: Mouton de Gruyter, 1999), 61–89.

82. Haspelmath, "Lexical Borrowing."

83. A. Blank, "Why Do New Meanings Occur?"

84. A. Lehrer, "Notes on Lexical Gaps," *Journal of Linguistics* 6, no. 2 (1970): 257–261; N. Chomsky, *Aspects of the Theory of Syntax* (Cambridge, MA: MIT Press, 1965); N. Chomsky and M. Halle, "Some Controversial Questions in Phonological Theory," *Journal of Linguistics* 1, no. 2 (1965): 97–138.

85. A. Lehrer, *Semantic Fields and Lexical Structures* (Amsterdam: North-Holland, 1974), 105.

86. Tadmor, "Loanwords in the World's Languages."

87. P. Ekman, "An Argument for Basic Emotions," *Cognition & Emotion* 6, nos. 3–4 (1992): 169–200.

88. E. Berscheid, "Love in the Fourth Dimension," *Annual Review of Psychology* 61 (2010): 1–25, 6.

89. J. A. Lee, "A Typology of Styles of Loving," *Personality and Social Psychology Bulletin* 3, no. 2 (1977): 173–182.

90. J. Blenkinsopp and M. Shademan Pajouh, "Lost in Translation? Culture, Language and the Role of the Translator in International Business," *Critical Perspectives on International Business* 6, no. 1 (2010): 38–52.

91. M. McClaren, *Interpreting Cultural Differences: The Challenge of International Communication* (Dereham: Peter Francis, 1998), 128.

92. C. Taylor, *Philosophy and the Human Sciences: Philosophical Papers*, vol. 2 (Cambridge: Cambridge University Press, 1985), 23–24.

93. A. Wierzbicka, *Emotions across Languages and Cultures: Diversity and Universals* (Cambridge: Cambridge University Press, 1999), 8.

94. L. Wittgenstein, *Last Writings on the Philosophy of Psychology*, vol. 1 (Chicago: University of Chicago Press, 1990).

95. T. Lomas, "Recontextualising Mindfulness: Theravada Buddhist Perspectives on the Ethical and Spiritual Dimensions of Awareness," *Psychology of Religion and Spirituality* (2016).

96. S. Scheibe, A. M. Freund, and P. B. Baltes, "Toward a Developmental Psychology of Sehnsucht (Life Longings): The Optimal (Utopian) Life," *Developmental Psychology* 43, no. 3 (2007): 778–795.

97. J. Oldstone-Moore, *Taoism: Origins, Beliefs, Practices, Holy Texts, Sacred Places* (Oxford: Oxford University Press, 2003).

98. R. D. Fowler, M. E. P. Seligman, and G. P. Koocher, "The APA 1998 Annual Report," *American Psychologist* 54, no. 8 (1999): 537–568.

99. A. H. Maslow, "Toward a Humanistic Psychology," *A Review of General Semantics* 13 (1956): 10–22.

100. S. Resnick, A. Warmoth, and I. A. Serlin, "The Humanistic Psychology and Positive Psychology Connection: Implications for Psychotherapy," *Journal of Humanistic Psychology* 41, no. 1 (2001): 73–101.

101. E. Diener, "Subjective Well-Being: The Science of Happiness and a Proposal for a National Index," *American Psychologist* 55, no. 1 (2000): 34–43.

102. C. D. Ryff, "Happiness Is Everything, or Is It? Explorations on the Meaning of Psychological Well-Being," *Journal of Personality and Social Psychology* 57, no. 6 (1989): 1069–1081.

103. E. Deci and R. Ryan, "Hedonia, Eudaimonia, and Well-Being: An Introduction," *Journal of Happiness Studies* 9, no. 1 (2008): 1–11.

104. C. D. Ryff, "Happiness Is Everything, or Is It?"

105. D. Becker and J. Marecek, "Dreaming the American Dream: Individualism and Positive Psychology," *Social and Personality Psychology Compass* 2, no. 5 (2008): 1767–1780.

106. J. Henrich, S. J. Heine, and A. Norenzayan, "Most People Are Not WEIRD," *Nature* 466, no. 7302 (2010): 29.

107. D. Becker and J. Marecek, "Dreaming the American Dream: Individualism and Positive Psychology," *Social and Personality Psychology Compass* 2, no. 5 (2008): 1767–1780.

108. S. Pope, "Expressive Individualism and True Self-Love: A Thomistic Perspective," *Journal of Religion* (1991): 384–399, 384.

109. T. Lomas, "Positive Social Psychology: A Multilevel Inquiry into Socio-Cultural Wellbeing Initiatives," *Psychology, Public Policy, and Law* 21, no. 3 (2015): 338–347.

110. R. Biswas-Diener, J. Vittersø, and E. Diener, "Most People Are Pretty Happy, but There Is Cultural Variation: The Inughuit, the Amish, and the Maasai," *Journal of Happiness Studies* 6, no. 3 (2005): 205–226.

111. J. Zhang, Y. Yang, and H. Wang, "Measuring Subjective Well-Being: A Comparison of China and the USA," *Asian Journal of Social Psychology* 12, no. 3 (2009): 221–225.

112. T. Lomas, "Positive Cross-Cultural Psychology: Exploring Similarity and Difference in Constructions and Experiences of Wellbeing," *International Journal of Wellbeing* 5, no. 4 (2015): 60–77; J. W. Berry, Y. H. Poortinga, M. H. Segall, and P. R. Dasen, *Cross-Cultural Psychology: Research and Applications*, 2nd ed. (Cambridge: Cambridge University Press, 2002), xix.

113. Biswas-Diener, Vittersø, and Diener, "Most People Are Pretty Happy, but There Is Cultural Variation."

114. R. Layard, *Happiness: Lessons from a New Science* (London: Penguin, 2005), 33.

115. M. Joshanloo, "Eastern Conceptualizations of Happiness: Fundamental Differences with Western Views," *Journal of Happiness Studies* 15, no. 2 (2014): 475–493; Y.

Uchida and Y. Ogihara, "Personal or Interpersonal Construal of Happiness: A Cultural Psychological Perspective," *International Journal of Wellbeing* 2, no. 4 (2012): 354–369; S. Oishi, "Culture and Well-Being: Conceptual and Methodological Issues," in *International Differences in Well-Being*, ed. E. Diener, J. F. Helliwell, and D. Kahneman (New York: Oxford University Press, 2010), 34–69.

116. http://www.worldatlas.com/nations/.

117. A. Strauss and J. Corbin, *Basics of Qualitative Research: Techniques and Procedures for Developing Grounded Theory*, 2nd ed. (Thousand Oaks, CA: Sage, 1998).

118. J. R. Cutcliffe, "Adapt or Adopt: Developing and Transgressing the Methodological Boundaries of Grounded Theory," *Journal of Advanced Nursing* 51, no. 4 (2005): 421–428.

119. C. Taylor, *Philosophical Papers,* vol. 2: *Philosophy and the Human Sciences* (Cambridge: Cambridge University Press, 1985).

120. T. Lomas, "Positive Cross-Cultural Psychology: Exploring Similarity and Difference in Constructions and Experiences of Wellbeing," *International Journal of Wellbeing* 5, no. 4 (2015): 60–77.

121. M. Dunn, S. J. Greenhill, S. C. Levinson, and R. D. Gray, "Evolved Structure of Language Shows Lineage-Specific Trends in Word-Order Universals," *Nature* 473, no. 7345 (2011): 79–82.

122. Z. B. Silva, "Saudade—A Key Portuguese Emotion," *Emotion Review* 4, no. 2 (2012): 203–211.

123. M. McClaren, *Interpreting Cultural Differences: The Challenge of International Communication* (Dereham: Peter Francis, 1998), 128.

Chapter 2: Feelings

1. F. Jackson, "Epiphenomenal Qualia," *Philosophical Quarterly* 32, no. 127 (1982): 127–136.

2. S.C. Widen and J. A. Russell, "Descriptive and Prescriptive Definitions of Emotion," *Emotion Review* 2, no. 4 (2010): 377–378.

3. C. E. Izard, "The Many Meanings/Aspects of Emotion: Definitions, Functions, Activation, and Regulation," *Emotion Review* 2, no. 4 (2010): 363–370.

4. A. Damasio, "Fundamental Feelings," *Nature* 413, no. 6858 (2001): 781.

5. T. Nagel, "What Is It Like to Be a Bat?" *Philosophical Review* 83, no. 4 (1974): 435–450.

6. F. Jackson, "Epiphenomenal Qualia," *Philosophical Quarterly* 32, no. 127 (1982): 127–136, 127.

7. M. Boiger and B. Mesquita, "The Construction of Emotion in Interactions, Relationships, and Cultures," *Emotion Review* 4, no. 3 (2012): 221–229.

8. J. A. Russell, "A Circumplex Model of Affect," *Journal of Personality and Social Psychology* 39 (1980): 1161–1178.

9. P. Ekman, "Basic Emotions," in *The Handbook of Cognition and Emotion*, ed. T. Dalgleish and T. Power (Sussex, UK: John Wiley & Sons, 1999), 45–60.

10. J. Posner, J. A. Russell, and B. S. Peterson, "The Circumplex Model of Affect: An Integrative Approach to Affective Neuroscience, Cognitive Development, and Psychopathology," *Development and Psychopathology* 17, no. 3 (2005): 715–734, 715.

11. P. Ekman, "An Argument for Basic Emotions," *Cognition & Emotion* 6, nos. 3–4 (1992): 169–200.

12. Z. Kövecses, *Metaphor and Emotion: Language, Culture, and Body in Human Feeling* (Cambridge: Cambridge University Press, 2003).

13. R. Harré, *The Social Construction of Emotions* (Oxford: Blackwell, 1986), 5.

14. C. Lutz, "The Domain of Emotion Words on Ifaluk," *American Ethnologist* 9, no. 1 (1982): 113–128; G. B. Palmer and R. Brown, "The Ideology of Honour, Respect, and Emotion in Tagalog," in *Speaking of Emotions: Conceptualisation and Expression*, ed. Athanasiadou and E. Tabakowska (Berlin: Walter de Gruyter, 1998), 331–356.

15. D. Matsumoto and H. S. Hwang, "Culture and Emotion: The Integration of Biological and Cultural Contributions," *Journal of Cross-Cultural Psychology* 43, no. 1 (2012): 91–118, 92.

16. L. F. Barrett, "Are Emotions Natural Kinds?" *Perspectives on Psychological Science* 1, no. 1 (2006): 28–58, 49.

17. L. F. Barrett, "Are You in Despair? That's Good," *New York Times*, June 3, 2016).

18. L. F. Barrett, J. Gross, T. C. Christensen, and M. Benvenuto, "Knowing What You're Feeling and Knowing What to Do about It: Mapping the Relation between Emotion Differentiation and Emotion Regulation," *Cognition & Emotion* 15, no. 6 (2001): 713–724.

19. L. F. Barrett, "Are You in Despair?"

20. S. M. Breugelmans, Z. Ambadar, J. B. Vaca, Y. H. Poortinga, B. Setiadi, P. Widiyanto, and P. Philippot, "Body Sensations Associated with Emotions in Raramuri Indians, Rural Javanese, and Three Student Samples," *Emotion* 5, no. 2 (2005): 166–174.

21. T. B. Kashdan, L. F. Barrett, and P. E. McKnight, "Unpacking Emotion Differentiation: Transforming Unpleasant Experience by Perceiving Distinctions in Negativity," *Current Directions in Psychological Science* 24, no. 1 (2015): 10–16.

22. M. A. Brackett, S. E. Rivers, M. R. Reyes, and P. Salovey, "Enhancing Academic Performance and Social and Emotional Competence with the RULER Feeling Words Curriculum," *Learning and Individual Differences* 22, no. 2 (2012): 218–224.

23. F. A. Fogarty, L. M. Lu, J. J. Sollers, S. G. Krivoschekov, R. J. Booth, and N. S. Consedine, "Why It Pays to Be Mindful: Trait Mindfulness Predicts Physiological Recovery from Emotional Stress and Greater Differentiation among Negative Emotions," *Mindfulness* 6, no. 2 (2015): 175–185.

24. B. L. Fredrickson, "Promoting Positive Affect," in *The Science of Subjective Well-Being*, ed. M. Eid and R. Larsen (New York: Guilford Press, 2008), 449–467.

25. http://www.paulekman.com/atlas-of-emotions.

26. W. Van Gordon, E. Shonin, M. Griffiths, and N. Singh, "There Is Only One Mindfulness: Why Science and Buddhism Need to Work Together," *Mindfulness* 6, no. 1 (2015): 49–56.

27. J. Kabat-Zinn, "Some Reflections on the Origins of MBSR, Skillful Means, and the Trouble with Maps," *Contemporary Buddhism* 12, no. 1 (2011): 281–306.

28. J. E. Houben, ed., *Ideology and Status of Sanskrit: Contributions to the History of the Sanskrit Language* (New York: Brill, 1996).

29. L. Hodous and W. E. Soothill, *A Dictionary of Chinese Buddhist Terms: With Sanskrit and English Equivalents and a Sanskrit-Pali Index* (London: Routledge, 2003).

30. R. R. Jackson, "Terms of Sanskrit and Pali Origin Acceptable as English Words," *Journal of the International Association of Buddhist Studies* 5, no. 2 (1982): 141–142.

31. R. Coningham, K. Acharya, K. Strickland, C. Davis, M. Manuel, I. Simpson, K. Gilliland, J. Tremblay, T. Kinnaird, and D. Sanderson, "The Earliest Buddhist Shrine: Excavating the Birthplace of the Buddha, Lumbini (Nepal)," *Antiquity* 87, no. 338 (2013): 1104–1123.

32. S. Batchelor, *The Awakening of the West: The Encounter of Buddhism and Western Culture* (Berkeley, CA: Parallax Press, 1994).

33. R. Gethin, "On Some Definitions of Mindfulness," *Contemporary Buddhism* 12, no. 1 (2011): 263–279.

34. Anālayo, *Satipaṭṭhāna: The Direct Path to Realization* (Birmingham: Windhorse Publications, 2003), 48.

35. Majjhima Nikaaya 10, B. Bodhi, "What Does Mindfulness Really Mean? A Canonical Perspective," *Contemporary Buddhism* 12, no. 1 (2011): 19–39.

36. E. Shonin, W. Van Gordon, and M. Griffiths, "Teaching Ethics in Mindfulness-Based Interventions," *Mindfulness* (2015): 1–3.

37. R. Gethin, "On Some Definitions of Mindfulness," *Contemporary Buddhism* 12, no. 1 (2011): 263–279.

38. T. W. Rhys Davids, *Buddhist Suttas* (Oxford: Clarendon Press, 1881), 9, 63.

39. T. W. Rhys Davids, *Dialogues of the Buddha*, vol. 2 (London: Henry Frowde, 1910).

40. J. Kabat-Zinn, "An Outpatient Program in Behavioral Medicine for Chronic Pain Patients Based on the Practice of Mindfulness Meditation: Theoretical Considerations and Preliminary Results," *General Hospital Psychiatry* 4, no. 1 (1982): 33–47.

41. Z. V. Segal, J. M. G. Williams, and J. D. Teasdale, *Mindfulness-Based Cognitive Therapy for Depression: A New Approach to Preventing Relapse* (New York: Guilford Press, 2002).

42. P. Grossman, L. Niemann, S. Schmidt, and H. Walach, "Mindfulness-based Stress Reduction and Health Benefits: A Meta-Analysis," *Journal of Psychosomatic Research* 57, no. 1 (2004): 35–43.

43. J. Kabat-Zinn, "Mindfulness-based Interventions in Context: Past, Present, and Future," *Clinical Psychology: Science and Practice* 10, no. 2 (2003): 144–156, 145.

44. S. L. Shapiro, L. E. Carlson, J. A. Astin, and B. Freedman, "Mechanisms of Mindfulness," *Journal of Clinical Psychology* 62, no. 3 (2006): 373–386.

45. M. Monier-Williams, *A Sanskrit-English Dictionary: Etymologically and Philologically Arranged with Special Reference to Cognate Indo-European languages* (Oxford: Clarendon Press, 1899).

46. T.-f. Kuan, *Mindfulness in Early Buddhism: New Approaches through Psychology and Textual Analysis of Pali, Chinese and Sanskrit Sources* (London: Routledge, 2007).

47. T. Stcherbatsky, *Central Conception of Buddhism and the Meaning of the word Dharma* (New Delhi: Asian Educational Services, 2003).

48. J. M. G. Williams and J. Kabat-Zinn, "Mindfulness: Diverse Perspectives on Its Meaning, Origins, and Multiple Applications at the Intersection of Science and Dharma," *Contemporary Buddhism* 12, no. 01 (2011): 1–18, 4.

49. S. Stanley, "Intimate Distances: William James' Introspection, Buddhist Mindfulness, and Experiential Inquiry," *New Ideas in Psychology* 30, no. 2 (2012): 201–211, 202.

50. A. T. Schmidt, "The Ethics and Politics of Mindfulness-Based Interventions," *Journal of Medical Ethics* 42 (2016): 450–454.

51. N. Johnson, *Barefoot Zen: The Shaolin Roots of Kung Fu and Karate* (York Beach, ME: Samuel Weiser Books, 2000).

52. A. Chiesa, R. Calati, and A. Serretti, "Does Mindfulness Training Improve Cognitive Abilities? A Systematic Review of Neuropsychological Findings," *Clinical Psychological Review* 31, no. 3 (2011): 449–464; Y. Y. Tang, Y. Ma, Y. Fan, H. Feng, J. Wang, S. Feng, Q. Lu, et al., "Central and Autonomic Nervous System Interaction Is Altered by Short-Term Meditation," *Proceedings of the National Academy of Sciences* 106, no. 22 (2009): 8865–8870.

53. P. Grossman, L. Niemann, S. Schmidt, and H. Walach, "Mindfulness-Based Stress Reduction and Health Benefits: A Meta-Analysis," *Journal of Psychosomatic Research* 57, no. 1 (2004): 35–43.

54. M. Monier-Williams, *A Sanskrit-English Dictionary: Etymologically and Philologically Arranged with Special Reference to Cognate Indo-European languages* (Oxford: Clarendon Press, 1899); D. Keown, *A Dictionary of Buddhism* (Oxford: Oxford University Press, 2003).

55. C. Sanchez, *Budo for Budoka* (Tokyo: Seishin-Kumiai, 2013), 54.

56. N. J. Johnson, *Barefoot Zen: The Shaolin Roots of Kung Fu and Karate* (New York: Weiser Books, 2000), 215.

57. S. Odin, *Tragic Beauty in Whitehead and Japanese Aesthetics* (London: Lexington Books, 2016), 307.

58. D. M. McMahon, *Happiness: A History* (New York: Atlantic Monthly Press, 2006).

59. J. L. Bowman, *A Reference Guide to Stoicism: A Compilation of the Principle Stoic Writings on Various Topics* (Bloomington: AuthorHouse, 2014), 44.

60. D. M. Fresco, M. T. Moore, M. H. M. van Dulmen, Z. V. Segal, S. H. Ma, J. D. Teasdale, and J. M. G. Williams, "Initial Psychometric Properties of the Experiences Questionnaire: Validation of a Self-Report Measure of Decentering," *Behavior Therapy* 38, no. 3 (2007): 234–246.

61. A. L. De Gaetano, "Some New Trends in Italian Poetry of Our Times," *Italica* 38, no. 2 (1961): 116–129.

62. M. Christodoulidou, "Siga in Interaction," *Pragmatics* 18, no. 2 (2008): 189–213.

63. D. M. McMahon, *Happiness: A History* (New York: Atlantic Monthly Press, 2006).

64. C. S. Carver and M. F. Scheier, "Origins and Functions of Positive and Negative affect: A Control-Process View," *Psychological Review* 97, no. 1 (1990): 19–35.

65. Y.-K. Ng and L. S. Ho, "Introduction: Happiness as the Only Ultimate Objective of Public Policy," in *Happiness and Public Policy*, ed. Y.-K. Ng and L. S. Ho (London: Springer, 2006), 1–16.

66. http://www.italki.com/question/41057/.

67. C. D. Ryff, "Happiness Is Everything, or Is It? Explorations on the Meaning of Psychological Well-Being," *Journal of Personality and Social Psychology* 57, no. 6 (1989): 1069–1081; E. Diener, "Subjective Well-Being: The Science of Happiness and a Proposal for a National Index," *American Psychologist* 55, no. 1 (2000): 34–43.

68. D. M. McMahon, "From the Happiness of Virtue to the Virtue of Happiness: 400 BC–AD 1780," *Daedalus* 133, no. 2 (2004): 5–17, 7.

69. S. Oishi, "Culture and Well-Being: Conceptual and Methodological Issues," in *International Differences in Well-Being*, ed. E. Diener, J. F. Helliwell, and D. Kahneman (New York: Oxford University Press, 2010), 34–69.

70. Z. R. Mulla and V. R. Krishnan, "Karma Yoga: A Conceptualization and Validation of the Indian Philosophy of Work," *Journal of Indian Psychology* 24, no. 1 (2006): 26–43; H. C. Boucher, "Understanding Western-East Asian Differences and Similarities in Self-Enhancement," *Social and Personality Psychology Compass* 4, no. 5 (2010): 304–317; E. Midlarsky, A. Venkataramani-Kothari, and M. Plante, "Domestic Violence in the Chinese and South Asian Immigrant Communities," *Annals of the New York Academy of Sciences* 1087, no. 1 (2006): 279–300.

71. M. Booth, "Hygge—Why the Craze for Danish Cosiness Is Based on a Myth," *Guardian*, September 4, 2016.

72. R. Orange, "Hunting for Hygge, a New Ingredient in Denmark's Recipe for Happiness," *Guardian*, September 3, 2016; B. Rothstein, "Happiness and the Welfare State," *Social Research* (2010): 441–468.

73. K. Keating, *The Hug Therapy Book* (London: Hazelden, 1994).

74. Orange, "Hunting for Hygge."

75. http://www.afroginthefjord.com.

76. A. J. De Boinod. *The Meaning of Tingo: And Other Extraordinary Words from Around the World* (London: Penguin, 2007).

77. J. Ayto, *Word Origins* (London: A&C Black, 2009).

78. K. Bergström, B. Söderfeldt, H. Berthelsen, K. Hjalmers, and S. Ordell, "Overall Job Satisfaction among Dentists in Sweden and Denmark: A Comparative Study, Measuring Positive Aspects of Work," *Acta Odontologica Scandinavica* 68, no. 6 (2010): 344–353.

79. http://www.paulekman.com/atlas-of-emotions.

80. N. Coupland, "Wales and Welsh: Boundedness and Peripherality," in *Language, Borders and Identity*, ed. N. Watt and C. Llamas (Edinburgh: Edinburgh University Press, 2014), 137–153, 148.

81. http://www.thelandreader.com/glossary/cwtch.

82. A. J. Nader, *Traumatic Verses: On Poetry in German from the Concentration Camps, 1933–1945* (London: Camden House, 2007), 66; G. L. Hachmeister, *Italy in the German Literary Imagination: Goethe's "Italian Journey" and Its Reception by Eichendorff, Platen, and Heine* (London: Camden House, 2002), 66.

83. B. Cassin, E. Apter, J. Lezra, and M. Wood, *Dictionary of Untranslatables: A Philosophical Lexicon* (Princeton, NJ: Princeton University Press, 2014).

84. T. Von Uexküll, "The Sign Theory of Jakob von Uexküll," in *Classics of Semiotics*, ed. M. Krampen, K. Oehler, R. Posner, T. Sebeok, and T. von Uexküll (New York: Springer, 1987), 147–179, 175.

85. J. Whiteoak, "Making 'Gemutlichkeit': Antecedents of 'Bavarian-style' Musical Entertainment in Australia," paper presented at the Music on the Edge: Selected Papers from the 2007 IASPM Australia/New Zealand Conference, Australia, 2008.

86. S. Freud, "The Uncanny," in *The Standard Edition of the Complete Psychological Works of Sigmund Freud* (New York: Vintage Classics, 1955).

87. M. Parsons, *Living Psychoanalysis: From Theory to Experience* (London: Routledge, 2014), 16.

88. C. W. Lin, S. L. Chen, and R. Y. Wang, "Savouring and Perceived Job Performance in Positive Psychology: Moderating Role of Positive Affectivity," *Asian Journal of Social Psychology* 14, no. 3 (2011): 165–175, 166.

89. P. E. Jose, B. T. Lim, and F. B. Bryant, "Does Savoring Increase Happiness? A Daily Diary Study," *Journal of Positive Psychology* 7, no. 3 (2012): 176–187.

90. M. I. Posner and S. E. Petersen, "The Attention System of the Human Brain," *Annual Review of Neuroscience* 13, no. 1 (1990): 25–42.

91. A.-L. Granlund, "Comparing Emotional Intensity between Languages: A Parallel Corpus Investigation on the Swedish Word Njuta and Its English Equivalents," BA thesis, Malmö University, 2006.

92. S. Harrow and T. A. Unwin, "Introduction," in *Joie de Vivre in French Literature and Culture: Essays in Honor of Michael Freeman*, ed. S. Harrow and T. A. Unwin (Paris: Rodopi, 2009), 17–33, 19.

93. M. K. Pukui and S. H. Elbert, *Hawaiian Dictionary: Hawaiian-English, English-Hawaiian* (Hawaii: University of Hawaii Press, 1986), 218.

94. E. Becker, *Overbooked: The Exploding Business of Travel and Tourism* (New York: Simon & Schuster, 2016), 386.

95. P. Durkin, *Borrowed Words: A History of Loanwords in English* (Oxford: Oxford University Press, 2014).

96. G. P. Del Negro, *The Passeggiata and Popular Culture in an Italian Town: Folklore and Performance of Modernity* (Montreal: McGill-Queen's Press, 2005), 16.

97. W. Benjamin, *Charles Baudelaire: A Lyric Poet in the Era of High Capitalism*, trans. H. Zohn (London: NRB, 1983).

98. M. Ueda, *The Master Haiku Poet Matsuo Basho* (Kodansha International: Kodansha International, 1982).

99. W. M. Gesler, "Therapeutic Landscapes: Medical Issues in Light of the New Cultural Geography," *Social Science & Medicine* 34, no. 7 (1992): 735–746; W. M. Gesler, *Healing Places* (Oxford: Rowman & Littlefield, 2003).

100. B. J. Park, Y. Tsunetsugu, T. Kasetani, T. Kagawa, and Y. Miyazaki, "The Physiological Effects of Shinrin-Yoku (Taking in the Forest Atmosphere or Forest Bathing): Evidence from Field Experiments in 24 Forests across Japan," *Environmental Health and Preventive Medicine* 15, no. 1 (2010): 18–26.

101. I. Nakamura, H. Takahashi, and Y. Sato, "Diversity and Breeding of Flowering Cherry in Japan," *Advances in Horticultural Science* 28, no. 4 (2014): 236–243.

102. E. Diener, "Subjective Well-Being: The Science of Happiness and a Proposal for a National Index," *American Psychologist* 55, no. 1 (2000): 34–43.

103. B. Grantham, "Craic in a Box: Commodifying and Exporting the Irish Pub," *Continuum: Journal of Media & Cultural Studies* 23, no. 2 (2009): 257–267.

104. H. T. Reis, S. D. O'Keefe, and R. D. Lane, "Fun Is More Fun When Others Are Involved," *Journal of Positive Psychology* (2016).

105. https://www.fastchinese.org/word?word=瘾-癮-yin3.

106. P. Ekman and D. Cordaro, "What Is Meant by Calling Emotions Basic," *Emotion Review* 3, no. 4 (2011): 364–370.

107. J. Wafer, *The Taste of Blood: Spirit Possession in Brazilian Candomblé* (Philadelphia: University of Pennsylvania Press, 2010), 35.

108. http://gogreece.about.com/cs/glossary/g/kefi.htm.

109. P. Riak, "A Cultural Interpretation of Greek Dance," *Journal of the Hellenic Diaspora* 33, nos. 1–2 (2007): 39–59, 42.

110. Ibid.

111. C. Allerton, "Making Guests, Making 'Liveliness': The Transformative Substances and Sounds of Manggarai Hospitality," *Journal of the Royal Anthropological Institute* 18, no. s1 (2012): S49–S62, S50.

112. C. Geertz, *The Interpretation of Cultures: Selected Essays* (New York: Basic Books, 1973), 446.

113. P. Manuel, K. Bilby, and M. Largey, *Caribbean Currents: Caribbean Music from Rumba to Reggae* (New York: Temple University Press, 2012).

114. S. Nevanlinna, "To Make Merry: Notes on the Origin and Meaning of the Idiomatic Expression 'To Make Merry' in Middle English," *Neuphilologische Mitteilungen* 81, no. 1 (1980): 34–41.

115. B. Ehrenreich, *Dancing in the Streets: A History of Collective Joy* (New York: Macmillan, 2007).

116. E. A. Roberts, *A Comprehensive Etymological Dictionary of the Spanish Language with Families of Words Based on Indo-European Roots*, vol. 1 (New York: Xlibris, 2014), 683.

117. H. Raftari, "Happiness in View of Aristotle and Avicenna," *International Journal of Social Science and Humanity* 5, no. 8 (2015): 714–719.

118. K.-E. Bühler, "Euphoria, Ecstacy, Inebriation, Abuse, Dependence, and Addiction: A Conceptual Analysis," *Medicine, Health Care and Philosophy* 8, no. 1 (2005): 79–87.

119. P. Michaelsen, "Ecstasy and Possession in Ancient Israel: A Review of Some Recent Contributions," *Scandinavian Journal of the Old Testament* 3, no. 2 (1989): 28–54.

120. B. McGinn, "Love, Knowledge, and Mystical Union in Western Christianity: Twelfth to Sixteenth Centuries," *Church History* 56, no. 1 (1987): 7–24.

121. R. Wilmot, "Euphoria," *Journal of Drug Issues* 15, no. 2 (1985): 155–191.

122. A. Bazan and S. Detandt, "On the Physiology of Jouissance: Interpreting the Mesolimbic Dopaminergic Reward Functions from a Psychoanalytic Perspective," *Frontiers in Human Neuroscience* 7, no. 709 (2013).

123. Ş. Susam-Sarajeva, *Theories on the Move: Translation's Role in the Travels of Literary Theories* (Amsterdam: Rodopi, 2006), 180.

124. J. Lacan, *Ecrits*, trans. B. Fink (New York: W. W. Norton, 2006).

125. B. Fink, *The Lacanian Subject: Between Language and Jouissance* (Princeton, NJ: Princeton University Press, 1997).

126. J. Bernstein, *Food for Thought: Transnational Contested Identities and Food Practices of Russian-Speaking Jewish Migrants in Israel and Germany* (Frankfurt: Campus Verlag, 2010), 58.

127. A. I. Miller, *Insights of Genius: Imagery and Creativity in Science and Art* (London: Springer, 2012).

128. F. S. Go, "Mothers, Maids and the Creatures of the Night: The Persistence of Philippine Folk Religion," *Philippine Quarterly of Culture and Society* 7, no. 3 (1979): 186–203.

129. G. Rouget, *Music and Trance: A Theory of the Relations between Music and Possession* (Chicago: University of Chicago Press, 1985), 281.

130. K. Wilber, J. Engler, D. P. Brown, and J. Chirban, *Transformations of Consciousness: Conventional and Contemplative Perspectives on Development* (Boston: New Science Library, 1986).

131. P. Cary, *Inner Grace: Augustine in the Traditions of Plato and Paul* (Oxford: Oxford University Press, 2008).

132. D. M. McMahon, *Happiness: A History* (New York: Atlantic Monthly Press, 2006).

133. B. MacLachlan, *The Age of Grace: Charis in Early Greek Poetry* (Princeton, NJ: Princeton University Press, 2014).

134. P. Tillich, *A History of Christian Thought* (New York: Simon & Schuster, 1967).

135. B. K. S. Iyengar, *Astadala Yogamala (Collected Works)*, vol. 8 (New Delhi: Allied Publishers, 2010), 153.

136. S. Singh, "Indian Perspectives on Happiness," *Indian Journal of Positive Psychology* 3, no. 4 (2012): 452–454.

137. S. Banth and C. Talwar, "Anasakti: The Hindu Ideal and Its Relationship to Well-Being and Orientations to Happiness," *Journal of Religion and Health* 51, no. 3 (2012): 934–946.

138. P. Harvey, *An Introduction to Buddhism: Teachings, History and Practices* (Cambridge: Cambridge University Press, 2012).

139. W. Lai, "Sinitic Speculations on Buddha-Nature: The Nirvāṇa School (420–589)," *Philosophy East and West* 32, no. 2 (1982): 135–149.

140. R. Gethin, *The Buddhist Path to Awakening: A Study of the Bodhi-Pakkhiya Dhamma* (Oxford: Oneworld, 2001).

141. I. Ivtzan, T. Lomas, K. Hefferon, and P. Worth, *Second Wave Positive Psychology: Embracing the Dark Side of Life* (London: Routledge, 2015); T. Lomas and I. Ivtzan, "Second Wave Positive Psychology: Exploring the Positive-Negative Dialectics of Wellbeing," *Journal of Happiness Studies* 17, no. 4 (2016): 1753–1768.

142. C. D. Ryff and B. Singer, "Ironies of the Human Condition: Well-Being and Health on the Way to Mortality," in *A Psychology of Human Strengths*, ed. L. G. Aspinwall and U. M. Staudinger (Washington, DC: American Psychological Association, 2003), 271–287.

143. T. Lomas, "Positive Psychology—The Second Wave," *Psychologist* 29 (2016): 536–539.

144. N. D. Weinstein, S. E. Marcus, and R. P. Moser, "Smokers' Unrealistic Optimism about Their Risk," *Tobacco Control* 14, no. 1 (2005): 55–59.

145. J. K. Norem and N. Cantor, "Defensive Pessimism: Harnessing Anxiety as Motivation," *Journal of Personality and Social Psychology* 51, no. 6 (1986): 1208–1217.

146. R. S. Lazarus, "The Lazarus Manifesto for Positive Psychology and Psychology in General," *Psychological Inquiry* 14, no. 2 (2003): 173–189.

147. C. S. Lewis, *The Four Loves* (New York: A Harvest Book/Harcourt Brace, 1988), 121.

148. J. Oldstone-Moore, *Taoism: Origins, Beliefs, Practices, Holy Texts, Sacred Places* (Oxford: Oxford University Press, 2003), 6.

149. H. Wilhelm, *The I Ching or Book of Changes*, trans. C. F. Baynes (1950; Princeton, NJ: Princeton University Press, 1977).

150. T. Lomas, "The Art of Second Wave Positive Psychology: Harnessing Zen Aesthetics to Explore the Dialectics of Flourishing," *International Journal of Wellbeing* 6, no. 2 (2016): 14–29.

151. Wilhelm, *The I Ching or Book of Changes*; cited in R. Atkinson, *Remembering 1969: Searching for the Eternal in Changing Times* (Wilmette, IL: Bahá'í, 2008), 59.

152. T. Fang, "Yin Yang: A New Perspective on Culture," *Management and Organization Review* 8, no. 1 (2012): 25–50.

153. Y.-L. Fung, *A Short History of Chinese Philosophy* (New York: Free Press, 1948), 19.

154. L.-J. Ji, R.E. Nisbett, and Y. Su, "Culture, Change, and Prediction," *Psychological Science* 12, no. 6 (2001): 450–456, 450.

155. C. R. Snyder, *Handbook of Hope: Theory, Measures, and Applications* (San Diego: Academic Press, 2000); C. R. Snyder, L. Irving, and J. Anderson, "Hope and Health: Measuring the Will and the Ways," in *Handbook of Social and Clinical Psychology*, ed. C. R. Snyder and D. R. Forsyth (Elmsford, NY: Pergamon, 1991), 285–305, 287.

156. R. S. Lazarus, "The Lazarus Manifesto for Positive Psychology and Psychology in General," *Psychological Inquiry* 14, no. 2 (2003): 173–189.

157. H. Baumgartner, R. Pieters, and R. P. Bagozzi, "Future-Oriented Emotions: Conceptualization and Behavioral Effects," *European Journal of Social Psychology* 38, no. 4 (2008): 685–696, 695.

158. De Boinod, *The Meaning of Tingo*.

159. http://icelandmag.visir.is/article/what-does-thetta-reddast-mean.

160. S. Einarsdóttir, G. Vilhjálmsdóttir, S. B. Smáradóttir, and G. B. Kjartansdóttir, "A Culture-Sensitive Approach in the Development of the Career Adapt-Abilities Scale in Iceland: Theoretical and Operational Considerations," *Journal of Vocational Behavior* 89 (2015): 172–181.

161. A. Nazzal, "The Pragmatic Functions of the Recitation of Qur'anic Verses by Muslims in Their Oral Genre: The Case of Insha'Allah, 'God's Willing,'" *Pragmatics* 15, nos. 2–3 (2005): 251–273.

162. V. Apresjan, "The Myth of the 'Russian Soul' through the Mirror of Language," *Folklorica* 14, no. 14 (2009): 91–121, 101.

163. N. Eltaiba and M. Harries, "Reflections on Recovery in Mental Health: Perspectives from a Muslim Culture," *Social Work in Health Care* 54, no. 8 (2015): 725–737.

164. F. Masini and P. Pietrandrea, "Magari," *Cognitive Linguistics* 21, no. 1 (2010): 75–121.

165. H. Willoughby, "The Sound of Han: P'ansori, Timbre and a Korean Ethos of Pain and Suffering," *Yearbook for Traditional Music* 32 (2000): 17–30, 17.

166. O. Holm, E. Greaker, and A. Strömberg, "Experiences of Longing in Norwegian and Swedish 4- and 5-year-old Children," *Journal of Psychology* 136, no. 6 (2002): 608–612, 608.

167. B. Feldman, "Saudade: Longing and Desire in the Brazilian Soul," *San Francisco Jung Institute Library Journal* 20, no. 2 (2001): 51–56, 51.

168. S. Scheibe, A. M. Freund, and P. B. Baltes, "Toward a Developmental Psychology of Sehnsucht (Life Longings): The Optimal (Utopian) Life," *Developmental Psychology* 43, no. 3 (2007): 778–795, 779.

169. N. Coupland, H. Bishop, and P. Garrett, "Home Truths: Globalisation and the Iconising of Welsh in a Welsh-American Newspaper," *Journal of Multilingual and Multicultural development* 24, no. 3 (2003): 153–177, 164.

170. Feldman, "Saudade," 55; Z. B. Silva, "Saudade: A Key Portuguese Emotion," *Emotion Review* 4, no. 2 (2012): 203–211, 203.

171. Rob MacFarlane on Twitter, May 4, 2017, https://twitter.com/RobGMacfarlane/status/860011185495736320.

172. J. I. Suárez, "Portugal's 'Saudosismo' Movement: An Esthetics of Sebastianism," *Luso-Brazilian Review* 28, no. 1 (1991): 129–140.

173. A. Wierzbicka, "Soul and Mind: Linguistic Evidence for Ethnopsychology and Cultural History," *American Anthropologist* 91, no. 1 (1989): 41–58, 41.

174. V. Nabokov, in Aleksandr Pushkin, *Eugene Onegin: A Novel in Verse*, vol. 2: *Commentary and Index* (Princeton, NJ: Princeton University Press, 1990), 141.

175. T. Sager, "Freedom as Mobility: Implications of the Distinction between Actual and Potential Travelling," *Mobilities* 1, no. 3 (2006): 465–488.

176. B. Gabriel, "The Unbearable Strangeness of Being: Edgar Reitz's Heimat and the Ethics of the Unheimlich," in *Postmodernism and the Ethical Subject*, ed. B. Gabriel and S. Ilcan (New York: McGill-Queen's University Press, 2004), 149–202, 155.

177. R. Diriwächter, "Heimweh or Homesickness: A Nostalgic Look at the Umwelt That No Longer Is," in *Relating to Environments: A New Look at Umwelt*, ed. R. S. Chang (Charlotte, NC: Information Age, 2009), 163–184.

178. P. O. Shields, "A Case for Wanderlust: Travel Behaviors of College Students," *Journal of Travel & Tourism Marketing* 28, no. 4 (2011): 369–387.

179. M. Metsämäki, "Persuasive Discourse in EFL Debate," *Theory and Practice in Language Studies* 2, no. 2 (2012): 205–213.

180. A. V. Horwitz and J. C. Wakefield, *The Loss of Sadness* (Oxford: Oxford University Press, 2007).

181. J. Decety, K. J. Michalska, and K. D. Kinzler, "The Contribution of Emotion and Cognition to Moral Sensitivity: A Neurodevelopmental Study," *Cerebral Cortex* 22, no. 1 (2012): 209–220.

182. M. E. Sachs, A. Damasio, and A. Habibi, "The Pleasures of Sad Music: A Systematic Review," *Frontiers in Human Neuroscience* 9 (2015): 404.

183. L. Taruffi and S. Koelsch, "The Paradox of Music-Evoked Sadness: An Online Survey," *PLoS One* 9, no. 10 (2014): e110490.

184. A. I. Miller, *Insights of Genius: Imagery and Creativity in Science and Art* (London: Springer, 2012).

185. N. Cave, "The Secret Life of the Love Song," public lecture, Vienna, September 25, 1999.

186. J. W. v. Goethe, *Die Leiden des Jungen Werthers* [The sorrows of young Werther] (Leipzig: Weygand'sche Buchhandlung, 1774).

187. H. H. Rudnick, "Weltschmerz, or The Pain of Living," in *Life Creative Mimesis of Emotion: From Sorrow to Elation: Elegiac Virtuosity in Literature*, ed. A.-T. Tymieniecka (Dordrecht: Springer Netherlands, 2000), 155–166, 155.

188. R. L. Woolfolk, "The Power of Negative Thinking: Truth, Melancholia, and the Tragic Sense of Life," *Journal of Theoretical and Philosophical Psychology* 22, no. 1 (2002): 19–27, 23.

189. *The Tale of the Heike*, trans. R. Tyler (London: Penguin, 2012); cited in M. Smethurst, "Ninagawa's Production of Euripides' *Medea*," *American Journal of Philology* 123, no. 1 (2002): 1–34.

190. D. T. Suzuki, *Zen and Japanese Culture* (1959; Princeton, NJ: Princeton University Press, 1973).

191. N. Panpothong and S. Phakdeephasook, "The Wide Use of Mai-Pen-Rai 'It's Not Substantial' in Thai Interactions and Its Relationship to the Buddhist Concept of Tri Laksana," *Journal of Pragmatics* 69 (2014): 99–107.

192. M. Epstein, "The Deconstruction of the Self: Ego and 'Egolessness' in Buddhist Insight Meditation," *Journal of Transpersonal Psychology* 20, no. 1 (1988): 61–69.

193. P. Breiter and A. Chah, *Everything Arises, Everything Falls Away: Teachings on Impermanence and the End of Suffering* (Boston: Shambhala Publications, 2005).

194. Cited in D. Keene, *Essays in Idleness: The Tsurezuregusa of Kenkō* (New York: Columbia University Press, 1967), 7.

195. L. Prusinski, "Wabi-Sabi, Mono no Aware, and Ma: Tracing Traditional Japanese Aesthetics through Japanese History," *Studies on Asia* 2, no. 1 (2013): 21–45, 23.

196. A. W. Watts, *The Way of Zen* (London: Penguin Books, 1957).

197. Prusinski, "Wabi-Sabi," 25.

198. B. Park, "Buddhism and Japanese Aesthetics," *Philosophy East and West* 55, no. 4 (2005).

199. J. Tanizaki, *In Praise of Shadows* (1933; New York: Random House, 2001), 11–12.

200. Cited in Keene, *Essays in Idleness*, 115.

201. D. Hirota, *Wind in the Pines: Classic Writings of the Way of Tea as a Buddhist Path* (Fremont: Asian Humanities Press, 1995), 226.

202. Cited in Hirota, *Wind in the Pines*, 226.

203. G. Keulemans, "The Geo-Cultural Conditions of Kintsugi," *Journal of Modern Craft* 9, no. 1 (2016): 15–34.

204. H. Hammitzsch, *Zen in the Art of the Tea Ceremony*, trans. P. Lemesurier (New York: Arkana, 1979), 46.

205. M. Ueda, *The Master Haiku Poet Matsuo Basho* (New York: Kodansha International, 1982).

206. Cited in W. A. Dyrness and V.-M. Kärkkäinen, *Global Dictionary of Theology* (Nottingham: IVP Academic, 2008), 66.

207. T. Lomas, N. Etcoff, W. V. Gordon, and E. Shonin, "Zen and the Art of Living Mindfully: The Health-Enhancing Potential of Zen Aesthetics," *Journal of Religion and Health* (2017), online publication ahead of print.

208. R. E. Purser, "Zen and the Art of Organizational Maintenance," *Organizational Aesthetics* 2, no. 1 (2013): 34–58, 39.

209. G. Parkes, "Japanese Aesthetics," in *Stanford Encyclopedia of Philosophy*, ed. E. N. Zalta, 2011, http://plato.stanford.edu/entries/japanese-aesthetics/.

210. D. Kaula, "On Noh Drama," *Tulane Drama Review* (Sept. 1960): 69–70, 69.

211. A. T. Tsubaki, "Zeami and the Transition of the Concept of Yūgen: A Note on Japanese Aesthetics," *Journal of Aesthetics and Art Criticism* 30, no. 1 (1971): 55–67.

212. D. T. Suzuki, *Zen and Japanese Culture* (1959; Princeton, NJ: Princeton University Press, 1973), 220–221.

213. K.n. Chōmei, "An Account of My Hut," in *Anthology of Japanese Literature*, ed. D. Keene (1912; New York: Grove Press, 1968); cited in W. A. Dyrness and V.-M. Kärkkäinen, *Global Dictionary of Theology* (Nottingham: IVP Academic, 2008), 65.

214. S. Hisamatsu, *Zen and the Fine Arts*, trans. G. Tokiwa (New York: Kodansha International, 1971).

215. Kaula, "On Noh Drama," 69.

216. A. H. Maslow, *The Farther Reaches of Human Nature* (London: Maurice Bassett, 1972).

217. P. T. P. Wong, "Meaning-Seeking, Self-Transcendence, and Well-Being," in *Logotherapy and Existential Analysis*, ed. A. Batthyany (Vienna: Proceedings of the Viktor Frankl Institute, 2016), 311–322.

218. M. A. Sells, *Mystical Languages of Unsaying* (Chicago: University of Chicago Press, 1994).

219. Watts, *The Way of Zen*.

Chapter 3: Relationships

1. J. F. Helliwell, "How's Life? Combining Individual and National Variables to Explain Subjective Well-Being," *Economic Modeling* 20, no. 2 (2003): 331–360; J. F. Helliwell and R. D. Putnam, "The Social Context of Well-Being," *Philosophical Transactions of the Royal Society of London, Series B: Biological Sciences* 359, no. 1449 (2004): 1435–1446.

2. R. Veenhoven, "The Four Qualities of Life Ordering Concepts and Measures of the Good Life," in *The Exploration of Happiness*, ed. A. Delle Fave (Netherlands: Springer, 2013), 195–226.

3. R. Biswas-Diener and E. Diener, "Making the Best of a Bad Situation: Satisfaction in the Slums of Calcutta," in *Culture and Well-Being*, ed. E. Diener (Dordrecht: Springer, 2009), 261–278, 202.

4. S. Lindenberg and B. S. Frey, "Alternatives, Frames, and Relative Prices: A Broader View of Rational Choice Theory," *Acta Sociologica* 36, no. 3 (1993): 191–205.

5. E. Diener, C. L. Gohm, E. Suh, and S. Oishi, "Similarity of the Relations between Marital Status and Subjective Well-Being Across Cultures," *Journal of Cross-Cultural Psychology* 31, no. 4 (2000): 419–436.

6. D. G. Blanchflower and A. J. Oswald, "Well-Being Over Time in Britain and the USA," *Journal of Public Economics* 88, nos. 7–8 (2004): 1359–1386.

7. A. H. Maslow, "A Theory of Human Motivation," *Psychological Review* 50, no. 4 (1943): 370–396.

8. W. A. Arrindell and F. Luteijn, "Similarity between Intimate Partners for Personality Traits as Related to Individual Levels of Satisfaction with Life," *Personality and Individual Differences* 28, no. 4 (2000): 629–637.

9. S. Vanassche, G. Swicegood, and K. Matthijs, "Marriage and Children as a Key to Happiness? Cross-National Differences in the Effects of Marital Status and Children on Well-Being," *Journal of Happiness Studies* 14, no. 2 (2013): 501–524.

10. P. Lloyd-Sherlock, B. Corso, and N. Minicuci, "Widowhood, Socio-Economic Status, Health and Wellbeing in Low and Middle-Income Countries," *Journal of Development Studies* (2015): 1–15.

11. P. Bourdieu, "The Forms of Capital," in *Handbook of Theory and Research for the Sociology of Education*, ed. J. G. Richardson (New York: Greenwood, 1986), 241–258, 248.

12. R. V. Patulny and G. L. H. Svendsen, "Exploring the Social Capital Grid: Bonding, Bridging, Qualitative, Quantitative," *International Journal of Sociology and Social Policy* 27, nos. 1–2 (2007): 32–51.

13. J. Fien and P. Skoien, " 'I'm Learning ... How You Go about Stirring Things Up— in a Consultative Manner': Social Capital and Action Competence in Two Community Catchment Groups," *Local Environment* 7, no. 3 (2002): 269–282.

14. G. Veenstra, "Explicating Social Capital: Trust and Participation in the Civil Space," *Canadian Journal of Sociology/Cahiers canadiens de sociologie* (2002): 547–572.

15. W. Tsai and S. Ghoshal, "Social Capital and Value Creation: The Role of Intrafirm Networks," *Academy of Management Journal* 41, no. 4 (1998): 464–476.

16. W. Poortinga, "Community Resilience and Health: The Role of Bonding, Bridging, and Linking Aspects of Social Capital," *Health & Place* 18, no. 2 (2012): 286–295.

17. M. T. Hyyppä and J. Mäki, "Why Do Swedish-Speaking Finns Have Longer Active Life? An Area for Social Capital Research," *Health Promotion International* 16, no. 1 (2001): 55–64; M. T. Hyyppä and J. Mäki, "Social Participation and Health in a Community Rich in Stock of Social Capital," *Health Education Research* 18, no. 6 (2003): 770–779.

18. R. D. Putnam, "Tuning In, Tuning Out: The Strange Disappearance of Social Capital in America," *Political Science and Politics* 28, no. 4 (1995): 664–683, 664; R. N. Bellah, R. Madsen, W. M. Sullivan, A. Swidler, and S. M. Tipton, *Habits of the Heart: Individualism and Commitment in American Life* (Berkeley, CA: University of California Press, 1996).

19. D. Becker and J. Marecek, "Dreaming the American Dream: Individualism and Positive Psychology," *Social and Personality Psychology Compass* 2, no. 5 (2008): 1767–1780.

20. C. Geertz, *Local Knowledge* (London: Fontana Press, 1983), 59.

21. H. C. Triandis, "Individualism-Collectivism and Personality," *Journal of Personality* 69, no. 6 (2001): 907–924, 907.

22. M. E. Spiro, "Is the Western Conception of the Self 'Peculiar' within the Context of the World Cultures?" *Ethos* 21, no. 2 (1993): 107–153.

23. V. Taras, B. L. Kirkman, and P. Steel, "Examining the Impact of Culture's Consequences: A Three-Decade, Multilevel, Meta-Analytic Review of Hofstede's Cultural Value Dimensions," *Journal of Applied Psychology* 95, no. 3 (2010): 405–439.

24. H. R. Markus and S. Kitayama, "Culture and the Self: Implications for Cognition, Emotion, and Motivation," *Psychological Review* 98, no. 2 (1991): 224–253.

25. R. E. Nisbett, K. Peng, I. Choi, and A. Norenzayan, "Culture and Systems of Thought: Holistic versus Analytic Cognition," *Psychological Review* 108, no. 2 (2001): 291–310.

26. R. M. Ryan and E. L. Deci, "Self-Regulation and the Problem of Human Autonomy: Does Psychology Need Choice, Self-Determination, and Will?" *Journal of Personality* 74, no. 6 (2006): 1557–1586; A. D. Cast and P. J. Burke, "A Theory of Self-Esteem," *Social Forces* 80, no. 3 (2002): 1041–1068; C. Taylor, *Sources of the Self: The Making of the Modern Identity* (Cambridge, MA: Harvard University Press, 1989); A. R. Mele, *Autonomous Agents: From Self-Control to Autonomy* (Oxford: Oxford University Press, 1995).

27. A. Harrington, "A Science of Compassion or a Compassionate Science: What Do We Expect from a Cross-Cultural Dialogue with Buddhism," in *Visions of Compassion: Western Scientists and Tibetan Buddhists Examine Human Nature*, ed. R. J. Davidson and A. Harrington (Oxford: Oxford University Press, 2002), 18–30.

28. D. Becker and J. Marecek, "Dreaming the American Dream: Individualism and Positive Psychology," *Social and Personality Psychology Compass* 2, no. 5 (2008): 1767–1780.

29. S. Lyubomirsky, K. M. Sheldon, and D. Schkade, "Pursuing Happiness: The Architecture of Sustainable Change," *Review of General Psychology* 9, no. 2 (2005): 111–131.

30. D. Lykken and A. Tellegen, "Happiness Is a Stochastic Phenomenon," *Psychological Science* 7, no. 3 (1996): 186–189.

31. B. Ehrenreich, *Smile or Die: How Positive Thinking Fooled America and the World* (London: Granta, 2009); N. L. Sin and S. Lyubomirsky, "Enhancing Well-Being and Alleviating Depressive Symptoms with Positive Psychology Interventions: A Practice-Friendly Meta-Analysis," *Journal of Clinical Psychology* 65, no. 5 (2009): 467–487; R. A. Emmons and M. E. McCullough, "Counting Blessings versus Burdens: An Experimental Investigation of Gratitude and Subjective Well-Being in Daily Life," *Journal of Personality and Social Psychology* 84, no. 2 (2003): 377–389.

32. B. Ehrenreich, *Smile or Die: How Positive Thinking Fooled America and the World* (London: Granta, 2009).

33. Equality and Human Rights Commission, *Equality, Human Rights and Good Relations in 2010* (London: Equality and Human Rights Commission, 2010).

34. C. Lund, A. Breen, A.J. Flisher, R. Kakuma, J. Corrigall, J.A. Joska, L. Swartz, and V. Patel, "Poverty and Common Mental Disorders in Low and Middle Income Countries: A Systematic Review," *Social Science & Medicine* 71, no. 3 (2010): 517–528; C. E. Ross, "Neighborhood Disadvantage and Adult Depression," *Journal of Health and Social Behavior* 41, no. 2 (2000): 177–187; D. Becker and J. Marecek, "Dreaming the American Dream: Individualism and Positive Psychology," *Social and Personality Psychology Compass* 2, no. 5 (2008): 1767–1780, 1771.

35. R. G. Wilkinson and K. Pickett, *The Spirit Level: Why More Equal Societies Almost Always Do Better* (London: Allen Lane, 2010).

36. B. I. Murstein, "A Taxonomy of Love," in *The Psychology of Love*, ed. R. Sternberg and M. Barnes (New Haven, CT: Yale University Press, 1988), 13–37, 33.

37. E. Berscheid, "Love in the Fourth Dimension," *Annual Review of Psychology* 61 (2010): 1–25, 6.

38. J. A. Lee, *The Colors of Love: An Exploration of the Ways of Loving* (Don Mills, Ontario: New Press, 1973); J.A. Lee, "A Typology of Styles of Loving," *Personality and Social Psychology Bulletin* 3, no. 2 (1977): 173–182.

39. R. J. Sternberg, "A Triangular Theory of Love," *Psychological Review* 93, no. 2 (1986): 119–135.

40. T. A. Shimp and T. J. Madden, "Consumer–Object Relations: A Conceptual Framework Based Analogously on Sternberg's Triangular Theory of Love," *Advances in Consumer Research* 15, no. 1 (1988): 163–168.

41. Y.-O. Whang, J. Allen, N. Sahoury, and H. Zhang, "Falling in Love with a Product: The Structure of a Romantic Consumer–Product Relationship," *Advances in Consumer Research* 31 (2004), 320–327.

42. I. Sotiropoulou, "Women in Alternative Economy, or What Do Women Do without Official Currency?" *Women's Studies International Forum* 47, Part B (2014): 339–348, 344.

43. Cited in A. Hofstadter and R. Kuhns, *Philosophies of Art and Beauty: Selected Readings in Aesthetics from Plato to Heidegger* (Chicago: University of Chicago Press, 2009), 61.

44. E. V. Walter, *Placeways: A Theory of the Human Environment* (London: UNC Press Books, 1988), 120.

45. N. El-Bizri, "'Ontopoiesis' and the Interpretation of Plato's 'Khora,'" in *Imaginatio Creatrix*, ed. A.-T. Tymieniecka (London: Springer, 2004), 25–45.

46. J. Graham, "He Apiti Hono, He Tātai Hono: That Which Is Joined Remains an Unbroken Line: Using Whakapapa (Genealogy) as the Basis for an Indigenous Research Framework," *Australian Journal of Indigenous Education* 34 (2005): 86–95.

47. C. I. Magallanes, "Use of Tangata Whenua and Mana Whenua in New Zealand Legislation: Attempts at Cultural Recognition," *Victoria University of Wellington Law Review* 42 (2011): 259.

48. E. Hemingway, *Death in the Afternoon* (New York: Scribner, 1932).

49. K. Sale, "There's No Place Like Home," *Ecologist* 31 (2001): 40–43, 43.

50. N. Sinclair, "Preface to Kyffin Williams' *The Land & the Sea*" (Cardiff: Gomer Press, 1998); cited in D. Snowden, "Complex Acts of Knowing: Paradox and Descriptive Self-Awareness," *Journal of Knowledge Management* 6, no. 2 (2002): 100–111, 110.

51. A. W. Price, *Love and Friendship in Plato and Aristotle* (Oxford: Clarendon Press, 1989).

52. A. Hofstadter and R. Kuhns, *Philosophies of Art and Beauty: Selected Readings in Aesthetics from Plato to Heidegger* (Chicago: University of Chicago Press, 2009).

53. Aristotle, *Rhetoric*, trans. W. R. Roberts, in *Basic Works* (New York: The Modern Library Press, 1954), II, 4.

54. V. G. Vassiliou and G. Vassiliou, "The Implicative Meaning of the Greek Concept of Philotimo," *Journal of Cross-Cultural Psychology* 4, no. 3 (1973): 326–341, 326.

55. O. Kent, "A Theory of Havruta Learning," *Journal of Jewish Education* 76, no. 3 (2010): 215–245.

56. S. E. Smith, S. Munt, and A.K.-T. Yip, *Cosmopolitan Dharma: Race, Sexuality, and Gender in British Buddhism* (Leiden: Brill, 2016), 9.

57. Aristotle, *Nicomachean Ethics*, ed. R. Crisp (Cambridge: Cambridge University Press, 350BCE/2000), IX 8; A.W. Adkins, "The Connection between Aristotle's Ethics and Politics," *Political Theory* 12, no. 1 (1984): 29–49.

58. K. D. Neff, "Self-Compassion: An Alternative Conceptualization of a Healthy Attitude toward Oneself," *Self and Identity* 2, no. 2 (2003): 85–101.

59. J. Annas, "Self-Love in Aristotle," *Southern Journal of Philosophy* 27, no. S1 (1989): 1–18.

60. J.-J. Rousseau, *The Social Contract* (1762; New York: Cosimo Classics, 2008).

61. A. W. Kruglanski, J. J. Bélanger, M. Gelfand, R. Gunaratna, M. Hettiarachchi, F. Reinares, E. Orehek, J. Sasota, and K. Sharvit, "Terrorism—A (Self) Love Story: Redirecting the Significance Quest Can End Violence," *American Psychologist* 68, no. 7 (2013): 559–575.

62. P. Force, *Self-Interest before Adam Smith: A Genealogy of Economic Science* (Cambridge: Cambridge University Press, 2003).

63. R. P. Hanley, "Commerce and Corruption Rousseau's Diagnosis and Adam Smith's Cure," *European Journal of Political Theory* 7, no. 2 (2008): 137–158.

64. D. Isaacs, "Parental Love," *Journal of Paediatrics and Child Health* 51, no. 3 (2015): 241–242.

65. D. S. Browning, "Science and Religion on the Nature of Love," in *Altruism and Altruistic Love: Science, Philosophy, and Religion in Dialogue*, ed. S. G. Post, L. G. Underwood, J. P. Schloss, and W. B. Hurlbut (Oxford: Oxford University Press, 2002), 335–345, 335.

66. M. J. Montgomery and G. T. Sorell, "Differences in Love Attitudes across Family Life Stages," *Family Relations* (1997): 55–61.

67. F. R. Myers, *Pintupi Country, Pintupi Self: Sentiment, Place, and Politics among Western Desert Aborigines* (Los Angeles: University of California Press, 1991), 146.

68. http://www.paulekman.com/atlas-of-emotions.

69. A. Schepard, "Kvell[ing] for Family Court Review on Its Fiftieth Birthday," *Family Court Review* 51, no. 1 (2013): 1–6.

70. M. Mohr, "Filial Piety with a Zen Twist: Universalism and Particularism Surrounding the Sutra on the Difficulty of Reciprocating the Kindness of Parents," *Journal of Religion in Japan* 2, no. 1 (2013): 35–62, 35.

71. C. G. Ravasi, "Towards a Biblical Theology of Emotions," in *Issues in Science and Theology: Do Emotions Shape the World?*, ed. D. Evers, M. Fuller, A. Runehov, and K.-W. Sæther (New York: Springer, 2016), 159–176, 165.

72. G. Taylor, "Readability of OHS Documents—A Comparison of Surface Characteristics of OHS Text between Some Languages," *Safety Science* 50, no. 7 (2012): 1627–1635, 1629.

73. S. L. Robinson and B. G. Hayes, "Social Responsibility: A Cautionary Tale for Counsellors," *Journal of Humanistic Counseling* 41, no. 2 (2002): 159–163.

74. J.-P. G. Potet, *Tagalog Borrowings and Cognates*, 3rd ed. (Raleigh, NC: Lulu, 2015), 198.

75. A. Hetsroni, "Associations between Television Viewing and Love Styles: An Interpretation Using Cultivation Theory," *Psychological Reports* 110, no. 1 (2012): 35–50.

76. O. R. Aragón, M. S. Clark, R. L. Dyer, and J. A. Bargh, "Dimorphous Expressions of Positive Emotion: Displays of Both Care and Aggression in Response to Cute Stimuli," *Psychological Science* 26, no. 3 (2015): 259–273, 260.

77. T. Rose, "From Méphistophélès to Méliès," in *Between Opera and Cinema*, ed. J. Joe and T. Rose (New York: Routledge, 2002), 1–18, 17.

78. E. Underhill, *Mysticism: A Study in the Nature and Development of Man's Spiritual Consciousness* (London: Aeterna Press, 1941/2015).

79. D. Schultze, "Wisdom in the Margins: Text and Paratext in The Seven Points of True Love and Everlasting Wisdom," *Études anglaises* 66, no. 3 (2013): 341–356.

80. D. R. Kinsley, "Creation as Play in Hindu Spirituality," *Studies in Religion/Sciences Religieuses* 4, no. 2 (1974): 108–119.

81. D. B. Sarwer, S. C. Kalichman, J. R. Johnson, J. Early, and S. A. Ali, "Sexual Aggression and Love Styles: An Exploratory Study," *Archives of Sexual Behavior* 22, no. 3 (1993): 265–275, 265.

82. K. Evans, J. McGrath, and R. Milns, "Searching for Schizophrenia in Ancient Greek and Roman Literature: A Systematic Review," *Acta Psychiatrica Scandinavica* 107, no. 5 (2003): 323–230.

83. A. Breton, *Mad Love (L'Amour Fou)*, trans. M. A. Caws (Lincoln: University of Nebraska Press, 1937).

84. B. H. Spitzberg and W. R. Cupach, *The Dark Side of Close Relationships* (London: Routledge, 1998).

85. E. J. Bakker, "Pragmatics: Speech and Text," in *A Companion to the Ancient Greek Language*, ed. E. J. Bakker (Oxford: Wiley-Blackwell, 2010), 151–167, 151.

86. E. Fromm, *The Art of Loving: The Centennial Edition* (New York: Bloomsbury, 1956/2000).

87. B. Breen, "'The Elks Are Our Horses': Animals and Domestication in the New France Borderlands," *Journal of Early American History* 3, nos. 2–3 (2013): 181–206.

88. Cited in C. M. Bowra, *The Greek Experience* (New York: W. P. Publishing, 1958), 61.

89. S. Mintz, *The Prime of Life: A History of Modern Adulthood* (Cambridge, MA: Harvard University Press, 2015), 76.

90. K. Williams, "Language Learning: Its Moral and Civic Remit," *Pedagogy, Culture & Society* (2016): 1–13.

91. P. A. Kottman, "Defying the Stars: Tragic Love as the Struggle for Freedom in Romeo and Juliet," *Shakespeare Quarterly* 63, no. 1 (2012): 1–38.

92. R. K. Brown and R. E. Brown, "Faith and Works: Church-Based Social Capital Resources and African American Political Activism," *Social Forces* 82, no. 2 (2003): 617–641.

93. C. Hitchens, *Arguably: Selected Prose* (London: Atlantic Books, 2011).

94. *The Bible*, Revised Standard Version, 1 Corinthians, 13:13.

95. S. E. Smith, S. Munt, and A. K.-T. Yip, *Cosmopolitan Dharma: Race, Sexuality, and Gender in British Buddhism* (Leiden: Brill, 2016), 9.

96. W. Z. Harvey, "Grace or Loving-Kindness," in *20th Century Jewish Religious Thought*, ed. A. A. Cohen and P. Mendes-Flohr (Philadelphia: Jewish Publication Society, 2009), 299–303, 299.

97. Cited in W. R. Bowen, *Engineering Ethics: Challenges and Opportunities* (New York: Springer Science & Business Media, 2014), 83.

98. A. S. Ahmed, *Millennium and Charisma among Pathans: A Critical Essay in Social Anthropology* (London: Routledge, 1976/2011), 58.

99. J. S. Murphy and J. Gray, "Manaakitanga in Motion: Indigenous Choreographies of Possibility," *Biography* 36, no. 1 (2013): 242–278, 242.

100. R. Blundell, V. Gibbons, and S. Lillis, "Cultural Issues in Research, A Reflection," *New Zealand Medical Journal* 123, no. 1309 (2010): 97–105, 99.

101. S. H. Blumberg, "To Know Before Whom You Stand: A Philosophy for a Spiritual and Moral Liberal Jewish Education for the 21st Century," in *International Handbook of the Religious, Moral and Spiritual Dimensions in Education*, ed. M. de Souza, K. Engebretson, G. Durka, R. Jackson, and A. McGrady (New York: Springer, 2006), 717–729, 724.

102. A. P. Ross, *Recalling the Hope of Glory: Biblical Worship from the Garden to the New Creation* (Grand Rapids, MI: Kregel Academic, 2006), 51.

103. S. Kierkegaard, *Fear and Trembling and the Sickness unto Death*, trans. M. Lowrie (Princeton, NJ: Princeton University Press, 1843).

104. D. Keltner and J. Haidt, "Approaching Awe, a Moral, Spiritual, and Aesthetic Emotion," *Cognition & Emotion* 17, no. 2 (2003): 297–314, 297.

105. L. E. Nelson, "The Ontology of Bhakti: Devotion as Paramapuruṣārtha in Gauḍīya Vaisnavism and Madhusūdana Sarasvatī," *Journal of Indian Philosophy* 32, no. 4 (2004): 345–392.

106. J. D. Mlecko, "The Guru in Hindu Tradition," *Numen* 29, no. 1 (1982): 33–61.

107. D. Kaufmann, A. Kraay, and M. Mastruzzi, "Governance Matters VIII: Aggregate and Individual Governance Indicators, 1996–2008," *World Bank Policy Research Working Paper*, no. 4978 (2009).

108. R. A. Easterlin, "Does Economic Growth Improve the Human Lot? Some Empirical Evidence," in *Nations and Households in Economic Growth: Essays in Honor of Moses Abramovitz*, ed. R. David and R. Reder (New York: Academic Press, 1974), 89–125.

109. R. G. Wilkinson and K. Pickett, *The Spirit Level: Why More Equal Societies Almost Always Do Better* (London: Allen Lane, 2010).

110. C. Izquierdo, "When 'Health' Is Not Enough: Societal, Individual and Biomedical Assessments of Well-Being among the Matsigenka of the Peruvian Amazon," *Social Science & Medicine* 61, no. 4 (2005): 767–783.

111. G. Danesi, "Commensality in French and German Young Adults: An Ethnographic Study," *Hospitality & Society* 1, no. 2 (2012): 153–172.

112. G. M. Yeager, "Gabriel René-Moreno and the Intellectual Context of Late Nineteenth-Century South America," *Social Science Quarterly* 59, no. 1 (1978): 77–92.

113. B. Espejo, M. T. Cortés, B. M. del Río, J. A. Giménez, and C. Gómez, "Traits That Define the Different Alcohol Intensive Consume Type During the Practice of 'Botellon,'" *Spanish Journal of Psychology* 15, no. 1 (2012): 256–264.

114. H. G. Koenig, "Research on Religion, Spirituality, and Mental Health: A Review," *Canadian Journal of Psychiatry* 54, no. 5 (2009): 283–291.

115. M. Foucault, *Religion and Culture*, ed. J. Carrette (London: Routledge, 2013).

116. D. F. Polish, "Aspects of Esther: A Phenomenological Exploration of the Megillah of Esther and the Origins of Purim," *Journal for the Study of the Old Testament* 24, no. 85 (1999): 85–106.

117. J. H. Prouser, "Lots of Strange Bedfellows: Toward a Plausible Translation for 'Purim,'" *Conservative Judaism* 64, no. 2 (2013): 72–79.

118. Y. Levy, *Journey Through Grief: A Sephardic Manual for the Bereaved and Their Community* (Newark: KTAV Publishing House, 2003).

119. D. Pelcovitz, "Counseling Congregants in Crisis," in *A Practical Guide to Rabbinic Counseling*, ed. Y. N. Levitz and A. J. Twerski (Jerusalem: Feldheim, 2005), 66–90.

120. J. Stern, *Problems and Parables of Law: Maimonides and Nahmanides on Reasons for the Commandments (Ta'Amei Ha-Mitzvot)* (New York: SUNY Press, 2012).

121. D. S. Muzzey, "Medieval Morals," *International Journal of Ethics* 17, no. 1 (1906): 29–47, 29.

122. G. C. Hazard Jr., "Law, Morals, and Ethics," *Southern Illinois University Law Journal* 19 (1994): 447–458, 453.

123. E. Shulman, "Early Meanings of Dependent-Origination," *Journal of Indian Philosophy* 36, no. 2 (2008): 297–317.

124. V. Eltschinger, "The Four Nobles' Truths and Their 16 Aspects: On the Dogmatic and Soteriological Presuppositions of the Buddhist Epistemologists' Views on Niścaya," *Journal of Indian Philosophy* 42, nos. 2–3 (2014): 249–273.

125. B. Bodhi, *The Noble Eightfold Path: The Way to the End of Suffering* (Kandy, Sri Lanka: Buddhist Publication Society, 2010).

126. U. Sangharakshita and D. Subhuti, *Seven Papers*, 2nd ed. (London: Triratna Buddhist Community, 2013), 49.

127. D. Keown, *A Dictionary of Buddhism* (Oxford: Oxford University Press, 2003).

128. Cited in D. T. Jones, "The Five Niyāmas as Laws of Nature: An Assessment of Modern Western Interpretations of Theravāda Buddhist Doctrine," *Journal of Buddhist Ethics* 19 (2012): 545–582, 548.

129. S. Aurobindo, *The Complete Works of Sri Aurobindo* (Pondicherry: Sri Aurobindo Ashram Publication Department, 1939–1940).

130. C. Kang, "Buddhist and Tantric Perspectives on Causality and Society," *Journal of Buddhist Ethics* 16 (2009): 69–103, 73.

131. R. Schulz, R. S. Hebert, M. A. Dew, S. L. Brown, M. F. Scheier, S. R. Beach, S. J. Czaja, L. M. Martire, D. Coon, and K. M. Langa, "Patient Suffering and Caregiver Compassion: New Opportunities for Research, Practice, and Policy," *Gerontologist* 47, no. 1 (2007): 4–13, 6.

132. M. Metsämäki, "Persuasive Discourse in EFL Debate," *Theory and Practice in Language Studies* 2, no. 2 (2012): 205–213.

133. K. H. Schwind, "Like Watching a Motorway Crash: Exploring the Embarrassment Humor of *The Office*," *Humor* 28, no. 1 (2015): 49–70.

134. R. Bishop, "Freeing Ourselves from Neo-Colonial Domination in Research: A Maori Approach to Creating Knowledge," *International Journal of Qualitative Studies in Education* 11, no. 2 (1998): 199–219.

135. K. Hara, "The Concept of Omoiyari (Altruistic Sensitivity) in Japanese Relational Communication," *Intercultural Communication Studies* 15, no. 1 (2006): 24–32, 24.

136. T. Colleman, "The Semantic Range of the Dutch Double Object Construction: A Collostructional Perspective," *Constructions and Frames* 1, no. 2 (2009): 190–221.

137. Webster's New World Dictionary, *Webster's II New College Dictionary, 3rd ed.* (Boston: Houghton Mifflin, 2005), 622.

138. M. Cleary and J. Horsfall, "Kindness and Its Relevance to Everyday Life: Some Considerations for Mental Health Nurses," *Issues in Mental Health Nursing* 37, no. 3 (2016): 206–208.

139. S. C. Heilman, "Tzedakah: Orthodox Jews and Charitable Giving," in *Contemporary Jewish Philanthropy in America*, ed. B. A. Kosmin and P. Ritterband (Lanham, MD: Rowman & Littlefield, 1991), 133–144; A. M. Sadeq, "Waqf, Perpetual Charity and Poverty Alleviation," *International Journal of Social Economics* 29, nos. 1–2 (2002): 135–151.

140. S. Shah and V. Ramamoorthy, "Business Responsibility through the Ages: A Journey from Scriptural Insights, with Noble Philanthropists, to Committed Institutions and Leaders," in *Soulful Corporations*, ed. S. Shah and V. E. Ramamoorthy (London: Springer, 2014), 123–154.

141. M. Feingold, "Philanthropy, Pomp, and Patronage: Historical Reflections upon the Endowment of Culture," *Daedalus* (1987): 155–178.

142. C. Su, R. K. Mitchell, and M. J. Sirgy, "Enabling Guanxi Management in China: A Hierarchical Stakeholder Model of Effective Guanxi," *Journal of Business Ethics* 71, no. 3 (2007): 301–319, 301.

143. Ibid.

144. M. Mohr, "Filial Piety with a Zen Twist: Universalism and Particularism Surrounding the Sutra on the Difficulty of Reciprocating the Kindness of Parents," *Journal of Religion in Japan* 2, no. 1 (2013): 35–62, 35.

145. T. Lomas, T. Cartwright, T. Edginton, and D. Ridge, "New Ways of Being a Man: 'Positive' Hegemonic Masculinity in Meditation-Based Communities of Practice," *Men and Masculinities* 19, no. 3 (2016): 289–310; T. Lomas, T. Cartwright,

T. Edginton, and D. Ridge, "A Religion of Wellbeing? The Appeal of Buddhism to Men in London, UK," *Psychology of Religion and Spirituality* 6, no. 3 (2014): 198–207.

146. A. Németh, "Ta'ârof as a Writer's Tool in Twentieth Century Persian Literary Orose," *Iranian Studies* 41, no. 2 (2008): 183–211, 183.

147. A. Raifee, *Colloquial Persian* (London: Routledge, 2013), 154.

148. A. T. Wolf, "Healing the Enlightenment Rift: Rationality, Spirituality and Shared Waters," *Journal of International Affairs* (2008): 51–73.

149. E. Trillas and M. Navarro, "An Essay on the Ancient Ideal of 'Enraonar,'" *Archives of Philosophy and History of Soft Computing* 1 (2015): 1–28, 1.

150. D. Brenneis, "Telling Troubles: Narrative, Conflict and Experience," *Anthropological Linguistic* (1988): 279–291; T. Vaioleti, "Talanoa: Differentiating the Talanoa Research Methodology from Phenomenology, Narrative, Kaupapa Maori and Feminist Methodologies," *Te Reo* 56 (2013): 191.

151. T. Derico, *Oral Tradition and Synoptic Verbal Agreement: Evaluating the Empirical Evidence for Literary Dependence* (Eugene, OR: Pickwick Publications, 2016), 93.

152. A. Landa, "Shalom and Erene: Fully Caring for the Afflicted Person," *Christian Journal for Global Health* 1, no. 2 (2014): 16–18.

153. J. Davis, "Mazel Tov: The Bar Mitzvah as a Multigenerational Ritual of Change and Continuity," *Rituals in Families and Family Therapy* (1988): 177–208.

154. A. Colorni, *Israel for Beginners* (Jerusalem: Gefen, 2011), 11.

155. V. G. Spiridon, "Issues in Translating Common Japanese Phrases," *Linguistic and Philosophical Investigations*, no. 13 (2014): 557–561.

156. E. Becker, *Overbooked: The Exploding Business of Travel and Tourism* (New York: Simon & Schuster, 2016), 386.

157. J. Kaomea, "A Curriculum of Aloha? Colonialism and Tourism in Hawaii's Elementary Textbooks," *Curriculum Inquiry* 30, no. 3 (2000): 319–344.

158. M.-R. Ungunmerr-Baumann, *Dadirri: Inner Deep Listening and Quiet Still Awareness* (Darwin: Emmaus Productions, 2002), 1.

159. R. West, L. Stewart, K. Foster, and K. Usher, "Through a Critical Lens: Indigenist Research and the Dadirri Method," *Qualitative Health Research* 22, no. 11 (2012): 1582–1590.

160. M. Kahn-John and M. Koithan, "Living in Health, Harmony, and Beauty: The Diné (Navajo) Hózhó Wellness Philosophy," *Global Advances in Health and Medicine* 4, no. 3 (2015): 24–30, 24.

161. W. M. Clements, "'A Continual Beginning, and Then an Ending, and Then a Beginning Again': Hopi Apocalypticism in the New Age," *Journal of the Southwest* 46, no. 4 (2004): 643–660.

162. H. C. Triandis, G. Marín, J. Lisansky, and H. Betancourt, "Simpatía as a Cultural Script of Hispanics," *Journal of Personality and Social Psychology* 47, no. 6 (1984): 1363–1375, 1363.

163. C. Geertz, *The Religion of Java* (Chicago: University of Chicago Press, 1976), 31.

164. W. L. Cleveland, *The Making of an Arab Nationalist: Ottomanism and Arabism in the Life and Thought of Sati'al-Husri* (Princeton, NJ: Princeton University Press, 2015), 104.

165. M. Carotenuto and K. Luongo, *Obama and Kenya: Contested Histories and the Politics of Belonging* (Ohio: Ohio University Press, 2016), 157.

166. C. Levisen, *Cultural Semantics and Social Cognition: A Case Study on the Danish Universe of Meaning* (Berlin: Walter de Gruyter, 2013), 30.

167. L. Shevtsova, "Forward to the Past in Russia," *Journal of Democracy* 26, no. 2 (2015): 22–36.

168. I. Huvila, *Information Services and Digital Literacy: In Search of the Boundaries of Knowing* (Oxford: Cliandos, 2012), 58.

169. A. Sandemose, *En Flyktning Krysser Sitt Spor (A Fugitive Crosses His Tracks)*, trans. E. Gay-Tifft (New York: A. A. Knopf, 1936).

170. C. Levisen, *Cultural Semantics and Social Cognition: A Case Study on the Danish Universe of Meaning* (Berlin: Walter de Gruyter, 2013).

171. D. Bakan, *The Duality of Human Existence* (Chicago: Rand McNally, 1966).

Chapter 4: Development

1. R. Veenhoven, "Is Happiness Relative?" *Social Indicators Research* 24 (1991): 1–34.

2. S. Ahmed, "The Happiness Turn," *New Formations* 63 (2007): 7–14.

3. Cited in S. I. Friedland, "Outcomes and the Ownership Conception of Law School Courses," *William Mitchell Law Review* 38, no. 3 (2012): 947–975, 957.

4. M. Heidegger, *Being and Time*, trans. J. MacQuarrie and E. Robinson (London: Blackwell, 1927); E. C. Boedeker Jr., "Individual and Community in Early Heidegger: Situating Das Man, the Man-Self, and Self-Ownership in Dasein's Ontological Structure," *Inquiry* 44, no. 1 (2001): 63–99.

5. J. A. Ciaffa, "Toward an Understanding of Heidegger's Conception of the Inter-Relation between Authentic and Inauthentic Existence," *Journal of the British Society for Phenomenology* 18, no. 1 (1987): 49–59.

6. D. Bakan, *The Duality of Human Existence* (Chicago: Rand McNally, 1966).

7. K. Wilber, *Sex, Ecology, Spirituality: The Spirit of Evolution* (Boston: Shambhala Publications, 1995), 256.

8. L. M. Wierenga, M. Langen, B. Oranje, and S. Durston, "Unique Developmental Trajectories of Cortical Thickness and Surface Area," *NeuroImage* 87 (2014): 120–126.

9. M. Pasupathi, "Issues of Age and Health," in *Handbook of Diversity Issues in Health Psychology*, ed. P. M. Kato and T. Mann (New York: Springer, 1996), 39–48; M. Runge, J. Rittweger, C. R. Russo, H. Schiessl, and D. Felsenberg, "Is Muscle Power Output a Key Factor in the Age-Related Decline in Physical Performance? A Comparison of Muscle Cross Section, Chair-Rising Test and Jumping Power," *Clinical Physiology and Functional Imaging* 24, no. 6 (2004): 335–340.

10. D. H. Salat, R. L. Buckner, A. Z. Snyder, D. N. Greve, R. S. Desikan, E. Busa, J. C. Morris, A. M. Dale, and B. Fischl, "Thinning of the Cerebral Cortex in Aging," *Cerebral Cortex* 14, no. 7 (2004): 721–730.

11. D. G. Blanchflower and A. J. Oswald, "Is Well-Being U-Shaped Over the Life Cycle?" *Social Science & Medicine* 66, no. 8 (2008): 1733–1749.

12. T. Lomas, K. Hefferon, and I. Ivtzan, "Positive Developmental Psychology: A Review of Literature Concerning Well-Being throughout the Lifespan," *Journal of Happiness & Well-Being* 4, no. 2 (2016): 143–164.

13. T. B. Kashdan, R. Biswas-Diener, and L. A. King, "Reconsidering Happiness: The Cost of Distinguishing Between Hedonics and Eudaimonia," *Journal of Positive Psychology* 3, no. 4 (2008): 219–233.

14. E. Diener, "Subjective Well-Being: The Science of Happiness and a Proposal for a National Index," *American Psychologist* 55, no. 1 (2000): 34–43; C. D. Ryff, "Happiness Is Everything, or Is It? Explorations on the Meaning of Psychological Well-Being," *Journal of Personality and Social Psychology* 57, no. 6 (1989): 1069–1081.

15. Ryff, "Happiness Is Everything, or Is It?"

16. Aristotle, *Nicomachean Ethics*, ed. R. Crisp (Cambridge: Cambridge University Press, 2000), 11.

17. A. H. Maslow, *Motivation and Personality: With New Material by Ruth Cox and Robert Frager*, ed. R. Frager (1954; New York: Harper & Row, 1987).

18. Ryff, "Happiness Is Everything, or Is It?"

19. D. van Dierendonck, "The Construct Validity of Ryff's Scales of Psychological Well-Being and Its Extension with Spiritual Well-Being," *Personality and Individual Differences* 36, no. 3 (2004): 629–643.

20. C. Peterson and M. E. P. Seligman, *Character Strengths and Virtues: A Handbook and Classification* (Washington, DC: American Psychological Association, 2004); C. Peterson and N. Park, "Classifying and Measuring Strengths of Character," in *Oxford Handbook of Positive Psychology*, ed. S. J. Lopez and G. R. Snyder (New York: Oxford University Press, 2009), 25–33, 29.

21. R. E. McGrath, "Character Strengths in 75 Nations: An Update," *Journal of Positive Psychology* 10, no. 1 (2015): 41–52.

22. A. M. Wood, P. A. Linley, J. Maltby, T. B. Kashdan, and R. Hurling, "Using Personal and Psychological Strengths Leads to Increases in Well-Being Over Time: A Longitudinal Study and the Development of the Strengths Use Questionnaire," *Personality and Individual Differences* 50, no. 1 (2011): 15–19.

23. G. A. du Plessis and G. P. de Bruin, "Using Rasch Modelling to Examine the International Personality Item Pool (IPIP) Values in Action (VIA) Measure of Character Strengths," *Journal of Psychology in Africa* 25, no. 6 (2015): 512–521.

24. K. Dahlsgaard, C. Peterson, and M. E. Seligman, "Shared Virtue: The Convergence of Valued Human Strengths across Culture and History," *Review of General Psychology* 9, no. 3 (2005): 203–213.

25. A. W. Adkins, "The Connection between Aristotle's Ethics and Politics," *Political Theory* 12, no. 1 (1984): 29–49.

26. M. McDonnell, *Roman Manliness: "Virtus" and the Roman Republic* (Cambridge: Cambridge University Press, 2006).

27. N. S. Sarma, "Etymology as an Aid to Understanding Chemistry Concepts," *Journal of Chemistry Education* 81, no. 10 (2004): 1437.

28. J. Rivera, "Finding Aristotle's Golden Mean: Social Justice and Academic Excellence," *Journal of Education* 186, no. 1 (2005): 79–85.

29. A. C. Wicks, S. L. Berman, and T. M. Jones, "The Structure of Optimal Trust: Moral and Strategic Implications," *Academy of Management Review* 24, no. 1 (1999): 99–116.

30. S. H. Blumberg, "To Know Before Whom You Stand: A Philosophy for a Spiritual and Moral Liberal Jewish Education for the 21st century," in *International Handbook of the Religious, Moral and Spiritual Dimensions in Education*, ed. M. de Souza, K. Engebretson, G. Durka, R. Jackson and A. McGrady (New York: Springer, 2006), 717–729, 724.

31. B. J. Baer and N. Olshanskaya, *Russian Writers on Translation: An Anthology* (New York: Routledge, 2014), 106.

32. S. K. Hookham, *The Buddha Within: Tathagatagarbha Doctrine According to the Shentong Interpretation of the Ratnagotravibhaga* (New York: SUNY Press, 1991).

33. A. Buddharakkhita, *The Dhammapada: The Buddha's Path of Wisdom* (London: Buddhist Publication Society, 2008), 44, verses 95–96.

34. T. Angelovska and A. Hahn, "Written L3 (English): Transfer Phenomena of L2 (German) Lexical and Syntactic Properties," in *Cross-linguistic Influences in Multilingual Language Acquisition*, ed. D. Gabrys-Barker (Berlin: Springer, 2012), 23–40, 37.

35. Y. Maemura, "Humor and Laughter in Japanese Groups: The Kuuki of Negotiations," *Humor* 27, no. 1 (2014): 103–119.

36. R. Chavasse, "Latin Lay Piety and Vernacular Lay Piety in Word and Image: Venice, 1471–Early 1500s," *Renaissance Studies* 10, no. 3 (1996): 319–342.

37. F. Max-Müller, "The Dhammapada," in *Sacred Books of the East* (Oxford: Clarendon Press, 1881); M. Soeng, "The Art of Not Deceiving Yourself," in *Buddhist Thought and Applied Psychological Research: Transcending the Boundaries*, ed. D. K. Nauriyal, M. S. Drummond, and Y. B. Lal (London: Routledge, 2006), 302–313; S. Thera, *The Way of Mindfulness: The Satipatthana Sutta and Its Commentary* (Asgiriya, Kandy: Saccanubodia Samiti, 1941); J. Peacock, "Sati or Mindfulness? Bridging the Divide," in *After Mindfulness: New Perspectives on Psychology and Meditation*, ed. M. Mazzano (Basingstoke: Palgrave Macmillan, 2014), 3–22; K. R. Rao, "Purposeful Living," in *Value Management in Professions: Present Scenario, Future Strategies*, ed. N. K. Shastree, B. R. Dugar, J. P. N. Mishra, and A. K. Dhar (New Delhi: Ashok Kumar Mittal, 2007), 63–71, 63; J. R. Carter, "Buddhist Ethics?" in *The Blackwell Companion to Religious Ethics*, ed. W. Schweiker (Oxford: Blackwell, 2005), 278–285, 280.

38. T. Lomas, "Recontextualising Mindfulness: Theravada Buddhist Perspectives on the Ethical and Spiritual Dimensions of Awareness," *Psychology of Religion and Spirituality* 9, no. 2 (2017): 209–219.

39. R. E. Allinson, "Hillel and Confucius: The Prescriptive Formulation of the Golden Rule in the Jewish and Chinese Confucian Ethical Traditions," *Dao* 3, no. 1 (2003): 29–41, 29.

40. Analects 15:24, cited in R. E. Allinson, "Hillel and Confucius: The Prescriptive Formulation of the Golden Rule in the Jewish and Chinese Confucian Ethical Traditions," *Dao* 3, no. 1 (2003): 29–41, 29.

41. Talmud, tractate Shabbat 31a.

42. C. Kang, "Buddhist and Tantric Perspectives on Causality and Society," *Journal of Buddhist Ethics* 16 (2009): 69–103, 73.

43. E.A. Kinsella and A. Pitman, eds., *Phronesis as Professional Knowledge: Practical Wisdom in the Professions* (Boston: Springer Science & Business Media, 2012).

44. R. H. Trowbridge and M. Ferrari, "Sophia and Phronesis in Psychology, Philosophy, and Traditional Wisdom," *Research in Human Development* 8, no. 2 (2011): 89–94, 89.

45. E. Weisskopf-Joelson, "Some Suggestions Concerning Weltanschauung and Psychotherapy," *Journal of Abnormal and Social Psychology* 48, no. 4 (1953): 601–604.

46. T. Nagel, *The View from Nowhere* (Oxford: Oxford University Press, 1989).

47. R. A. Makkreel, *Dilthey: Philosopher of the Human Studies* (Princeton: Princeton University Press, 1992); A. Higgins, "Mixed Messages and No Progress in Greek Crisis," *New York Times*, July 2, 2015.

48. C. v. Ehrenfels, *On Gestalt Qualities*, trans. B. Smith (1890; Munich: Philosophia Verlag, 1988), 83.

49. F. Perls, *Gestalt Therapy Verbatim* (New York: Bantam Books, 1969), 71; S. E. Palmer, "Modern Theories of Gestalt perception," *Mind & Language* 5, no. 4 (1990): 289–323.

50. H. P. Wolvekamp, "The Concept of the Organism as an Integrated Whole," *Dialectica* 20, no. 2 (1966): 196–214, 196.

51. W. H. Calhoun and R. R. Shrader, *Ganzheit Psychology* (Pittsburgh: RoseDog Books, 2010), front cover.

52. A. L. Blumenthal, "A Reappraisal of Wilhelm Wundt," *American Psychologist* 30, no. 11 (1975): 1081–1088.

53. A. Elpidorou and L. Freeman, "Affectivity in Heidegger: Moods and Emotions in Being and Time," *Philosophy Compass* 10, no. 10 (2015): 661–671.

54. K. Withy, "Situation and Limitation: Making Sense of Heidegger on Thrownness," *European Journal of Philosophy* 22, no. 1 (2014): 61–81.

55. M. Joronen, "Heidegger on the History of Machination: Oblivion of Being as Degradation of Wonder," *Critical Horizons* 13, no. 3 (2012): 351–376, 354.

56. N. Kompridis, "On World Disclosure: Heidegger, Habermas and Dewey," *Thesis Eleven* 37, no. 1 (1994): 29–45, 29.

57. F. R. Dallmayr, "Ontology of Freedom: Heidegger and Political Philosophy," *Political Theory* 12, no. 2 (1984): 204–234.

58. R. M. Ryan and E. L. Deci, "Self-Determination Theory and the Facilitation of Intrinsic Motivation, Social Development, and Well-Being," *American Psychologist* 55, no. 1 (2000): 68–78.

59. J. P. Lynch and G. B. Miles, "In Search of Thumos: Toward an Understanding of a Greek Psychological Term," *Prudentia* 12, no. 1 (1980): 3–10, 3.

60. M. Johansson and L. Nordrum, "Swedish Hinna Viewed through Its English Correspondences—Have Time or Be Able To?" *Nordic Journal of English Studies* 15, no. 3 (2016): 171–199, 186.

61. S. C. Saraydar, "No Longer Shall You Kill: Peace, Power and the Iroquois Great Law," *Anthropology and Humanism Quarterly* 15, no. 1 (1990): 20–28.

62. A. L. Duckworth, C. Peterson, M. D. Matthews, and D. R. Kelly, "Grit: Perseverance and Passion for Long-Term Goals," *Journal of Personality and Social Psychology* 92, no. 6 (2007): 1087–1101.

63. K. Lucas and P. M. Buzzanell, "Blue-Collar Work, Career, and Success: Occupational Narratives of Sisu," *Journal of Applied Communication Research* 32, no. 4 (2004): 273–292, 273.

64. E. Lahti, "Above and Beyond Perseverance: An Exploration of Sisu" (2013), master's thesis, University of Pennsylvania; J. Sinkkonen, "The Land of Sauna, Sisu, and Sibelius—An Attempt at a Psychological Portrait of Finland," *International Journal of Applied Psychoanalytic Studies* 10, no. 1 (2013): 49–52.

65. H. Nassar, "Darwish and the Need for a New Poetry of Resistance for the Arab Spring," *Near East Quarterly* 4 (2011): 1–7, 4.

66. D. J. Clines, "Job and the Spirituality of the Reformation," in *The Bible, the Reformation and the Church: Essays in Honor of James Atkinson*, ed. W. P. Stephens (Sheffield: Sheffield Academic Press, 1995), 49–72.

67. J. Hoeksema, "Elative Compounds in Dutch," in *Cross-Linguistic Comparison of Intensified Adjectives and Adverbs*, ed. G. Oebel (Hamburg: Verlag Dr. Kovac, 2012), 97–142.

68. D. Hirasuna, *The Art of Gaman: Arts and Crafts from the Japanese American Internment Camps 1942–1946* (Berkeley: Ten Speed Press, 2013), front flap.

69. C. Burgess, "Japanese National Character Stereotypes in the Foreign Media in the Aftermath of the Great East Japan Earthquake: Myth or Reality?" *Tsuda Review* 56 (2012): 23–56.

70. Y. Tono, M. Yamazaki, and K. Maekawa, *A Frequency Dictionary of Japanese* (New York: Routledge, 2013), 31.

71. H. Schemann and P. Knight, *English/German Dictionary of Idioms: Supplement to the German/English Dictionary of Idioms* (New York: Routledge, 2013), 437.

72. I. J. Crossfield, "Observations of Exoplanet Atmospheres," *Publications of the Astronomical Society of the Pacific* 127, no. 956 (2015): 941.

73. J. A. Guggenheim, "Evolution of Chutzpah as a Legal Term: The Chutzpah Championship, Chutzpah Award, Chutzpah Doctrine, and Now, the Supreme Court," *Kentucky Law Journal* 87 (1998): 417.

74. J. Coker, "The Therapy of Nietzsche's 'Free Spirit,'" *International Studies in Philosophy* 29, no. 3 (1997): 63–88.

75. H. North, *Sophrosyne: Self-Knowledge and Self-Restraint in Greek Literature* (Ithaca: Cornell University Press, 1966).

76. R. J. Laird, "Mindset (γνώμη) in John Chrysostom," in *The Oxford Handbook of Maximus the Confessor*, ed. P. Allen and B. Neil (Oxford: Oxford University Press, 2015), 194–211, 200.

77. D. M. McMahon, *Happiness: A History* (New York: Atlantic Monthly Press, 2006).

78. C. S. Queen and S. B. King, *Engaged Buddhism: Buddhist Liberation Movements in Asia* (New York: SUNY Press, 1996); A. Ok-Sun, "A Critique of the Early Buddhist Texts: The Doctrine of Woman's Incapability of Becoming an Enlightened One," *Asian Journal of Women's Studies* 8, no. 3 (2002): 7–34.

79. M. Guiliano, *Women, Work and the Art of Savoir Faire: Business Sense and Sensibility* (New York: Simon & Schuster, 2009).

80. L. de Sousa, "'Above the Law, Below Ethics': Some Findings on Portuguese Attitudes towards Corruption," in *The Social Construction of Corruption in Europe*, ed. D. Tänzler, K. Maras, and A. Giannakopoulos (New York: Routledge, 2016), 245–264, 259.

81. K. S. Rosenn, "The Jeito: Brazil's Institutional Bypass of the Formal Legal System and Its Developmental Implications," *American Journal of Comparative Law* (1971): 514–549.

82. J. Pine, *The Art of Making Do in Naples* (Minneapolis: Universityof Minnesota Press, 2012); F. Allum, "Becoming a Camorrista: Criminal Culture and Life Choices in Naples," *Journal of Modern Italian Studies* 6, no. 3 (2001): 324–347.

83. M. Brockmann, L. Clarke, and C. Winch, *Knowledge, Skills and Competence in the European Labour Market: What's in a Vocational Qualification?* (New York: Routledge, 2011), 37.

84. J. De Romilly, "Eunoia in Isocrates or the Political Importance of Creating Good Will," *Journal of Hellenic Studies* 78 (1958): 92–101.

85. G. W. Bertram and R. Celikates, "Towards a Conflict Theory of Recognition: On the Constitution of Relations of Recognition in Conflict," *European Journal of Philosophy* 23, no. 4 (2015): 838–861.

86. J. Yoneoka, "What Is a Kokusaijin? A 10 Year Study," *Language Teacher* 24, no. 9 (2000): 7–13.

87. P. B. Baltes and M. M. Baltes, "Savoir Vivre in Old Age," *National Forum* 78, no. 2 (1998): 13–18.

88. P. Lopate, "Against Joie de Vivre," *Ploughshares* (1986): 11–32, 11.

89. S. Harrow and T. A. Unwin, "Introduction," in *Joie de Vivre in French Literature and Culture: Essays in Honor of Michael Freeman*, ed. S. Harrow and T. A. Unwin (Paris: Rodopi, 2009), 17–33, 19.

90. C. Noy, *A Narrative Community: Voices of Israeli Backpackers* (Detroit: Wayne State University Press, 2006), 134.

91. M. F. Steger, S. Oishi, and T. B. Kashdan, "Meaning in Life Across the Life Span: Levels and Correlates of Meaning in Life from Emerging Adulthood to Older Adulthood," *Journal of Positive Psychology* 4, no. 1 (2009): 43–52.

92. N. Yamamoto-Mitani and M. Wallhagen, "Pursuit of Psychological Well-Being (Ikigai) and the Evolution of Self-Understanding in the Context of Caregiving in Japan." *Culture, Medicine, and Psychiatry* 26, no. 4 (2002): 399–417, 399.

93. T. Sone, N. Nakaya, K. Ohmori, T. Shimazu, M. Higashiguchi, M. Kakizaki, N. Kikuchi, S. Kuriyama, and I. Tsuji, "Sense of Life Worth Living (Ikigai) and Mortality in Japan: Ohsaki Study," *Psychosomatic Medicine* 70, no. 6 (2008): 709–715.

94. A. Koch, "Sexual Healing: Regulating Male Sexuality in Edo-Period Books on 'Nurturing Life,'" *International Journal of Asian Studies* 10, no. 2 (2013): 143–170.

95. T. Boes, "Modernist Studies and the Bildungsroman: A Historical Survey of Critical Trends," *Literature Compass* 3, no. 2 (2006): 230–243; M. Swales, *The German Bildungsroman from Wieland to Hesse* (Princeton, NJ: Princeton University Press, 2015).

96. H. Hesse, *Siddhartha*, trans. H. Rosner (1922; New York: New Directions, 1922).

97. S. Katz, "Secular Morality," in *Morality and Health*, ed. A. Brandt and P. Rozin (New York: Routledge, 1997), 297–330.

98. P. Sheldrake, *A Brief History of Spirituality* (Malden, MA: Wiley-Blackwell, 2007).

99. M. T. Dempsey, "Biblical Hermeneutics and Spiritual Interpretation: The Revelatory Presence of God in Karl Barth's Theology of Scripture," *Biblical Theology Bulletin: A Journal of Bible and Theology* 37, no. 3 (2007): 120–131.

100. H. G. Koenig, "Research on Religion, Spirituality, and Mental Health: A Review," *Canadian Journal of Psychiatry* 54, no. 5 (2009): 283–291.

101. B. Saler, "Religio and the Definition of Religion," *Cultural Anthropology* 2, no. 3 (1987): 395–399.

102. J. Burton, *Monastic and Religious Orders in Britain, 1000–1300* (Cambridge: Cambridge University Press, 1994).

103. B. A. Kosmin and A. Keysar, *American Religious Identification Survey (ARIS 2012)* (Hartford: ISSSC, Trinity College, 2013).

104. H. G. Koenig, "Research on Religion, Spirituality, and Mental Health: A Review," *Canadian Journal of Psychiatry* 54, no. 5 (2009): 283–291, 283.

105. K. T. Nyima and S. Gyaltsap, *Vajra Wisdom: Deity Practice in Tibetan Buddhism* (Boston: Shambhala Publications, 2013).

106. T. Lomas, T. Cartwright, T. Edginton, and D. Ridge, "A Religion of Wellbeing? The Appeal of Buddhism to Men in London, UK," *Psychology of Religion and Spirituality* 6, no. 3 (2014): 198–207.

107. J. Feather, "The Necessity of Sacrifice for Consciousness: Attitude and Meaning," *Psychological Perspectives* 56, no. 3 (2013): 334–341.

108. E. Durkheim, *The Elementary Forms of Religious Life*, trans. C. Cosman (Oxford: Oxford University Press, 1912/2001), 47.

109. S. Boym, "From the Russian Soul to Post-Communist Nostalgia," *Representations*, no. 49 (1995): 133–166.

110. P. C. Hill, K. I. Pargament, R. W. Hood, M. E. McCullough Jr, J. P. Swyers, D. B. Larson, and B. J. Zinnbauer, "Conceptualizing Religion and Spirituality: Points of Commonality, Points of Departure," *Journal for the Theory of Social Behavior* 30, no. 1 (2000): 51–77; W. Braud, "Experiencing Tears of Wonder-Joy: Seeing with the Heart's Eye," *Journal of Transpersonal Psychology* 33, no. 2 (2001): 99–112.

111. E. D. Goldstein, "Sacred Moments: Implications on Well-Being and Stress," *Journal of Clinical Psychology* 63, no. 10 (2007): 1001–1019.

112. B. Holdrege, *Veda and Torah: Transcending the Textuality of Scripture* (New York: SUNY Press, 1995).

113. S. Radhakrishnan, "The Vedanta Philosophy and the Doctrine of Maya," *International Journal of Ethics* 24, no. 4 (1914): 431–451.

114. D. Y. Ho, "Selfhood and identity in Confucianism, Taoism, Buddhism, and Hinduism: Contrasts with the West," *Journal for the Theory of Social Behavior* 25, no. 2 (1995): 115–139, 124.

115. A. D. Aczel, *The Mystery of the Aleph: Mathematics, the Kabbalah, and the Search for Infinity* (New York: Simon & Schuster, 2001).

116. A. Kaplan, *Sefer Yetzirah: The Book of Creation in Theory and Practice* (Boston: Weiser Books, 1997).

117. M. Gimbutas, *The Gods and Goddesses of Old Europe, 7000 to 3500 BC: Myths, Legends and Cult Images* (Berkeley: University of California Press, 1974).

118. L. S. Sussman, "The Birth of the Gods: Sexuality, Conflict and Cosmic Structure in Hesiod's Theogony," *Ramus* 7, no. 1 (1978): 61–77.

119. S. Sen, "The Vedic-Upanisadic Concept of Brahman (The Highest God)," in *Concepts of the Ultimate*, ed. L. J. Tessier (London: Springer, 1989), 83–97.

120. *Catechism of the Catholic Church Revised* (London: Burns & Oates, 1994), 60.

121. M. Barker, *The Great Angel: A Study of Israel's Second God* (London: Westminster John Knox Press, 1992).

122. K. Ottosson, "The Anticausative and Related Categories in the Old Germanic Languages," *Diachronic and Typological Perspectives on Verbs* (2013): 329–382.

123. A. Allamani, S.-S. Einstein, and T. M. Godlaski, "A Review of the Many Meanings of an Unseizable Concept," *Substance Use & Misuse* 48, no. 12 (2013): 1081–1084.

124. D. Y. Ho, "Selfhood and Identity in Confucianism, Taoism, Buddhism, and Hinduism: Contrasts with the West," *Journal for the Theory of Social Behavior* 25, no. 2 (1995): 115–139, 124.

125. L. Poonamallee, "Advaita (Non-Dualism) as Metatheory: A Constellation of Ontology, Epistemology, and Praxis," *Integral Review* 6 (2010): 190–200.

126. M. Epstein, "The Deconstruction of the Self: Ego and 'Egolessness' in Buddhist Insight Meditation," *Journal of Transpersonal Psychology* 20, no. 1 (1988): 61–69.

127. R. F. Gombrich, *How Buddhism Began: The Conditioned Genesis of the Early Teachings* (London: Routledge, 2006).

128. C. B. Becker, "Rebirth and Afterlife in Buddhism," in *Perspectives on Death and Dying: Cross-Cultural and Multi-Disciplinary Views*, ed. J. Berger (Philadelphia: Charles Press, 1989), 108–125.

129. V. Saroglou, "Believing, Bonding, Behaving, and Belonging: The Big Four Religious Dimensions and Cultural Variation," *Journal of Cross-Cultural Psychology* 42, no. 8 (2011): 1320–1340.

130. R. Descartes, *Meditations on First Philosophy: With Selections from the Objections and Replie*, trans. M. Moriarty (1641; Oxford: Oxford University Press, 2008).

131. G. Wildegren, "Researches in Syrian Mysticism: Mystical Experiences and Spiritual Exercises," *Numen: International Review for the History of Religions* 8 (1961): 161–198, 169.

132. R. Cardoso, E. de Souza, L. Camano, and J. Roberto Leite, "Meditation in Health: An Operational Definition," *Brain Research Protocols* 14, no. 1 (2004): 58–60.

133. A. Lutz, H. A. Slagter, J. D. Dunne, and R. J. Davidson, "Attention Regulation and Monitoring in Meditation," *Trends in Cognitive Sciences* 12, no. 4 (2008): 163–169.

134. S. Young, "Purpose and Method of Vipassana Meditation," *Humanistic Psychologist* 22, no. 1 (1994): 53–61.

135. A. Raffone and N. Srinivasan, "The Exploration of Meditation in the Neuroscience of Attention and Consciousness," *Cognitive Processing* 11, no. 1 (2010): 1–7, 2.

136. A. Chiesa, "Vipassana Meditation: Systematic Review of Current Evidence," *Journal of Alternative and Complementary Medicine* 16, no. 1 (2010): 37–46.

137. T. Gyatso, "Science at the Crossroads," *EXPLORE: The Journal of Science and Healing* 2, no. 2 (2006): 97–99, 98.

138. G. Giustarini, "The Role of Fear (Bhaya) in the Nikāyas and in the Abhidhamma," *Journal of Indian Philosophy* 40, no. 5 (2012): 511–531.

139. V. Raghavan, *The Power of the Sacred Name: Indian Spirituality Inspired by Mantras*, ed. W. J. Jackson (Bloomington, IN: World Wisdom, 2011), xvii.

140. G. Wildegren, "Researches in Syrian Mysticism: Mystical Experiences and Spiritual Exercises," *Numen: International Review for the History of Religions* 8 (1961): 161–198, 169.

141. J. W. Carson, F. J. Keefe, T. R. Lynch, K. M. Carson, V. Goli, and A. M. Fras, "Loving-Kindness Meditation for Chronic Low Back Pain," *Journal of Holistic Nursing* 23, no. 3 (2005): 287–304.

142. C. H. Durousseau, "Yah: A Name of God," *Jewish Bible Quarterly* 42, no. 1 (2014): 21–26.

143. Vessantara, *Meeting the Buddhas: A Guide to Buddhas, Bohisattvas, and Tantric Deities* (Birmingham: Windhorse Publications, 2002).

144. J. Varenne, *Yoga and the Hindu Tradition* (Chicago: University of Chicago Press, 1977).

145. G. Feuerstein, *The Yoga Tradition: Its History, Literature, Philosophy, and Practice* (New Delhi: Bhavana Books, 2002).

146. M. T. Quilty, R. B. Saper, R. Goldstein, and S. B. S. Khalsa, "Yoga in the Real World: Perceptions, Motivators, Barriers, and Patterns of Use," *Global Advances in Health and Medicine* 2, no. 1 (2013): 44–49.

147. S. E. Henning, "Academia Encounters the Chinese Martial Arts," *China Review International* 6, no. 2 (1999): 319–332.

148. L. Galante, *Tai Chi: The Supreme Ultimate* (Boston: Weiser Books, 1981).

149. Y. H. Zhang and K. Rose, *A Brief History of Qi* (Brookline: Paradigm Publications, 2001).

150. K. Dahlsgaard, C. Peterson, and M. E. Seligman, "Shared Virtue: The Convergence of Valued Human Strengths across Culture and History," *Review of General Psychology* 9, no. 3 (2005): 203–213, 209.

151. T. Lomas, "Self-Transcendence through Shared Suffering: A Transpersonal Theory of Compassion," *Journal of Transpersonal Psychology* 27, no. 2 (2015): 168–187.

152. G. Armstrong and M. Young, "Fanatical Football Chants: Creating and Controlling the Carnival," *Culture, Sport Society* 2, no. 3 (1999): 173–211; J. Lutz, "Flow and Sense of Coherence: Two Aspects of the Same Dynamic?" *Global Health Promotion* 16, no. 3 (2009): 63–67.

153. R. J. Castillo, "Culture, Trance, and the Mind-Brain," *Anthropology of Consciousness* 6, no. 1 (1995): 17–34.

154. Epstein, "The Deconstruction of the Self."

155. G. W. F. Hegel, *The Phenomenology of Spirit*, trans. A. V. Miller (1807; Oxford: Clarenden Press, 1977), 163–164.

156. K. Wilber, *Sex, Ecology, Spirituality: The Spirit of Evolution* (Boston: Shambhala Publications, 1995).

157. Galatians, 2:20, *The Catholic Comparative New Testament* (New York: Oxford University Press, 2005), 1260.

158. G. Du Pre, "Science and the Skandhas," in *Buddhism and Science*, ed. B. P. Kirthisinghe (Delhi: Motilal Banarsidass, 1993), 119–127.

159. Epstein, "The Deconstruction of the Self."

160. D. Hume, *A Treatise of Human Nature* (Oxford: Clarendon Press, 1739); W. James, "The Knowing of Things Together," *Psychological Review* 2, no. 2 (1895): 105–124.

161. M. Siderits, *Studies in Buddhist Philosophy*, ed. J. Westerhoff (Oxford: Oxford University Press, 2016), 92.

162. P. De Silva, "Theoretical Perspectives on Emotions in Early Buddhism," in *Emotions in Asian Thought: A Dialogue in Comparative Philosophy*, ed. J. Marks and R. T. Ames (New York: SUNY Press, 1995), 109–121.

163. R. L. Goldstone, J. R. de Leeuw, and D. H. Landy, "Fitting Perception in and to Cognition," *Cognition* 135 (2015): 24–29, 24.

164. G. Maehle, *Ashtanga Yoga: Practice and Philosophy* (Novato, CA: New World Library, 2007), 3.

165. W. S. Waldron, "How Innovative Is the Alayavijñāna?" *Journal of Indian Philosophy* 22, no. 3 (1994): 199–258.

166. E. Conze, "Text, Sources, and Bibliography of the Prajñāpāramitā-Hṛdaya," *Journal of the Royal Asiatic Society* 80, no. 1–2 (1948): 33–51.

167. H.-C. Shih, "The Significance of Tāthāgatagarbha: A Positive Expression of Śūnyatā," *NTU Philosophical Review*, no. 11 (1988): 227–246.

168. Y. Wakui-Khaw, "Who Do You Say That I Am? A Japanese Response to the Person and the Work of Christ," *Stimulus: The New Zealand Journal of Christian Thought and Practice* 21, no. 3 (2014): 14–21; M. Abe, "Śūnyatā as Formless Form: Plato and Mahāyāna Buddhism," in *Zen and Comparative Studies*, ed. S. Heine (New York: Springer, 1997), 139–148; C. Kang, "Buddhist and Tantric Perspectives on Causality and Society," *Journal of Buddhist Ethics* 16 (2009): 69–103.

Chapter 5: A Map of Well-Being

1. A. Strauss and J. Corbin, *Basics of Qualitative Research: Techniques and Procedures for Developing Grounded Theory*, 2nd ed. (Thousand Oaks, CA: Sage, 1998).

2. V. Braun and V. Clarke, "Using Thematic Analysis in Psychology," *Qualitative Research in Psychology* 3, no. 2 (2006): 77–101.

3. E. Diener, "Subjective Well-Being: The Science of Happiness and a Proposal for a National Index," *American Psychologist* 55, no. 1 (2000): 34–43; C. D. Ryff, "Happiness Is Everything, or Is It? Explorations on the Meaning of Psychological Well-Being," *Journal of Personality and Social Psychology* 57, no. 6 (1989): 1069–1081.

4. Ryff, "Happiness Is Everything, or Is It?"

5. M. E. P. Seligman, *Flourish: A Visionary New Understanding of Happiness and Well-Being* (New York: Simon & Schuster, 2012).

6. M. L. Kern, L. E. Waters, A. Adler, and M. A. White, "A Multidimensional Approach to Measuring Well-Being in Students: Application of the PERMA Framework," *Journal of Positive Psychology* 10, no. 3 (2015): 262–271.

7. D. J. Disabato, F. R. Goodman, T. B. Kashdan, J. L. Short, and A. Jarden, "Different Types of Well-Being? A Cross-Cultural Examination of Hedonic and Eudaimonic Well-Being," *Psychological Assessment* 28, no. 5 (2016): 471–482.

8. D. van Dierendonck, "The Construct Validity of Ryff's Scales of Psychological Well-Being and Its Extension with Spiritual Well-Being," *Personality and Individual Differences* 36, no. 3 (2004): 629–643.

9. F. Jackson, "Epiphenomenal Qualia," *Philosophical Quarterly* 32, no. 127 (1982): 127–136, 127.

10. M. Boiger and B. Mesquita, "The Construction of Emotion in Interactions, Relationships, and Cultures," *Emotion Review* 4, no. 3 (2012): 221–229.

11. J. A. Russell, "A Circumplex Model of Affect," *Journal of Personality and Social Psychology* 39 (1980): 1161–1178.

12. P. Ekman, "Basic Emotions," in *The Handbook of Cognition and Emotion*, ed. T. Dalgleish and T. Power (Sussex, UK: John Wiley, 1999), 45–60.

13. L. F. Barrett, "Are Emotions Natural Kinds?" *Perspectives on Psychological Science* 1, no. 1 (2006): 28–58, 49.

14. I. Ivtzan, T. Lomas, K. Hefferon, and P. Worth, *Second Wave Positive Psychology: Embracing the Dark Side of Life.* (London: Routledge, 2015); T. Lomas and I. Ivtzan, "Second Wave Positive Psychology: Exploring the Positive-Negative Dialectics of Wellbeing," *Journal of Happiness Studies* 17, no. 4 (2016): 1753–1768.

15. T. Fang, "Yin Yang: A New Perspective on Culture," *Management and Organization Review* 8, no. 1 (2012): 25–50.

16. T. Lomas, T. Cartwright, T. Edginton, and D. Ridge, "A Religion of Wellbeing? The Appeal of Buddhism to Men in London, UK," *Psychology of Religion and Spirituality* 6, no. 3 (2014): 198–207.

17. J. F. Helliwell, "How's Life? Combining Individual and National Variables to Explain Subjective Well-Being," *Economic Modeling* 20, no. 2 (2003): 331–360; J. F. Helliwell and R. D. Putnam, "The Social Context of Well-Being," *Philosophical Transactions of the Royal Society of London, Series B: Biological Sciences* 359, no. 1449 (2004): 1435–1446.

18. J. A. Lee, *The Colors of Love: An Exploration of the Ways of Loving* (Don Mills, Ontario: New Press, 1973); J. A. Lee, "A Typology of Styles of Loving," *Personality and Social Psychology Bulletin* 3, no. 2 (1977): 173–182; R. J. Sternberg, "A Triangular Theory of Love," *Psychological Review* 93, no. 2 (1986): 119–135.

19. D. Bakan, *The Duality of Human Existence* (Chicago: Rand McNally, 1966).

20. K. Wilber, *Sex, Ecology, Spirituality: The Spirit of Evolution* (Boston: Shambhala Publications, 1995), 256.

21. C. Taylor, *Sources of the Self: The Making of the Modern Identity* (Cambridge, MA: Harvard University Press, 1989), 60.

22. T. Lomas, "Positive Social Psychology: A Multilevel Inquiry into Socio-Cultural Wellbeing Initiatives," *Psychology, Public Policy, and Law* 21, no. 3 (2015): 338–347.

23. C. Peterson and M. E. P. Seligman, *Character Strengths and Virtues: A Handbook and Classification* (Washington, DC: American Psychological Association, 2004).

24. K. Dahlsgaard, C. Peterson, and M. E. Seligman, "Shared Virtue: The Convergence of Valued Human Strengths across Culture and History," *Review of General Psychology* 9, no. 3 (2005): 203–213.

25. Aristotle, *Nicomachean Ethics*, ed. R. Crisp (350 BCE; Cambridge: Cambridge University Press, 2000), 11.

26. A. C. Wicks, S. L. Berman, and T. M. Jones, "The Structure of Optimal Trust: Moral and Strategic Implications," *Academy of Management Review* 24, no. 1 (1999): 99–116.

27. B. Schwartz, "Self-Determination: The Tyranny of Freedom," *American Psychologist* 55, no. 1 (2000): 79–88.

28. R. Cardoso, E. de Souza, L. Camano, and J. Roberto Leite, "Meditation in Health: An Operational Definition," *Brain Research Protocols* 14, no. 1 (2004): 58–60.

29. Dahlsgaard, Peterson, and Seligman, "Shared Virtue," 209.

30. Galatians, 2:20, *The Catholic Comparative New Testament* (New York: Oxford University Press, 2005), 1260.

31. M. Dunn, S. J. Greenhill, S. C. Levinson, and R. D. Gray, "Evolved Structure of Language Shows Lineage-Specific Trends in Word-Order Universals," *Nature* 473, no. 7345 (2011): 79–82.

32. R. S. Schreiber, "The 'How To' of Grounded Theory: Avoiding the Pitfalls," in *Using Grounded Theory in Nursing*, ed. R. S. Schreiber and P. N. Stern (New York: Springer, 2001), 55–83, 60.

33. F. Finlay and B. Gough, *Reflexivity: A Practical Guide for Researchers in Health and Social Sciences* (Oxford: Blackwell Science, 2003).

34. B. Temple and R. Edwards, "Interpreters/Translators and Cross-Language Research: Reflexivity and Border Crossings," *International Journal of Qualitative Methods* 1, no. 2 (2002): 1–12.

35. T. Nagel, *The View from Nowhere* (Oxford: Oxford University Press, 1989).

36. J. Luft, *Of Human Interactions: The Johari Model* (Palo Alto, CA: Mayfield, 1969).

37. J. R. Searle, *Construction of Social Reality* (London: Free Press, 1995).

38. Strauss and Corbin, *Basics of Qualitative Research*, 2nd ed.

39. S. Scheibe, A. M. Freund, and P. B. Baltes, "Toward a Developmental Psychology of Sehnsucht (Life Longings): The Optimal (Utopian) Life," *Developmental Psychology* 43, no. 3 (2007): 778–795, 779.

40. S. Messick, "Validity of Psychological Assessment: Validation of Inferences from Persons' Responses and Performances as Scientific Inquiry into Score Meaning," *American Psychologist* 50, no. 9 (1995): 741–749.

41. M. Bullinger, "German Translation and Psychometric Testing of the SF-36 Health Survey: Preliminary Results from the IQOLA Project," *Social Science & Medicine* 41, no. 10 (1995): 1359–1366.

42. C. Taylor, *Philosophy and the Human Sciences: Philosophical Papers*, vol. 2 (Cambridge: Cambridge University Press, 1985), 23–24.

43. U. Tadmor, "Loanwords in the World's Languages: Findings and Results," in *Loanwords in the World's Languages: A Comparative Handbook*, ed. M. Haspelmath and U. Tadmor (Berlin: De Gruyter Martin, 2009), 55–75.

44. G. H. Cannon and A. S. Kaye, *The Arabic Contributions to the English Language: An Historical Dictionary* (Berlin: Otto Harrassowitz Verlag, 1994).

45. T. B. Kashdan, L. F. Barrett, and P. E. McKnight, "Unpacking Emotion Differentiation: Transforming Unpleasant Experience by Perceiving Distinctions in Negativity," *Current Directions in Psychological Science* 24, no. 1 (2015): 10–16.

46. M. A. Brackett, S. E. Rivers, M. R. Reyes, and P. Salovey, "Enhancing Academic Performance and Social and Emotional Competence with the RULER Feeling Words Curriculum," *Learning and Individual Differences* 22, no. 2 (2012): 218–224.

47. C. Saarni, *The Development of Emotional Competence* (London: Guilford Press, 1999); F. A. Fogarty, L. M. Lu, J. J. Sollers, S. G. Krivoschekov, R. J. Booth, and N. S. Consedine, "Why It Pays to Be Mindful: Trait Mindfulness Predicts Physiological Recovery from Emotional Stress and Greater Differentiation among Negative Emotions," *Mindfulness* 6, no. 2 (2015): 175–185.

48. J. Kabat-Zinn, "An Outpatient Program in Behavioral Medicine for Chronic Pain Patients Based on the Practice of Mindfulness Meditation: Theoretical Considerations and Preliminary Results," *General Hospital Psychiatry* 4, no. 1 (1982): 33–47; Z. V. Segal, J. M. G. Williams, and J. D. Teasdale, *Mindfulness-Based Cognitive Therapy for Depression: A New Approach to Preventing Relapse* (New York: Guilford Press, 2002); J. W. Carson, F. J. Keefe, T. R. Lynch, K. M. Carson, V. Goli, and A. M. Fras, "Loving-Kindness Meditation for Chronic Low Back Pain," *Journal of Holistic Nursing* 23, no. 3 (2005): 287–304; B. L. Fredrickson, M. A. Cohn, K. A. Coffey, J. Pek, and S. M. Finkel, "Open Hearts Build Lives: Positive Emotions, Induced through Loving-Kindness Meditation, Build Consequential Personal Resources," *Journal of Personality and Social Psychology* 95, no. 5 (2008): 1045–1062.

49. S. L. Shapiro, L .E. Carlson, J. A. Astin, and B. Freedman, "Mechanisms of Mindfulness," *Journal of Clinical Psychology* 62, no. 3 (2006): 373–386.

50. S. R. Bishop, M. Lau, S. Shapiro, L. Carlson, N. D. Anderson, J. Carmody, Z. V. Segal, et al., "Mindfulness: A Proposed Operational Definition," *Clinical Psychology: Science and Practice* 11, no. 3 (2004): 230–241.

51. Part II, verse 9, cited in T. Lomas and Jnanavaca, "Types of Mindfulness, Orders of Conditionality, and Stages of the Spiritual Path," in *Buddhist Foundations of Mindfulness*, ed. E. Shonin, W. van Gordon, and N. N. Singh (London: Springer, 2015), 287–310, 287.

52. S. T. Katz, *Mysticism and Religious Traditions* (Oxford: Oxford University Press, 1983).

53. K. W. Brown and R. M. Ryan, "The Benefits of Being Present: Mindfulness and Its Role in Psychological Well-Being," *Journal of Personality and Social Psychology* 84, no. 4 (2003): 822–848.

54. W. James, *Principles of Psychology* (1890; New York: Holt, 1923), 424. Italics in the original.

55. B. Bodhi, "What Does Mindfulness Really Mean? A Canonical Perspective," *Contemporary Buddhism* 12, no. 1 (2011): 19–39.

56. M. E. Addis, "Gender and Depression in Men," *Clinical Psychology: Science and Practice* 15, no. 3 (2008): 153–168.

57. K. Bluth, R. A. Campo, S. Pruteanu-Malinici, A. Reams, M. Mullarkey, and P. C. Broderick, "A School-Based Mindfulness Pilot Study for Ethnically Diverse At-Risk Adolescents," *Mindfulness* 7, no. 1 (2016): 90–104; S. Beshai, L. McAlpine, K. Weare, and W. Kuyken, "A Non-Randomised Feasibility Trial Assessing the Efficacy of a Mindfulness-Based Intervention for Teachers to Reduce Stress and Improve Well-Being," *Mindfulness* 7, no. 1 (2015): 198–208; W. B. Britton, B. Shahar, O. Szepsenwol, and W. J. Jacobs, "Mindfulness-Based Cognitive Therapy Improves Emotional Reactivity to Social Stress: Results from a Randomized Controlled Trial," *Behavior Therapy* 43, no. 2 (2012): 365–380; S. H. Ma and J. D. Teasdale, "Mindfulness-Based Cognitive Therapy for Depression: Replication and Exploration of Differential Relapse Prevention Effects," *Journal of Consulting and Clinical Psychology* 72, no. 1 (2004): 31–40; J. Piet and E. Hougaard, "The Effect of Mindfulness-Based Cognitive Therapy for Prevention of Relapse in Recurrent Major Depressive Disorder: A Systematic Reviewd and Meta-Analysis," *Clinical Psychology Review* 31, no. 6 (2011): 1032–1040.

Index